Introducing Social Semiotics

Introducing Social Semiotics is a lively introduction to the ways in which different aspects of modern society combine to create meaning. These 'semiotic resources' surrounding us include obvious modes of communication such as language, gesture, images and music, but also less obvious ones such as food, dress and everyday objects, all of which carry cultural value and significance.

Introducing Social Semiotics uses a wide variety of texts including photographs, adverts, magazine pages and film stills to explain how meaning is created through complex semiotic interactions. Practical exercises and examples as wide ranging as furniture arrangements in public places, advertising jingles, photojournalism and the rhythm of a rapper's speech provide readers with the knowledge and skills they need to be able to analyse and also produce successful multimodal texts and designs.

The book traces the development of semiotic resources through particular channels such as the history of the press and advertising; and explores how and why these resources change over time, for reasons such as advancing technology.

Featuring a full glossary of terms, exercises, discussion points and suggestions for further reading, *Introducing Social Semiotics* makes concrete the complexities of meaning making and is essential reading for anyone interested in how communication works.

Theo van Leeuwen is Professor at the Centre for Language and Communication Research at Cardiff University, UK.

Introducing Social Semiotics

Theo van Leeuwen

LONDON AND NEW YORK

First published 2005
by Routledge
2 Park Square, Milton Park, Abingdon, Oxon OX14 4RN

Simultaneously published in the USA and Canada
by Routledge
270 Madison Ave, New York, NY 10016

Routledge is an imprint of the Taylor & Francis Group

Typeset in Bell Gothic by Bookcraft Ltd, Stroud, Gloucestershire
Printed and bound in Great Britain by TJ International, Padstow, Cornwall

British Library Cataloguing in Publication Data
A catalogue record for this book is available from the British Library.

Library of Congress Cataloging in Publication Data Van Leeuwen, Theo, 1947–
Introducing social semiotics / Theo van Leeuwen. p. cm.
Includes bibliographical references.
1. Semiotics—Social aspects. I. Title.
P99.4.S62V36 2005
302.2-dc22   2004013007

ISBN 0-415-24943-0 (hbk)
ISBN 0-415-24944-9 (pbk)

Contents

Illustrations

Acknowledgements

The author and publishers would like to thank the following copyright holders for permission to reprint material:

Chapter 1

1.1 Woman in mirror from *Growing Up Female* with permission of Abigail Heyman.

1.2 Shower advertisement from *House Beautiful*, September 1998. Reprinted with the permission of Matki PLC.

1.3 Lenor Care advertisement with permission of Proctor and Gamble UK and Grey Advertising.

1.4 Rémy Martin advertisements by courtesy of E. Rémy Martin & Co.

1.5 Storm watches advertisement with permission of Storm.

Chapter 2

2.1 'Gulf War' 1991 by Moir, *Sydney Morning Herald*. Reprinted with the permission of Alan Moir.

2.2 Cover artwork for 'Grandpa's Party' by Monie Love used by permission of EMI Records and Me Company.

2.3 Post TV CD-ROMm reprinted with the permission of Post Tool Design.

2.4 Circuit typeface by Peter Grundy. Reprinted with the permission of Grundy & Northedge, Power Road Studios, 114 Power Road, London, W4 5PY www.grundynorthedge.com.

2.5 Parkett logo reprinted with permission from Parkett Publishers, Zurich-New York.

2.6 True Romance commercial with permission of Barnbrook Design.

2.7a Linguistic analysis from *An Introduction to Functional Grammar* by M.A.K. Halliday, Edward Arnold 1985. Reproduced by permission of Hodder Arnold.

2.7b from *Stage Two: Media Literacy (Write it Right, Literacy in Industry Research Project)*, published by the Disadvantaged Schools Program, Metropolitan East Region, NSW Department of School Education, 1994. Reprinted with permission of NSW Department of Education and Training.

2.8 'Students' concept map D of living liquid' from Kress et al., *Multimodal Teaching and Learning*. The Continuum Publishing Group, 2001. Reprinted with the permission of the publisher.

Chapter 3

3.2   Dress of an orthodox and a marginal Mennonite woman by Linda Arthur from *Religion, Dress and the Body*, Linda Arthur ed. 1994. Reprinted with the permission of the author.
3.3   Historic colours. Photographer Colin Poole with permission of PhotoWord Syndication Limited.

Chapter 4

4.1   Vietnam Execution with permission of Associated Press/ AP.
4.4   Starck Lemon Squeezer, 'Juicy Salif', Alessi 1990–1991. Reprinted with the permission of Agence Starck, Paris.

Extract from 'Toys as Communication Project' in chapter 4 reprinted with the permission of Professor Carmen R. Caldas-Coulthard.

Chapter 5

5.1   'Interrupting is bad for your heart' with permission of *Men's Health* magazine.
5.2b   The heart as pump from *Principles of Anatomy and Physiology* 8th Edition by Tortora and Grabowski, 1999. This material is used by permission of John Wiley & Sons, Inc.
5.3   Photographer Elliott Erwitt/Magnum Photos.
5.4   Photographer Elliott Erwitt/Magnum Photos.

Transcripts in chapter 5 and figures 5.7 and 5.8 from *Black Hawk Down* game reprinted with the permission of NovaLogic, Calabasas, CA.

Chapter 6

6.4   Carrière from *Dutch Cosmo*, October 2001. Reprinted by permission of Cosmopolitan Holland.

Chapter 7

7.1   'Child' from *Winter Trees* by Sylvia Plath. Copyright © 1963 Ted Hughes. Reprinted by permission of HarperCollins Publishers Inc and Faber and Faber Ltd.

Chapter 8

8.3   Salvador Dali, *St John of the Cross*, 1951. Reprinted by the permission of Glasgow Museums, The Burrell Collection.

8.4   Six Stills by Corinna Holthusen. With permission of Photo Selection and the artist.

8.5   Photographer Joseph Koudelka/Magnum Photos.

Chapter 10

10.1   Screen shot from *Body Adventure* CD-Rom. Body Adventure © Knowledge Adventures, Inc. and is used with the permission.

10.4   Plan of a Winnebago village according to informants of the upper phratry (figure 6, p.134). From *Structural Anthropology*. Volume 1 (Paper) by Claude Lévi-Strauss, translated by Claire Jacobson and Brooke Grundfest Schoepf (Peregrines, 1977). Copyright Basic Books, Inc, 1963. Reproduced by permission of Penguin Books Ltd. Copyright 1974 by Perseus Books Group. Reproduced with permission of Perseus Books Group in the format of textbook via the Copyright Clearance Center.

10.5   Omarakana village from *The sexual life of savages* by Bronislaw Malinowski with permission of Helena Wayne and the estate of Malinowski.

10.8   Lexmark cartridge packaging reprinted by the permission of Lexmark International, UK.

10.9   Alberto Giacometti, 'Hour of the Traces', 1930 © ADAGP, Paris, and DACS, London 2003. Photograph © Tate, London 2004.

Chapter 11

11.8–11.12 Screen shots and extracts from Microsoft *Dangerous Creatures* 1994 reprinted by permission from Microsoft Corporation.

Chapter 12

12.1   Extract from *You Just Don't Understand* by Deborah Tannen with permission of Time Warner Books UK.

Lyrics from 'I am a Rock' © 1965 Paul Simon. Used by permission of the Publisher: Paul Simon Music.

Excerpts from *Moulin Rouge* © 2001 Twentieth Century Fox. Written by Baz Luhrmann and Craig Pearce. All rights reserved.

Every effort has been made to obtain permission to reproduce copyright material. If any proper acknowledgement has not been made, or permission not received, we would invite copyright holders to inform us of the oversight.

Preface

This book is an attempt to write an accessible and, above all, *usable* introduction to social semiotics.

Although strongly inspired by Paris School semiotics, and especially by the work of Roland Barthes, which I first came across as a film school student in Amsterdam in the late 1960s, social semiotics has long since moved beyond an exclusive interest in structure and system.

- Just as in linguistics the focus changed from the 'sentence' to the 'text' and its 'context', and from 'grammar' to 'discourse', so in social semiotics the focus changed from the 'sign' to the way people use semiotic 'resources' both to produce communicative artefacts and events and to interpret them – which is also a form of semiotic production – in the context of specific social situations and practices.
- Rather than constructing separate accounts of the various semiotic modes – the 'semiotics of the image', the 'semiotics of music', and so on – social semiotics compares and contrasts semiotic modes, exploring what they have in common as well as how they differ, and investigating how they can be integrated in multimodal artefacts and events.
- Rather than describing semiotic modes as though they have intrinsic characteristics and inherent systematicities or 'laws', social semiotics focuses on how people regulate the use of semiotic resources – again, in the context of specific social practices and institutions, and in different ways and to different degrees.
- Finally, social semiotics is itself also a practice, oriented to observation and analysis, to opening our eyes and ears and other senses for the richness and complexity of semiotic production and interpretation, and to social intervention, to the discovery of new semiotic resources and new ways of using existing semiotic resources.

Although the approach to social semiotics presented here draws on a wide range of sources, the key impetus for its development was Halliday's social semiotic view of language (1978). In the second half of the 1980s and early 1990s, it was elaborated by the work of the Sydney Semiotics Circle, whose members included, among others, Jim Martin, Terry Threadgold, Paul Thibault, Radan Martinec, Anne Cranny-Francis, Jennifer Biddle and, above all, my long-time collaborator Gunther Kress – as well as, from a distance, Bob Hodge and Jay Lemke. In the 1990s I was influenced by my work with members of the critical discourse analysis group, especially Norman

Fairclough, Ruth Wodak, Teun van Dijk, Lilie Chouliaraki, Luisa Martin Rojo, Malcolm Coulthard and Carmen Caldas-Coulthard and, in different contexts, by my work on 'toys as communication' with Staffan Selander and on 'global media' with David Machin, and by discussions with Philip Bell, Adam Jaworski, Rick Iedema, Ron Scollon, Carey Jewitt, and Teal Triggs.

I must single out David Machin in particular. Our joint work over the past three years has not only produced several of the key examples I use in this book, it has also been a constant source of inspiration. The book would not have been the same without him.

Over the years I have taught the material presented in this book to students in linguistics, communication, interactive multimedia design, film studies, media studies and cultural studies, at Macquarie University, the London College of Printing and Cardiff University, as well as in short courses in a wide range of countries and institutions. This book is written for students, and it could not have existed without my own students' suggestions, comments, criticisms and extensions of the material. This includes present and past PhD students in London – especially Eleanor Margolies, Rob Flint, Cian Quayle and Maria Mencia – and Cardiff – especially Hanita Hassan, Lu Xing-Hua and Odysseas Constantinou. The book is also meant to be interdisciplinary and I hope that my many years of interdisciplinary teaching and research have helped me achieve at least something of this difficult aim.

Finally, I would like to thank Glen Stillar, Greg Myers, Per Ledin and Christabel Kirkpatrick for their useful comments on the manuscript, my editor, Louise Semlyen, for suggesting the book and waiting patiently for it, Julene Knox for all her work in chasing permissions for the illustrations, and Laura López-Bonilla for much appreciated moral support.

Theo van Leeuwen, March 2004

PART I

Semiotic principles

In part I, I discuss some of the principles that make social semiotics a new and distinctive approach to the practice and theory of semiotics. Where necessary, social semiotic concepts and methods are contrasted and compared to concepts from structuralist semiotics.

Above all, I hope two things will become clear in this part of the book:

1   Social semiotics is not 'pure' theory, not a self-contained field. It only comes into its own when it is applied to specific instances and specific problems, and it always requires immersing oneself not just in semiotic concepts and methods as such but also in some other field. When, in chapter 1, I explore the semiotics of office space, for instance, I need not just social semiotic concepts and methods but also concepts and methods from the theory and practice of office design and management. The same applies to the 'social' in 'social semiotics'. It can only come into its own when social semiotics fully engages with social theory. This kind of interdisciplinarity is an absolutely essential feature of social semiotics.

2   Social semiotics is a form of enquiry. It does not offer ready-made answers. It offers ideas for formulating questions and ways of searching for answers. This is why I end my chapters with questions rather than conclusions. These questions are not intended to invite readers to 'revise' the content of the preceding chapter but to encourage them to question it, to test it, to think it through independently – and to arrive at their own conclusions.

1 Semiotic resources

Semiotic resources

Books about semiotics often start with the question 'What is semiotics?' I would like to ask the question differently: 'What kind of *activity* is semiotics?', 'What do semioticians *do*?' And my answer is that semioticians do three things:

1 collect, document and systematically catalogue semiotic resources – including their history
2 investigate how these resources are used in specific historical, cultural and institutional contexts, and how people talk about them in these contexts – plan them, teach them, justify them, critique them, etc.
3 contribute to the discovery and development of new semiotic resources and new uses of existing semiotic resources.

The first two of these activities will be discussed and exemplified in this chapter, the third in chapter 2, where I deal with semiotic innovation.

The term 'semiotic resource' is therefore a key term in social semiotics. It originated in the work of Halliday who argued that the grammar of a language is not a code, not a set of rules for producing correct sentences, but a 'resource for making meanings' (1978: 192). In this book I extend this idea to the 'grammar' of other semiotic modes, and define semiotic resources as the actions and artefacts we use to communicate, whether they are produced physiologically – with our vocal apparatus; with the muscles we use to create facial expressions and gestures, etc. – or by means of technologies – with pen, ink and paper; with computer hardware and software; with fabrics, scissors and sewing machines, etc. Traditionally they were called 'signs'. For instance, a frown would be a sign of disapproval, the colour red a sign of danger, and so on. Signs were said to be the union of a signifier – an observable form such as a certain facial expression, or a certain colour – and a signified – a meaning such as disapproval or danger. The sign was considered the fundamental concept of semiotics. One of the most famous definitions of semiotics is that of Ferdinand de Saussure (1974 [1916]: 16) 'A science that studies the life of signs within society is conceivable ... I shall call it semiology (from Greek *semeion*, "sign").' In social semiotics the term 'resource' is preferred, because it avoids the impression that 'what a sign stands for' is somehow pre-given, and not affected by its use. As Hodge and Kress (1988: 18) have put it, in a discussion of the work of Vološinov – an important precursor of social semiotics – 'signs may not be divorced from the concrete forms of social intercourse

... and cannot exist, as such, without it'. So in social semiotics resources are signifiers, observable actions and objects that have been drawn into the domain of social communication and that have a *theoretical* semiotic potential constituted by all their past uses and all their potential uses and an *actual* semiotic potential constituted by those past uses that are known to and considered relevant by the users of the resource, and by such potential uses as might be uncovered by the users on the basis of their specific needs and interests. Such uses take place in a social context, and this context may either have rules or best practices that regulate how specific semiotic resources can be used, or leave the users relatively free in their use of the resource.

Semiotic resources are not restricted to speech and writing and picture making. Almost everything we do or make can be done or made in different ways and therefore allows, at least in principle, the articulation of different social and cultural meanings. Walking could be an example. We may think of it as non-semiotic behaviour, basic locomotion, something we have in common with other species. But there are many different ways of walking. Men and women walk differently. People from different parts of the world walk differently. Social institutions – the army, the church, the fashion industry – have developed their own special, ceremonial ways of walking. Through the way we walk, we express who we are, what we are doing, how we want others to relate to us, and so on. Different ways of walking can seduce, threaten, impress and much more. For this reason actors often start working on their roles by establishing how their characters might walk.

As soon as we have established that a given type of physical activity or a given type of material artefact constitutes a semiotic resource, it becomes possible to describe its semiotic *potential*, its potential for making meaning – for example, 'what kinds of walking can we observe, and what kinds of meanings can be made with them?' This is the first of the three semiotic activities described above, and it is one of the key contributions semioticians can make to interdisciplinary projects: inventorizing the different material articulations and permutations a given semiotic resource allows, and describing its semiotic potential, describing the kinds of meanings it affords. Again, the plural 'meanings' is crucial here, because just as dictionaries cannot predict the meaning which a word will have in a specific context, so other kinds of semiotic inventories cannot predict the meaning which a given facial expression – for example, a frown – or colour – for example, red – or style of walking will have in a specific context. We can say, for instance, that swaying hips have a potential for meaning something like the 'loosening up' or 'letting go' of some kind of restraint, but whether that 'letting go' will be used to convey sensuality or slovenliness depends on who 'lets go' of what, where and when, and on the other signs – other aspects of physical behaviour, style of dress, etc. – that accompany the swaying of the hips.

Closely related to the term 'semiotic potential' is the term 'affordance', which stems from the work of the psychologist Gibson (1979). According to Gibson, affordances are the potential uses of a given object. These, he says, stem directly from their observable properties. However, different observers might notice different affordances, depending on their needs and interests and on the specifics of the situation at hand. Perception is selective. And yet the other affordances are objectively there. Thus the meanings we find in the world, says Gibson, are both objective and subjective. This is evidently very similar to Halliday's concept of 'meaning potential', in which linguistic signifiers – words and sentences – have a signifying *potential* rather than specific meanings, and need to be studied in the social context. The difference is that the term 'meaning potential' focuses on meanings that have already been introduced into society, whether explicitly recognized or not, whereas 'affordance' also brings in meanings that have not yet been recognized, that lie, as it were, latent in the object, waiting to be discovered. No one can claim to know all the affordances of a given word or other semiotic 'object', yet as semioticians we do not need to restrict ourselves to what is, we can also set out to investigate what *could be*, as will be seen in the next chapter. The fact that resources have no objectively fixed meanings does not mean that meaning is a free-for-all. In social life people constantly try to fix and control the use of semiotic resources – and to justify the rules they make up – although more so in some domains than in others. The meaning of traffic signs, for instance, is fixed by precise rules, by a 'code'. It has to be, if we want to avoid accidents. In interpreting abstract art, on the other hand, we are usually given more freedom of interpretation.

Studying the semiotic potential of a given semiotic resource is studying how that resource has been, is, and can be used for purposes of communication, it is drawing up an inventory of past and present and maybe also future resources and their uses. By nature such inventories are never complete, because they tend to be made for specific purposes. Inventories of words, such as the dictionary or the thesaurus, may be made for the purposes of specialists, or of 'authors, translators, advertising copywriters and crossword-solvers' (sleeve notes of the *Roget's Thesaurus*), or of the 'general reader'. The same applies to other types of semiotic inventories. In chapter 4 I will describe an inventory of the ways in which children's toys can be designed to move or be moved. They can, for instance, be hard or soft – and therefore squeezable; they can be rigid or articulated – for example, the head and limbs of Barbie dolls and Action Men; they can be static or mobile – for example, toy cars; if they are mobile, they can be propelled in different ways – by hand, through a clockwork mechanism, through wind power – and so on. This inventory was drawn up in the context of a research project which looked at children's toys from the point of view of learning. The premise was that children – and adults – learn not only from looking and listening but also from manipulating objects. The inventory was therefore made from the point of view of a very specific relevance criterion. It had to be a systematic inventory of both the signifiers and the signifieds, both the physical properties of the objects and what could be learnt from them. For instance, from taking a toy apart children can learn what parts make up a given object, and from playing with a wind-powered toy – for example, a kite – children can learn about natural energy. It was a good example of the way new ideas – we called it the 'semiotics of kinetic design' – can come out of a very specific applied project, in which semioticians work together with others in an interdisciplinary context, in this case with educationalists and psychologists.

At the same time, we cannot always know beforehand what resources we will need, and we therefore also need inventories that are not made with an immediate, urgent purpose in mind. Today the patient work of the scholars who documented and decoded ancient hieroglyphic scripts, such as those of the Maya and Aztec civilizations, has suddenly found a new use in the design of icons for computer interfaces (Honeywill, 1999). What seemed 'pure research', the pursuit of knowledge for its own sake, has suddenly turned out to be a valuable resource for solving eminently practical problems of global computer-mediated communication. More generally, the collectors' culture of the past few centuries is now a very useful resource for artists, designers and other innovators. When such collections are no longer kept, our semiotic storehouses will be much less well-stocked, and our capacity for innovation will diminish. In the rest of this chapter I will use a specific example to illustrate how social semioticians might go about the first two activities described above, inventorizing a semiotic resource, and describing its use in a specific context.

Semiotic inventories: framing in magazine advertisements

To make an inventory we first need a collection. Collections for social semiotic research projects could be put together in several ways. In the case of walking we could make a collection of videotapes of people walking, whether secretly filmed for the purpose of the research, or taken from feature films and documentaries. One such collection, produced by a team of psychologists, consisted of a hundred 15-second scenes from CCTV footage, showing people walking just seconds before committing a crime (*Observer*, 22 July 2001: 11). But it could also be a collection of *descriptions* of walking, for instance from historical sources such as the 1766 Army drill regulations from which Foucault quotes in his discussion of disciplining 'docile bodies':

> The length of the short step will be a foot, that of the ordinary step, the double step and the marching step will be two feet, the whole measured from one heel to the next; as for the duration, that of the small step and the ordinary step will last one second, during which two double steps would be performed. The duration of the marching step will be a little longer than one second. The oblique step will take one second; it will be at most eighteen inches from one heel to the next ... The ordinary step will be executed forwards, holding the head up high and the body erect, holding oneself in balance successively on a single leg, and bringing the other forwards, the ham taut, the point of the foot a little turned outwards and low, so that one may without affectation brush the ground on which one must walk and place one's foot in such a way that each part may come to rest there at the same time without striking the ground.
>
> (Foucault, 1979: 15)

Just what kind of collection will be most appropriate clearly depends on the purpose of the inventory. Is it for the use of actors playing in historical dramas? Or for the purpose of police investigations? Or should it be a broader, multi-purpose inventory?

In our book *Reading Images* (1996) Gunther Kress and I introduced the notion of 'framing' in the context of visual communication. By 'framing' we meant the disconnection of the elements of a visual composition, for instance by frame-lines, pictorial framing devices – boundaries formed by the edge of a building, a tree, etc. – empty space between elements, discontinuities of colour, and so on. The concept also included the opposite, the ways in which elements of a composition may be visually connected to each other, through the absence of disconnection devices, through vectors, through similarities of colour, visual shape, and so on. The significance of this, its semiotic potential, we argued, is that disconnected elements will be read as in some sense separate and independent, perhaps even contrasting units of meaning, whereas connected elements will be read as belonging together in one way or another, as continuous or complementary, for instance. The photograph by Abigail Heyman (1974) in figure 1.1 uses the frame of the mirror to show two things as 'separate and disconnected' in this way, the woman's face in the mirror – her 'real self', perhaps – and the paraphernalia she uses to make herself presentable to the world – her 'mask', perhaps. It is a very heavy frame, and that constructs the divide between her two 'selves' as a very deep one. But framing can of course also be used for other purposes and in other ways, to separate pictures from text – or text boxes from the main text – in the layout of a magazine, for instance.

In *Reading Images* we did not describe framing in a great deal of detail. More specifically, we did not discuss the semiotic potential of different *types* of framing. We lumped a whole set of framing resources together – frame-lines, empty space, various

Figure 1.1   Growing Up Female (Abigail Heyman, 1974)

Figure 1.2   Shower advertisement (*House Beautiful*, September 1998: 34)

kinds of discontinuity– without asking whether their semiotic potential is the same or different. So let us see whether we can refine the theory a bit and make this into a demonstration of semiotic work, of the process of making a collection and an inventory – and hence a snippet of semiotic theory.

It is always a good idea to begin with a small and quite specific pilot study, and then gradually to enlarge the collection by adding other kinds of examples. Magazine advertisements are often a good starting point for studying aspects of visual communication, because they are obtained easily and tend to use a wide range of semiotic resources. Thirty to 40 examples will be plenty for a first exploration, so long as they include a range of different forms of framing, and several examples of each – to avoid misunderstandings, I should say at the outset that one advertisement may combine several types of framing.

In figure 1.2 text and image occupy distinct territories. The page is clearly divided into two kinds of space – picture space and text space. There are no words in the picture space and no pictures in the text space. The two spaces look quite distinct and although there are no frame-lines, the edges of the picture space form distinct boundaries, distinct and abrupt transitions between the two spaces. Other examples in the collection may have actual frame-lines of different thickness, and some of these may be 'iconic', made to resemble the gilded frame of a painting, or the perforated edges of photographic negative, for example.

The advertisement in figure 1.3 illustrates three different types of framing. First, the picture is almost monochrome, restricted to different tints of blue, except for the child's face on the label and the flowers, which are a bluish pink. The lettering immediately below the picture is also blue, as is the lettering on the banner bottom right. There is therefore a kind of colour 'rhyme' between the picture and (some of) the text, and this colour rhyme creates a degree of connection.

Second, there is empty space between the text immediately below the picture – 'Prevents premature ageing' – and the rest of the text. This, together with the typography and the colour, separates that part of the text from the other parts, signifies it as different in some way – just as is the case with the text above and the text below the picture in figure 1.2. Framing can thus make some parts of the text more connected to the picture than other parts. A very common example of this is the caption underneath (or to the side of) photographic illustrations, which is also separated from the main text by empty space – as well as, sometimes by other devices, for example, font.

Figure 1.3   Lenor Care advertisement (*House Beautiful*, September 1998: 15)

Third, there is a slight overlap between that text and the picture: the 'p' of 'Prevents premature ageing' intrudes into the picture. In other words, text can partially overlap with the picture space, forming a kind of link between the two. It is also possible for pictures to 'break out of their frame' to different degrees. In many advertisements a small superimposed picture of the product overlaps the picture space and the text space.

In figure 1.4 the words are inside the picture space. Here text and image do not occupy distinct territories. All of the space is picture space and the text is positioned inside it.

The same applies to figure 1.5 but in the opposite way. Here pictorial elements are taken out of their pictorial world, de-contextualized, so to speak, and entered into the textual space, the white page – small drop shadows still hint at three dimensions, but then, lettering may also have drop shadows. Many advertisements include two pictures – one presenting the fantasy attached to the product, the other the product itself. Frequently, the former is usually large and framed, and the latter smaller and unframed, integrated in the text space.

So far we have put together a more or less unordered collection of different types of framing. For the sake of space I have included only one example of each, but all are

Figure 1.4 Rémy Martin advertisement (*Wired,* November 1997: 47) by courtesy of E. Rémy Martin & Co.

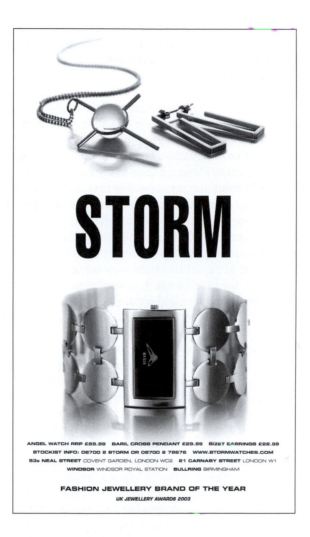

Figure 1.5   Storm advertisement (*Marie Claire*, May 2004: 174)

recognizable types that recur in many different advertisements. They also allow for modulation. There are not only kinds but also *degrees* of framing. Sometimes the picture space *gradually* changes into the text space. There are then still two distinct spaces but with a much less abrupt and clear-cut boundary between them. Finally, the few types of visual framing presented here do not exhaust all possible types. There is for instance also a difference between frames which are part of the represented world – 'diegetic', to use a term from film theory – as in the case of figure 1.1, and frames which are not, frames which have clearly been introduced by the image makers. The same is true for text. Text can be 'non-diegetic', superimposed on the image, or 'diegetic', part of the represented world, as with the label on the bottle in figure 1.4. My aim has not been to present a final product but to demonstrate how semiotic work is done. There is room for you to add further categories. However, given this set of observations, how can we now move towards a more systematic inventory? How can we encapsulate the semiotic potential opened up by the differences between these types of framing?

Let us try to order our observations. We have seen, first of all, how picture and text can be disconnected entirely, so that each lives in a quite separate and different world We now need to give this a name. Names are important. They allow us to hold on to the generalized essence of an observation, and to compare it to that of other observations. Let us call it 'segregation'. Next we have to try and describe its semiotic potential. Let us assume that segregation, whatever the precise context, is always likely to suggest that the segregated elements belong to two different orders. The context will then specify what these orders are. In the case of advertisements it is often the difference between fantasy – the dream world shown in the picture – and reality – the text that describes the actual product. Such an assumption is based on what segregation *is*. All we are assuming is that the actual *visual* segregation of two semiotic spaces can also *mean* the segregation, the keeping apart, of what is represented in these spaces.

Another way of disconnecting text and picture is by leaving empty space between them, by creating a kind of buffer zone or 'no-man's land' between them. Let us call this 'separation'. Let us then assume that, whatever the context, separation will always signify that the separated elements are the same or similar in some respects, and different in others. In the case of advertisements like figure 1.3, the separated parts may be different in terms of their communicative function, or in terms of their relation to the image. But they are all part of the verbal text, and in that sense they all belong to the same order of things.

It is also possible for picture and text to occupy the same space, to be 'integrated'. It can then either be that the text is integrated into the pictorial space – 'pictorial integration' – or that the picture is integrated into the textual space – 'textual integration'. In the case of advertising, pictorial integration absorbs text into the dream, the fantasy – 'reality text' is usually kept to a minimum and in very small print. Textual integration absorbs the picture into the real world – it is likely to show the actual advertised product or products only, rather than a whole scene.

We have also seen that frames may be porous. Part of the picture may break through the frame and spill out into the text space, or part of the text – or a superimposed picture of the product – may overlap with the picture and so link picture space and text space. We will call this 'overlap'. In the case of advertising, the overlap is likely to occur between the fantasy envisaged in the picture and the reality given by the text and the picture(s) of the product.

Finally it is possible for picture and text to 'rhyme', for instance through colour similarity. This signals that, although separate, they nevertheless have some quality in common. What that quality is then depends on the colour and its significance in the context. In figure 1.3 the colour is blue, and the connotation of this is glossed in the text as 'softness' and 'freshness'. The opposite is also possible. *Contrasts* can be enhanced by using opposite colours, opposite visual styles – for example, photography vs drawing – and so on.

   Let us summarize this inventory in the kind of 'system network' diagram (figure 1.6) that is often used in social semiotics to represent meaning potentials. The square brackets indicating 'either-or' choices and curly brackets 'both-and' choices.

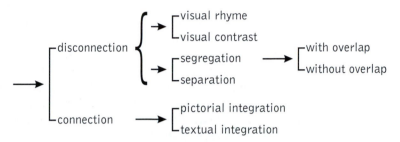

Figure 1.6   System network diagram: the framing of text and illustration in magazine advertisements

   We can also summarize the definitions of the terms we have introduced here:

Segregation	two or more elements occupy entirely different territories, and this indicates that they should be seen as belonging to different orders
Separation	two or more elements are separated by empty space, and this suggests that they should be seen as similar in some respects and different in others
Integration	text and picture occupy the same space – either the text is integrated in (for example, superimposed on) the pictorial space, or the picture in the textual space
Overlap	frames may be porous – for example, part of the picture may break through the frame or letters may be half in the pictorial space and half in the textual space
Rhyme	two elements, although separate, have a quality in common – what that quality is depends on the common feature (for example, a colour, a feature of form such as angularity or roundness, etc.)
Contrast	two elements differ in terms of a quality (as realized by a colour, or by formal features, etc.)

Note that there are *degrees* of framing, for example, a picture may gradually change into text space (fuzzy boundaries) – a frame may be thick or thin, etc.

   Two further points. First of all, the terms I have chosen for these types of framing are very general. They have to be, because they have to be applicable to a wide range of different contexts. They have to indicate a meaning potential, not a specific meaning, and their use will be different in different contexts. In advertising, framing will play a key role in playing with the boundaries between fantasy and reality. In other contexts different kinds of things will be disconnected or connected. In books and magazines, the text boxes might provide factual details or case stories, while the main text might give the broad outline, the general picture. Or the boxes might provide historical context, while the main text describes the present situation. In each case framing presents two things as belonging to different orders, as 'to be kept apart', whether it is the general and the detail, or history and the present. In traditional linear text such elements might be integrated.

Second, having completed a pilot study of the kind sketched here, the collection can now be extended, for instance by also including framing *within* the picture and *within* the text, and by including framing in other genres besides magazine advertising. It is my experience that this never yields a totally different set of categories. A few more categories may well have to be added, but on the whole it seems as if the same set of devices is used across a wide range of different types of text. There *is* something like a 'language' of visual communication, at least within the same broad cultural formation, but, and this is very important, it is drawn upon differently in different contexts. In different contexts people make different choices from the same overall semiotic potential and make different meanings with these choices. The set of semiotic choices that typify a given context is called a semiotic *register* (again, following Halliday, 1978).

This leads us to the second thing semioticians do. Semioticians not only inventorize semiotic resources, they also study registers. They also study how semiotic resources are used in the context of different social practices, and how people regulate their use in these contexts.

Semiotic inventories: framing in school and office buildings

In *Reading Images* (1996), Gunther Kress and I discussed framing as something specific to visual communication. Since then it has become clear to us that framing is a multimodal principle. There can be framing not only between the elements of a visual composition, or between the elements of a newspaper or magazine layout, but also between the people in an office, the seats in a train or restaurant (for example, private compartments vs sharing tables), the dwellings in a suburb, etc., and such instances of framing will be realized by similar kinds of semiotic resources – by 'frame-lines' (fences, partitions, etc.), empty space, discontinuities of all kinds, and so on. In time-based modes of communication 'framing' becomes 'phrasing' and is realized by semiotic resources such as the pauses and discontinuities of various kinds – rhythmic, dynamic, etc. – which separate the phrases of speech, of music, of actors' movements, etc. (see chapter 9). In other words, framing is a common semiotic principle, realized by different semiotic resources in different semiotic modes.

In this section I will therefore extend my inventory of types of framing into a new domain, the framing of interior space in offices and school buildings. This time my 'collection' comes from secondary sources – floor plans, descriptions and photographs of offices and schools in specialist literature (for offices: Browne, 1970; Boje, 1971; Eley and Marmot, 1995; Hartkopf et al., 1993; for schools: Bennett, 1978; McNicholas, 1978; Midwinter, 1978; Bennett et al., 1980). But it would of course also have been possible to collect such material first hand, by visiting offices and schools and documenting their design by means of floorplans, photographs and written notes.

Segregation

Partitions, ranging from curtains and flimsy screens to solid walls, can segregate spaces, and hence the people, groups and/or activities in them. Figure 1.7 shows the (somewhat simplified) layout of a unit designed for three teachers. Each teacher has a classroom-sized space ('home base') available. One of these spaces doubles as a (shared) practical ('wet') area. All can be segregated by curtains. Only the cloakroom and toilets have doors. There is also a shared 'quiet room' which can be segregated by means of sliding doors.

This example shows that the boundaries between segregated spaces can be of different 'thickness': walls, sliding doors, screens, or even 'thinner' partitions: the German designers who, in the 1950s, introduced the idea of the 'Bürolandschaft' ('office landscape') propagated the use of plants as dividers – outside, plants are of course often used for segregation, for example, hedges. This example therefore yields a new variable, something which we did not come across in considering magazine advertisements: the permanence or impermanence of frames.

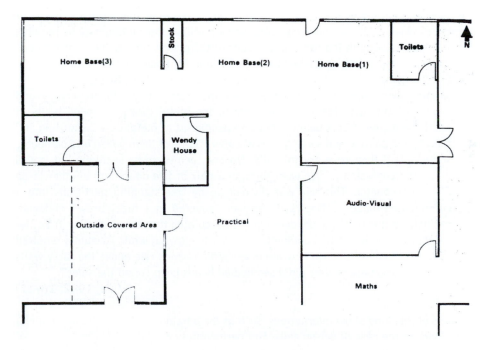

Figure 1.7   Semi-open teaching spaces (from Bennett et al., 1980: 53)

Permanence

Curtains and sliding doors can be opened or closed, and, when closed, locked or unlocked. This means that framing can be flexible and dynamic, and that a given framing device can be designed to allow several types of framing, segregation *and* separation, for instance, although never both at the same time. The free-standing partitions in open-plan offices can even be moved to a different position and many managers favour this because it affords flexibility, and allows 'any desired arrangement of work positions and sub-divisions with as frequent changes as required' (Boje, 1971: 8). On the other hand, partitions and furniture arrangements may also be permanent and bolted to the floor. Of course such arrangements can be undone. Even walls can be demolished. Nothing is entirely permanent. There are degrees of permanence. Nevertheless, some types of framing are designed to allow flexibility, while others are designed to fix social arrangements, to 'cast them in stone'. And that, clearly, is the semiotic potential of permanence and impermanence.

Permeability

Incarceration, being totally sealed off – or sealed in – is the limit case of segregation. But usually rooms have doors, and that allows some permeability, especially when the 'segregated' people can themselves decide whether or not to keep the doors open, as in the case of the offices of academics in universities. Even when doors remain locked or barred, or when partitions have no doors, some minimal interaction may be possible between spaces, as with the hatch in the door of the prison cell, or the gaps between the screens in this office, described by John Mole in his book *Brits at Work:*

> Monica, who worked in Personnel, took me from the plastic mahogany and subdued lighting of the executive floor to the metal desks and neon lights of Settlements, two floors below. About 30 people sat at metal desks, shuffling and ticking and passing and sorting piles of paper. Some of them gazed into computer screens as if they were crystal balls. No one seemed to be speaking but it was noisy and confusing ... We went through a pair of fire doors into another large office (Accounts). This one was divided up by free-standing partitions into a complicated maze ... The partitions were covered in a fuzzy brown material, repulsive to the touch, to deaden sound. I speculated that the work flow in Settlements was conducive to a completely open office layout while Accounts required small isolated units. Then why did disembodied hands rise above the furry walls with files and papers, why did disembodied heads peep round the sides?
>
> (Mole, 1992: 16–17)

Gaps of this kind allow interactions, such as the passing across of files and papers, or of food, in the case of prison cells. But permeability may be restricted to perception, either aural, or visual, or both. The so-called 'Prussian' school design, popular from 1873 onwards – both within and outside Germany – and still around today, has the top half of classroom walls glazed, to allow the headmaster to keep an eye on things. The partitions in open-plan offices, despite their sound-deadening fabrics, block vision, at least when the workers are sitting (their height tends to be around 1.60 m), but not sound – and complaints about noise are common in open-plan offices.

The semiotic potential of permeability lies in its capacity to limit interaction, to create obstacles to open interaction which can only be removed by those who hold the key. The semiotic potential of partial permeability – only vision, or only sound – lies in the differences between sound and vision. Vision creates a sharp division between its subject and object. The object of vision is precisely that, a 'thing', isolated, to be scrutinized with detachment, like a goldfish in a bowl. The subject of vision possesses and controls this object, while remaining at a distance: 'to see is to gather knowledge and to be in power' (Parret, 1995: 335). Sound, on the other hand, connects, and requires surrender to and immersion in participatory experience: 'it is above all through hearing that we live in communion with others' (De Buffon, 1971: 199).

Separation

Not only the parts of a text on a page but also the people in a space can be separated by empty space. Figure 1.8 shows an early (1935) landscaped office. Separation is achieved not only by empty space but also by the way the desks are angled. The roman numerals designate (I) Directors and secretaries, (II) Assistant sales manager and sales order clerks, (III) Buyers and stock controllers, (IV) Outside representatives, (V) Accounts, (VI) Typing and statistics, (VII) Reception, (VIII) Showroom salesmen.

Rhyme

Like the elements of magazine advertisements, segregated people or groups can be connected in terms of common visual qualities such as colour – or contrasted in similar ways. In the case of space this goes beyond the visual and extends to other physical qualities, for instance the material of which furniture is made, for example, the plastic mahogany and metal desks in the John Mole quote above, or lighting, as in the case of the subdued lighting and the neon lighting in the same quote. The semiotic potential of such physical differences is that they can indicate status (management vs workers), functions within the organization (Settlements vs Accounts), etc., in short, a range of common or contrasting aspects of identity.

Summarizing all this in a 'system network' diagram (figure 1.9):

Segregation	the segregation of interior spaces is, again, a matter of degree, ranging from curtains and flimsy screens to solid walls
Permanence	curtains and sliding doors can be opened or closed, and, when closed, locked or unlocked

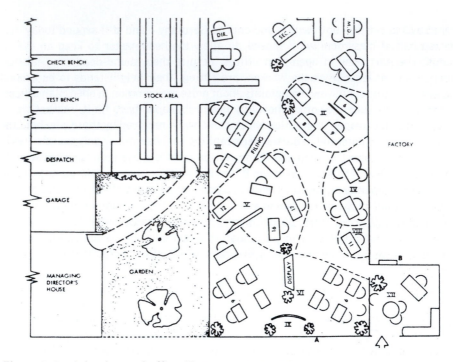

Figure 1.8   A landscaped office (Browne, 1970: 44)

Permeability	although total incarceration is possible, most walls have doors, which allows permeability (= 'overlap'). In offices people may be able to look over partitions when standing up, or hear what is going on in adjoining spaces
Separation	realized by empty space, furniture arrangement, etc.
Rhyme/contrast	realized by similarities and difference in colours and materials

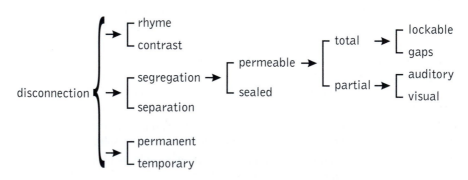

Figure 1.9   System network diagram: the framing of space in offices and schools

Comparing this diagram to the one in the preceding section shows that rhyme and contrast, as well as segregation and separation are *multimodal* semiotic principles. There are differences in terms of the elements involved – people and their activities as opposed to verbal and visual representations – and in terms of physical realization – partitions, fences etc. as opposed to frames, boxes etc. – but the semiotic work is the same: to connect or disconnect, to segregate or separate, to create similarity or contrast.

Both diagrams also include a distinction between clear-cut unambiguous bound-aries and fuzzy boundaries. But the terms I have used differ – 'overlap' in the one case, and 'permeability' in the other. Clearly another, slightly more general term is needed, a term which can encompass the many ways – some specific to magazine layout, some to interior design – in which boundaries can blur and categories overlap. A more detailed study of the semiotic strategies for creating such fuzzy boundaries could well make a significant contribution to semiotic and social life.

I also distinguished forms of 'partial permeability' – visual only, or auditory only – a distinction which, in the case of magazine advertisements was not necessary but might well be helpful, for instance, in thinking about audio-visual texts such as films and television programmes.

The use of semiotic resources: open-plan schools and offices

The same or similar framing resources were and are used in different social contexts and in different periods. The historical aspect is important here. It brings out more clearly than anything else how people use – and adapt, and transform – semiotic resources according to the interests and needs of the time and the setting.

In the nineteenth century, primary schools, although still voluntary, increased in number and began to receive government grants:

> Faced for the first time with the task of providing for mass education, administra-tors turned initially to a type of school which had been common in England since the Middle Ages. This consisted of one very large schoolroom in which a number of forms were taught at the same time, usually by one master and several assis-tants known as ushers.
>
> (Bennett et al., 1980: 13)

The most common design was the 'Lancaster model' introduced in the late eighteenth century and consisting of a schoolroom accommodating 320 children: 'rows of desks were arranged to face the master's platform, spaced so as to allow the monitors [another term for 'ushers'] to move freely between the rows' (Bennett et al., 1980: 14). It was a 'factory system', 'a piece of social machinery that was both simple and economical' (Lawson and Silver, 1973: 241). An alternative system was devised by Andrew Bell, an early nineteenth century clergyman. It involved curtaining off areas where the monitors could help groups of 10 to 20 pupils prepare for the recitations they had to give to the master.

When compulsory primary education was introduced in 1870, it was no longer possible to have only one certified teacher per school. The led to the idea of the 'class' as the main unit of organization and to the segregation of school buildings into class-rooms and corridors – or verandas or quadrangles. By the 1930s, influenced by the pioneering work of educators like Maria Montessori, the classroom system had already begun to be criticized. According to the Hadow Report on Primary Education (1931) teachers began to 'question the efficacy of class instruction and to look for something better' (quoted in Bennett et al., 1980: 17). The ideal infant school would be 'not a classroom but a playground, that is to say, not a limited space enclosed by four walls but an open area' (ibid.). In a 1959 Handbook for Primary Teachers, published by the Ministry of Education, teachers were encouraged to 'arrange the environment in the classroom and school so that children can learn for themselves, either individually or in small groups' (quoted in Bennett et al., 1980: 19). From this period on most new schools were built according to the open-plan model.

A similar development took place in the design of offices. Prior to the 1950s, rank determined how many people were to occupy one office and how much space each person would have. The UK civil service used eleven main standards, expressed as ranges to allow for the differences between buildings. A single department, the Prop-erty Services Agency presided over the allocation of space to 600,000 civil servants. In the 1950s the open-plan office broke through, largely through the work of the German Quickborner team of designers. Even in the civil service hierarchies were now flattened, and space allocations made, for instance, by individual ministries, rather than centrally. In other words, the same new pattern of framing, the same move from segregation towards separation and increased permeability and impermanence, was introduced in several separate settings at the same time.

Not all users of open spaces will be aware of these histories, however much they have shaped their everyday experience. So what do framing practices mean today, in a given context, for the people who have to live with them? How do *they* describe and evaluate the meanings of framing? How do they enforce or proscribe forms of framing, recom-mend or condemn them, justify or critique them? This can be studied through interviews with participants, but also through documents, such as government handbooks for teachers, office management textbooks, company documents, etc. My discussion in the remainder of this section relies on secondary materials, for the most part dating from the 1970s, the heyday of open-plan school and office design.

De-segregation

The de-segregation of offices space is 'read' differently by different participants. For many office workers it means losing their own office, or losing an office in which they had been able to work together with a small group in a relatively independent way, left alone to do their work, able to make private calls or chat without being overheard by supervisors. To them segregation means privacy, security, a sense of identity or small group solidarity, and the ability to get on with concentrated work. De-segregation means being constantly watched, supervised, controlled. Here are some of the questionnaire and interview responses quoted in Eley and Marmot:

> 'A total open plan system is not conducive to concentration. This needs urgent action. The noise at times is appalling. Interruptions are frequent and unnecessary.'

> 'The open plan concept has failed. People feel cramped for space, and the noise levels cause constant distractions.'

> 'Open plan is like trying to have a pee in an open field. There's nowhere to hide.'

> 'I think it is necessary for staff to have space that is their own ... I think that having one's own little reasonably secure space that can be personalised to a degree is psychologically very important to most people.'
>
> (Eley and Marmot, 1995: 19, 85, 86)

To the managers, on the other hand, de-segregation is a way of influencing behaviour, a way of creating 'team spirit', of making employees identify with the company as a whole. And they also see it as a way of decreasing conflict, and increasing control, flexibility, and productivity. According to a German management consultant, de-segregation creates 'a new type of office user', who 'speaks more softly, is more considerate, dresses correctly and carefully, and conducts arguments at a calmer pitch' (Boje, 1971: 64). Segregation, on the other hand, is seen as incompatible with company interests. According to one recent British management textbook, it is the 'bullies, the self-important and the truly antisocial' who 'create enclosures and empires quite irrelevant to the smooth working of the whole organisation' (Eley and Marmot, 1995: 89). Small groups in separate offices, likewise, 'have a particularly rigidifying effect, making it hard to create new groups, dissolve them and bring them together in different forms' (ibid., 78). Managers know that workers see this differently. But they have to press on regardless. When introducing the open-plan office, advises a management consultant, 'all stories should be listened to patiently, but without attributing dramatic significance to them. After three to six months these phenomena will have disappeared and output will settle down to a normal level or above' (Boje, 1971: 62).

What does open-plan framing mean in the case of schools? Again it depends on who you are listening to. Head teachers are likely to see open-plan framing as 'fostering socialisation and good attitudes to work' (Bennett, 1978: 47): 'It is good for children to see what others are doing'. 'In open plan children learn to respect other people and pool ideas' (Bennett et al, 1980: 194). In teachers it will foster co-operation, team work, flexibility and versatility. In a large survey (ibid., 1980) the majority of head teachers favoured open-plan framing – but only one third of teachers did. Teachers found the need for constant co-operation and negotiation demanding and exhausting, and saw it as eroding their autonomy. They also complained about noise and visual distraction, and the lack of any form of personal space: 'There are no nooks and crannies. Children can't get away from us and we can't get away from them' (Bennett et al., 1980: 194). Many teachers use blackboards and storage units to re-introduce some segregation between different groups; 'As privacy and security are lost alternative cover is arranged – thus the prevalence of the so-called regressive classroom' (Bennett et al., 1980: 33).

As for the children, their opinion is not often asked. Perhaps it should be. Surveys report that children, especially boys, do better in traditional schools, even in creative work. They also make more friends in traditional schools. Open-plan framing is said to work well for middle-class, 'high ability' and 'independent' children, but for others, including especially timid and insecure children, it is less beneficial (Bennett et al., 1980: 42–9).

Separation

From the point of view of managers, separation in offices promotes efficiency, because it makes it possible to 'place close together groups with a frequent need to contact each other' (as seen in figure 1.8). It allows subdivision without partitions, so that the sense of an overall team spirit can be preserved. According to Eley and Marmot (1995: 76–7):

> For a team to work together its members must be in communication. One way to achieve this is for all the members of the team to share a work room or space that helps to foster communication. ... High levels of interaction are encouraged in locations where lines of sight and access routes on the office floor link many workplaces.

Another management text speaks of 'optimum information flow, unhindered by doors' (Boje, 1971: 8). Needless to say, this does not necessarily accord with the views of office users, who, as we have seen, complain of distraction, noise and loss of individuality and privacy.

In schools separation is used to group children around different activities ('activity tables'). 'Open space between clusters of desks is used as a boundary-defining mechanism, and the effect is often reinforced by varying the orientation and arrangement of desks and tables' (Bennett et al., 1980: 29). Thus children can form separate groups while still 'seeing what the others are doing'.

Impermanence

Key features of the open-plan office are flexibility and cost efficiency:

> Internal flexibility over the largest possible floor area permits any desired arrangement of work positions and sub-divisions with as frequent changes as

required. When it is merely necessary to shift movable screens, storage units and the like, heavy conversion costs are avoided.

(Boje, 1971: 8)

Recent management ideas push the elimination or reduction of private and individual spaces in offices even further. This includes 'desk sharing', where office space is booked in the way one books a hotel room, work stations on wheels where permanent possessions are housed within mobile units to be wheeled to the most appropriate location, and so on. All this is meant to increase the efficient use of space, to make space more productive. No room, no desk must ever be unused. But it is unpopular with most workers:

We was robbed! Why are we the ones lumbered with this poor system? It wastes time, decreases feelings of personal involvement (I'm just a cog, I fit anywhere), reduces feelings of team involvement.

(quoted in Eley and Marmot, 1995: 19)

Open-plan schools also use flexible framing – curtains, sliding screens and so on (see figure 1.8). Fixed furniture arrangements have given way to lightweight loose furniture, and versatile screens and storage units. This 'offers teachers increased possibilities to adapt the space to their particular style of working' (Bennett et al., 1980: 179). Even a form of desk sharing exists, as some education authorities have a policy of providing 70 per cent seating, on the grounds that not all children will have to sit at the same time (ibid.: 180).

Conclusion

Detailed studies of the use of a given semiotic resource are interesting in their own right, but they also demonstrate a theoretical point. They show how the semiotic potential of framing is inflected on the basis of the interests and needs of a historical period, a given type of social institution, or a specific kind of participant in a social institution. On the one hand, my original gloss of the meaning of framing applies to all the instances I have discussed above: 'disconnected elements are read as in some sense separate and independent, perhaps even contrasting units, whereas connected elements are read as belonging together in some way, as continuous or complementary, for instance'. On the other hand, this basic meaning is inflected differently in different contexts. In early nineteenth century schools, connection means 'homogeneity', factory-style drill; in contemporary offices it means 'identifying with the company as a whole' – which does not exclude being involved in different activities. Again, one of the meanings of open-plan framing in contemporary offices is cost-efficiency and increased productivity; in schools this is less so, at least in the way the immediate participants talk about it – for education authorities cost efficiency and space saving have become important factors from the late 1940s onwards, hence in the same period that developed open-plan school buildings. And again, while for office workers segregation means security and privacy, for managers it means lack of control and company spirit. To this we can add cultural differences. The open-plan office, for instance, is reported to be much more widely accepted in the USA and Japan than in Europe, despite the work of the German *Bürolandschaft* designers. This clearly indicates different cultural attitudes towards individuality and team spirit, or, in the terms of the American sociologist Riesman, towards 'inner-directedness' and 'outer-directedness'.

Different inflections of the meaning of framing stem from different sources. Broad cultural and historical differences stem from what, in chapter 5, I will refer to as 'discursive formations', from the key 'themes' of a culture and period. Such themes will be used to model, and to evaluate and legitimate (or critique) a wide range of salient practices in the given culture or period. In the early days of the industrial society, the 'factory model', the discourse of discipline (in the sense of Foucault, 1979) was such a theme. In prisons, factories, schools, hospitals, even in orchestras, people's behaviour was regulated in similar ways, and these new practices were discussed and justified in similar terms. Today, in the 'information society', the 'corporate model' plays this role, and has spawned new ways of regulating people's behaviour, and a new discourse to justify this, the discourse of productivity and flexibility and teamwork which gradually erodes the 'inner-directed' spirit of autonomous, individual activity – for example, in many of the professions – to make place for more 'outer-directed', team-spirited and manager-led forms of activity.

Contextual differences, on the other hand, stem, at least in part, from the actual, more specific differences in the activities involved, the difference between office work and teaching and learning for instance – although it could be argued that, today, these two have come to resemble each other more.

Differences between different participants of the same practice, finally, between managers and workers, for instance, stem from the different interests of these participants, from who they are and what their role is in the given context – or sometimes, on who they identify with, on who they *want* to be – and they focus especially on evaluations and legitimations. What to the one is a gain, is a loss to the other. What the one values positively, the other values negatively.

Despite all these differences there is a common element – a common understanding of the basic meaning potential of the semiotic resource of framing, of what is at stake when we make or break frames. It is easy to overstate either commonality or difference. Social semiotics seeks to do justice to both.

Exercises

1   In *Reading Images* (1996: 183) Gunther Kress and I defined visual *salience* as the way in which the elements in a visual composition are made to attract the viewer's attention to different degrees because of the way they may be placed in

the foreground or background, and/or because of relative size, contrasts in tonal value or colour, differences in sharpness, and so on. Make a collection of a certain type of text – for example, magazine advertisements – and identify three different types of salience. Describe these types both in terms of their physical realization and their semiotic potential.

2   Would it be possible to apply the concept of salience to the exteriors of buildings? Give examples of the kinds of things that can be made salient, and of how they are made salient.

3   Find a discourse about salience, that is a text in which someone describes what is or should be made to attract the viewer's attention in a given context. It could be a director of photography talking about the lighting of a scene, a garden designer talking about where to plant certain flowers, a writer talking about what points to emphasize, or one of countless other possible examples. What reasons do they give for their use of the semiotic resource of salience?

4   Compare the framing of office space in an American and a European television police series.

5   Would it be possible to apply an idea from this chapter's account of the framing of interior spaces to the framing of advertisements, and develop 'permanent' or 'temporary' frames in advertisements – for example, on the web? How might this work? What advantages could it have?

2 Semiotic change

Semiotic innovation

Social semioticians not only inventorize semiotic resources and investigate how semiotic resources are used in specific contexts, they also contribute to the discovery and development of new semiotic resources and new ways of using existing semiotic resources. In other words, semioticians can contribute to semiotic change. Until recently, semiotic change has not been high on the semiotic agenda. One reason lies in de Saussure's (1974 [1916]) distinction between 'synchronic' and 'diachronic' semiotics. A synchronic description is a description of a state of affairs as it is at a given moment in time, a kind of snapshot or freeze frame. A diachronic description is a historical description, a description of how things change and evolve. Reacting against the predominance of diachronic descriptions of language in his day, de Saussure made a plea for describing language synchronically, as a system. He did not want to see this replace diachronic description, merely to complement it. But subsequently the pendulum swung the other way. Systematic, synchronic semiotics took off. Historical, diachronic semiotics had to take a backseat and virtually ground to a halt. This is a pity because studying how things came into being is a key to understanding why they are the way they are, and unfortunately people have a tendency to forget this and reconstruct history so that things come to be seen as part of a natural order rather than as invented for specific reasons which may well no longer exist.

Social semiotics attempts to combine the 'synchronic' system and the 'diachronic' narrative, as is hopefully evident from the way this book is written. Three aspects are singled out:

- *Social reasons for the change*
  As society changes, new semiotic resources and new ways of using existing semiotic resources may be needed. In this chapter I will discuss this by looking at a case study, typography. For a long time typography saw its role as one of trans-mitting the words of authors as clearly and legibly as possible, without adding anything of its own to the text. Today it is changing into a semiotic mode in its own right, and beginning to add its own, typographically realized meanings, alongside and simultaneously with those realized by the author's words. One aim of this chapter is to place this development in its social and historical context.
- *Resistance to change*
  Semiotic change often meets with resistance, because past ways of doing things may be 'hardwired' in technologies, or in the layout of buildings, or because people

with a vested interest in past ways of doing things see their traditional values threatened and try to hold back change. The new developments in typography threatened the traditional privileges and values of typographers in this way, and, as we will see, ever since these developments first emerged in the 1920s, typographers have criticized them as anathema to typography's true calling.

- *Principles of semiotic innovation*
  But the main business of this chapter is to explain how semiotic change is actually brought about – through metaphor and connotation. Because every semiotic resource and every use of every semiotic resource was once an innovation, metaphor and connotation are always there in the background, but this often gets forgotten – an aspect I will say more about when I discuss 'motivation' in the next chapter.

The new typography

Some semiotic practices are not really in need of innovation. They function quite adequately within well-defined boundaries and on the basis of long-established traditions and values. Until very recently, typography was such a field, essentially conservative, taking its cues from the tradition of the printed book even when dealing with other media, and looking back to the old masters of the trade for their inspiration and values, as in this example where the twentieth century American designer W.A. Dwiggins describes how he designed the Caledonia typeface:

> We turned to one of the types that Bulmer used, cut for him by William Martin around 1790 ... An attempt was made to add weight to the characters and still keep some of the Martin swing ... that quality in the curves, the way they get away from the straight stem with a calligraphic flick, and in the nervous angle on the underside of the arches as they descend to the right.
>
> (Quoted in McLean, 2000: 60)

In this context, the boundaries between typography, calligraphy and illustration were clear-cut. According to McLean (2000: 56), designer and author of the *Thames and Hudson Manual of Typography*:

> When rope is coiled to form the word 'Ship Ahoy', or branches writhe into 'Our Trees' ... that is illustration, not calligraphy.

Avant-garde experiments were not seen as particularly relevant because, like the art of the film editor, typography was considered a self-effacing art which should not get in the way of the words themselves. This did not exclude a connoisseur's appreciation of the fine details of different typefaces – debates could rage over small but crucial details such as whether to use serifs or not and, if so, what kind of serifs. According to Beatrice Warde, a writer on typography in the 1930s and 1940s:

> Printing demands a humility of mind, for the lack of which many of the fine arts are even now floundering in self-conscious and maudlin experiments. There is nothing simple or dull in achieving the transparent page. Vulgar ostentation is twice as easy as discipline. The 'stunt typographer' learns the fickleness of rich men who hate to read. Not for them are the long breaths held over serif and kern, they will not appreciate your splitting of hair-spaces. Nobody save other craftsmen will appreciate half your skill.
>
> (Warde, 1995: 77)

Above all, typography was not regarded as semiotic. It was grudgingly acknowledged that 'to a very limited extent, lettering may help to express a feeling or a mood that is in harmony with the meaning of the words' (McLean, 2000: 56), but for the most part 'lettering and calligraphy are abstract arts ... What moves us is something formal, and, in the last resort, inexplicable' (ibid.: 54).

In this context of centuries of such continuity and consistency, research was not necessary. Apprentices could learn all they needed to know from studying the masters:

> Research in legibility, even when carried out under the most 'scientific' conditions, has not yet come up with anything that typographic designers did not already know with their inherited experience of five hundred years of printing history ... No research so far published has been seriously helpful to designers.
>
> (McLean, 2000: 47)

The exception of course was the Bauhaus period in the 1920s, when designers such as Jan Tschichold analysed the basic letterform in an attempt to create a *Skelettschrift* ('skeleton lettering'), a rational and functional typeface appropriate to the modern, industrial era. Such typefaces did away with serifs and with 'entasis' – differences in thickness and thinness within letters – and included as many interchangeable components as possible – for example, the 'bowls' of 'a', 'b', 'p', 'd', 'g' and 'q' were all made identical, which they usually are not. McLean compared it unfavourably with more traditional design, and with a particular pre-war British typographer:

> This seductive theory had to be paid for in loss of legibility, since the effect was to reduce the differences ... Eric Gill's sans was different in that it was drawn by an artist and designer who was already deeply involved with the classical roman alphabet ... His letters contained subtleties and refinements which the German designers, preferring the logic (or dictatorship) of ruler and compasses, could not admit.
>
> (McLean, 2000: 67)

However, all this has changed. Suddenly typography is faced with a challenge and as a result research in a wide range of ideas and practices has become newly relevant, for instance research in previously marginal areas such as signwriting, film titles, etc., or into legibility itself. Typographers themselves now seek to do away with the boundaries between typography and the other graphic and photographic arts, and recognize the semiotic nature of typography. Bellantoni and Woolman (1999), for instance, say that the printed word has two levels of meaning, the 'word image', that is the idea represented by the word itself, constructed from a string of letters, and the 'typographic image', the 'holistic visual impression'. And Neuenschwander (1993: 13, 31) calls typography 'a fully developed medium of expression' possessing 'a complex grammar by which communication is possible', and quotes the Swiss designer Hans-Rudolf Lutz, who has said: 'Gestaltung ist auch Information' ('design is also information') (ibid.: 73).

The reason for all this is that new demands are made on typographic meaning. Typography is called upon to express new kinds of things, for instance the 'identities' of films, music, companies, etc.: 'Logos are twentieth century heraldry, serving as battle standards in the fight for profit' (Neuenschwander, 1993: 80). And typography is vitally involved in forging the new relationships between images, graphics and letterforms that are required in the age of computer-mediated communication, a form of communication which is on the one hand far more oriented towards writing than previous screen media such as film and television, but on the other hand also far more visually oriented than previous page media such as books. Even ordinary computer users must make meaningful choices from a wide array of letterforms, and combine them with images and graphic elements in meaningful ways. Where the new typography has not yet been able to make its mark, for example, in email, typographers are hard at work to introduce it. American artist Kathryn Marsan designed a program which interprets email writers' handwriting and then chooses a typeface and colour to convey their moods and personalities. Even aspects of the dynamics of the users' handwriting are typographically 'translated', for example, pressure on the user's pen will make the letters on the screen bolder. Marsan has clearly opted for an 'automatic' solution here, a program that makes choices *for* the user. It would also be possible, and I would prefer this, to teach the basics of the semiotics of typography to users in the same way as the basics of the semiotics of writing have already been taught for so long – and hopefully as something which, like writing, has room for both rules and creativity. How to do this is by no means settled. It is an object of ongoing semiotic research and innovation, and an area to which semioticians can make a real contribution.

Experiential metaphor

Metaphor is a key principle of semiotic innovation. Aristotle already knew it in the fourth century BC: 'Ordinary words convey only what we already know, it is from metaphor that we can best get hold of something new' (Aristotle, 1954: 1410b). Although this was, to Aristotle, less a matter of creating new ideas than of creating new ways of *expressing* ideas, we will see that metaphors are also vital in creating new ideas and new practices.

The essence of metaphor is the idea of 'transference', of transferring something from one place to another, on the basis of a perceived similarity between the two 'places'. In the Aristotelian view of metaphor – the view of metaphor as new *expression* – that something is a word which is transferred from one meaning to another, on the basis of a partial similarity between the two meanings. As it happens the word metaphor is itself a metaphor. It originally meant 'transport' – in Greece you can see it written on every lorry. Clearly the ancient Greeks perceived a similarity between transporting goods between places and transporting words between meanings. Here is another example. On the front page of my newspaper this morning I read 'Clarke savages Duncan Smith'. The verb 'savage' literally means 'to attack ferociously and wound' and it is usually said of animals. But the newspaper transports it from the domain of its usual application to another domain, that of politicians strongly criticizing each other, and it does this on the basis of an imputed similarity between the two domains – by virtue of the metaphor strong criticism is compared to a ferocious and bloody physical attack. This not only makes the headline vivid and dramatic, it also adds new meaning; it also interprets politics as a combat without rules, an 'anything goes' dogfight over power and influence.

The concept of metaphor is a multimodal concept and can be applied also to semiotic modes other than language. Political cartoons have often represented politicians as animals, or more precisely, as half-animal, half-human, since they have to be recognizable.

Figure 2.1   'Gulf War', by Moir, *Sydney Morning Herald*

The French semiotician Jacques Durand (1970) showed how metaphors and many other types of 'figurative language' can be and are applied in advertising images, and the same theme was explored in recent books on visual metaphors in art (Hausman, 1989) and advertising (Forceville, 1996).

The Aristotelian concept of metaphor as novel expression has been especially dominant in literary theory. According to Hawkes (1972: 17):

> We think of metaphor as a direct linguistic realisation of *personal* experience. Even banalities such as 'like a sledgehammer', 'a hot knife through butter', 'a bull in a china shop', aim at a 'vivid', 'striking' and 'physical' quality that relates *accurately* to events in the world.

He compares this to pre-Enlightenment Europe where 'metaphor reproduced the intelligible world'. The words of a twentieth century poet like Eliot, for instance, provide striking and accurate 'word pictures':

> I am aware of the damp souls of housemaids/Sprouting despondently at area gates,

while the words of poets like the early seventeenth century poet Thomas Campion are aimed not at creating word pictures but at making conventional references to aspects of the religious conception of reality that was dominant at the time, in this case to the Garden of Eden:

> There is a garden in her face/Where roses and white lilies grow/A heav'nly paradise is that place/Wherein all pleasant fruits do flow.

But Hawkes also points out that, from Vico onwards, many philosophers and poets saw metaphors as creating rather than depicting reality. Vico, in *New Science* (1725), saw abstract and analytical modes of thinking and writing as evolving out of the metaphors, symbols and myths which, long ago, created the reality we experience, and which are still deeply ingrained in the language we use today.

This idea has been taken up in a number of ways in the twentieth century, for instance by anthropologists (for example, Lévi-Strauss, 1962) and linguists, for example, Benjamin Whorf (1956), who argued that native American languages do not just say the same things differently but embody different outlooks on the world, different realities. More recently the theme has been taken up by Lakoff and Johnson, who see metaphor as 'one of the most basic mechanisms we have for understanding experience' (1980: 211), not only in ancient times, or small traditional societies, or before the Enlightenment, but also in today's world. Even in the context of highly rational endeavours such as science, ideas begin as metaphors, for instance the idea of 'wave' as applied to light, or, as we will see in detail in chapter 5, the idea of the heart as a pump.

Most metaphors may once have been innovative but are no longer. We do not even think of them as metaphors. They embody our everyday reality. They are the 'metaphors we live by', to use Lakoff and Johnson's telling phrase. The metaphorical meaning of 'savage', even though, if pressed, we can still recognize it as a metaphor, has become so common that it is included in my 1992 edition of the Collins dictionary as a standard meaning of the word – 'to criticize violently' is listed alongside 'to attack ferociously and wound'. Such metaphors are not isolated instances of felicitous expression, they are ingrained ways of thinking, part and parcel of contemporary journalism's jaded view of the political process. To journalists, and no doubt to many of their readers, they are not metaphors but the literal truth. Politicians *are* driven by ruthless ambition, the basic struggle for power and survival.

Lakoff and Johnson call such metaphors 'structural' – they entail a whole complex of ideas. The metaphor 'theories are buildings', for instance, entails such a complex of ideas, making it possible to say things like 'we've got the *framework* for a *solid* argument', 'If you don't *support* your argument with *solid* facts, the whole thing will *collapse*', and so on (Lakoff and Johnson, 1980: 98). In other words, the structure of a building can become a vehicle for understanding the structure of theories, at least in theory, because in fact only some parts of the building are commonly used in this way: the foundations and the outer shell. To speak of a theory as having rooms and corridors would be far more unusual than to speak of it as having a 'solid foundation'.

It is only when metaphors go beyond the beaten track that they begin to contribute to innovation, for instance by extending the 'used part' of a metaphor – for example, by saying 'these facts are the bricks and mortar of my theory' – or by extending the metaphor to the 'unused parts' – for example, by speaking of 'massive Gothic theories covered with gargoyles' (ibid: 53) – or by inventing wholly new metaphors – for example, 'Classical theories are patriarchs who father many children, most of whom fight incessantly' (ibid: 53). Because all metaphors are based on similarity, and as all similarities are partial, all metaphors tend to highlight some aspects of their domain of application and obscure others. New metaphors will therefore highlight new aspects, but they may also obscure aspects which previously were out in the open. New metaphors also tend to be structural, extending out to a whole network of ideas and associations, allowing new things to be noticed, new connections to be made, and new actions to be taken as a result. One of Lakoff and Johnson's examples of such a new metaphor is 'love is a collaborative work of art', and they note (ibid: 152) that it:

> ... picks out a certain range of our love experiences and defines a structural similarity between the entire range of highlighted experiences and the range of experiences involved in producing collaborative works of art ... for example, a frustrating love experience may be understood as being similar to a frustrating art experience not merely by virtue of being frustrating but as involving the kind of frustration peculiar to jointly producing works of art.

It is clear that metaphors of this kind can not only give us certain ways of understanding love but also help us plot new courses of action, for instance new ways of dealing with frustration.

We understand metaphors on the basis of our concrete experience: 'No metaphor can ever be comprehended or even adequately represented independently of its experiential basis' (Lakoff and Johnson, 1980: 19). This is a crucial point, not least because of its consequences for semiotic innovation: it suggests that new metaphors, and hence new concepts, new ideas and new practices can be founded on the affordances of direct, concrete experiences.

Such experiences may be physical, hence based on experiences shared by all humans, such as walking upright. Vocal tension is another example. When the throat muscles are tensed, the voice becomes higher, sharper and brighter, because in their tensed state the walls of the throat cavity dampen the sound less than they would in their relaxed state – an equivalent difference would be the difference between footsteps in a hollow tiled corridor and a heavily carpeted room. The sound that results from tensing not only *is* tense it also *means* tense and *makes* tense. We know when our voice is likely to become tense – when we feel threatened, for instance, or when we have to 'perform' and 'speak up', or when we have to stay in control and restrain our emotions, and this complex of experiences can then form the basis of the meaning potential of vocal tension. In other words, we can use our experience of vocal tension to understand other things, transfer it from the domain of direct human experience to the domain of more abstract cultural ideas, values and practices. Alan Lomax, in an overview of singing styles across the world, has noted that in cultures where the sexual repression of women is severe, a very high degree of tension in the female singing voice is considered beautiful:

> It is as if one of the assignments of the favoured singer is to act out the level of sexual tension which the customs of the society establish as normal. The content of this message may be painful and anxiety-producing, but the effect upon the culture member may be stimulating, erotic and pleasurable since the song reminds him of familiar sexual emotions and experiences.
>
> (Lomax, 1968: 194)

The experiential basis of metaphors may also lie in our physical interaction with our environment – moving, manipulating objects, and so on. Thus the experience of transporting goods can become the basis for (a certain way of) understanding communication, and the experience of building a house the basis for (a certain way of) understanding the theory of construction. Here a cultural element already enters. Although some aspects of the exploration of our environment are purely physical and hence universal – experiencing how heavy or light an object is, or how rough or smooth, etc., others are less so, for instance houses are built differently in different cultures.

Finally, we can understand metaphors on the basis of our interactions with people in our culture, in terms of social, political, economic and religious institutions, as in the case of Susan Sontag's discussion of the way illness can be understood on the basis of practices of colonialism and military conquest (the italics are mine):

> Cancer cells do not simply multiply, they are '*invasive*' ('malignant tumors *invade* even when they grow slowly', as one textbook puts it). Cancer cells '*colonise*' from the original tumor *to far sites* in the body, first *setting up tiny outposts* ('micrometastases', whose presence is assumed, though they cannot be detected). Rarely are the body's '*defences*' vigorous enough to obliterate a tumor that has *established* its own blood *supplies* and consists of billions of destructive cells. However '*radical*' the surgical *intervention,* however many 'scans' are taken of the body landscape, most remissions are temporary, and the prospect is that the 'tumor *invasion*' will *continue* or that '*rogue cells' will eventually regroup* and *mount a new assault* on the organism.
>
> (Sontag, 1979: 64–5)

In each case, concrete experiences, some purely physical, some culturally mediated, form the basis for metaphors that help us understand things which are both 'less clearly delineated' and more culturally specific, such as love, or medical knowledge. Clearly this principle can also be very important in creating understanding between different cultures, because it suggests that at least some cultural differences can be bridged by tracing the metaphors back to their experiential basis.

All this applies not just to metaphors but also to *metonyms* where, instead of an imputed similarity between the metaphor and its experiential basis, there is an imputed temporal or spatial relationship. The most common type of metonym is the *synecdoche*, in which a part stands for the whole, as when we say 'I need a pair of hands', instead of 'I need a person'. Other metonyms substitute the producer for the product – as when we say 'I saw a Picasso' – the object for its user –'the buses are on strike' – the institution for the people responsible – 'The University doesn't allow me to resit the exam', and so on. Like metaphors, metonyms highlight some aspects and repress others, thus indicating what is important for the purposes of the given context. For instance, if I say 'I need a pair of hands' I am not interested in the individuality of the helper, but only in his or her labour. Again, when advertisements for wool show sheep rather than wool, or labels on milk cartons cows rather than milk, this brings out an issue which is very important in advertising products of this kind, their 'naturalness'. As in all metaphors, one thing is highlighted, another obscured, for instance the fact that these products are mass-produced in factories and contain many ingredients which do not come from the sheep's wool or the cow's milk. Similar examples could be given from other fields. In my newspaper I read how the pound 'slides', 'climbs up', 'floats', 'jumps' and so on, as if it is an independent agent – a typical example of an 'object for user' substitution, which draws attention away from the acts of the speculators who cause the value of the pound to fluctuate in this way.

Let us now look at some examples of the way contemporary typographers use the principle of experiential metaphor in creating innovative designs.

A key physical characteristic of the letters in figure 2.2 is their irregularity. The letters differ in size and thickness, and indeed in shape – different a's for instance are drawn differently. And the distribution of 'weight' – thickness and thinness – goes against the norms of typography, in which it is usually the upright stems of the 'n', rather than the descending line in the middle which is thick. This is further accentuated by the 'irregular' proportions of the 'African' figures who flank the word 'party'. In our own direct experience, such irregularities stem from a lack of control, a lack of skill in applying the rules of calligraphy. But here it is done deliberately, to signify a kind of rebellion against the controlled strokes of the calligraphic pen. On the other hand, the layout of the whole *is* controlled and symmetrical, perhaps to signify that this rebellious form of expression is in fact kept under control by its overall packaging.

The ubiquitous MTV station identity animation has, on the one hand, a large and solid three-dimensional 'M' with very precise geometrical proportions. On the other hand, the 'T' and the 'V' are much rougher. Everyone who has any experience of making marks on paper with pen or pencil knows that forms like the 'M' can only be produced mechanically or with mechanical aids like rulers and compasses, and that the roughness of the 'T' and the 'V' can only derive from their being freely drawn by a human hand. Much of the contemporary music broadcast by MTV rests on such a combination of the

Figure 2.2   Cover of a Monie Love single (lettering by Ruth Rowland, design by Paul White, 1989)

'technological' – synthesizers and digital instruments – and the 'human' – the human voice and traditional instruments – and these letterforms could therefore be seen as an apt metaphor for the station's identity. The confused hand-drawn circles behind the letters are animated to become a turbulent tornado, swallowing up the letters. This is the drawing equivalent of action painting, wild scribbling. And again, it could be seen as standing for the anarchic energy of much modern music. The point is, on the typographic level of meaning, it is possible for us to understand these letterforms not on the basis of associations – in the way we understand gothic lettering on the basis of its association with historical or legal documents – but on the basis of our experience of producing pen or pencil marks on paper. This is not *the* – or the only – meaning of this logo, it is an illustration of the way in which we can *make* meaning and discuss plausible interpretations on the basis of shared, concrete experience.

In the 'Post TV' CD-ROM in figure 2.3 words are formed out of smoke, so that typographic meaning rests on texture and colour, rather than on the letterforms themselves. We know that smoke is evanescent, and this allows the metaphor to highlight the evanescent, 'rapid-fading' nature of language.

In all these examples semiotic innovation is based on concrete thinking, on thinking with and through direct, physical experiences such as observing smoke and making marks on paper. But these concrete experiences are then extended into metaphors for complex ideas, such as 'contained, acceptable rebelliousness', 'the human element in a "techno" world', or 'the ephemeral nature of words'.

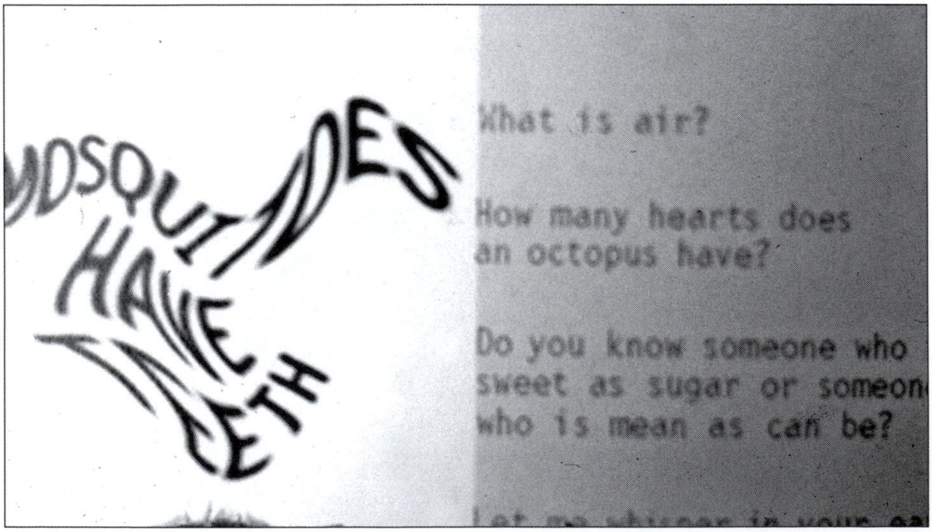

Figure 2.3 Post TV CD-ROM (Post Tool, 1997)

Connotation

The second mechanism of semiotic invention and innovation is connotation. As this term has been used in many different ways, it is perhaps a good idea to first disentangle it a bit. The distinction between denotation and connotation was first made by the nineteenth century philosopher John Stuart Mill, in his book *A System of Logic* (1843). He described words as having two kinds of meaning. The word 'white', for instance, first of all *denotes* the class of white things, 'as snow, paper, the foam of the sea, and so forth'. But it also *connotes* the abstract concept 'whiteness', by virtue of which all white things can be referred to with the one word 'white'. Other philosophers have used the terms 'extension' and 'intension' for what Mill calls denotation and connotation, while many linguists and semioticians have used 'reference' (for Mill's 'denotation') and 'sense' (for his 'connotation'). I will return to this distinction in a later chapter, because it has repercussions for social semiotic theory.

Turn of the century linguists began to develop theories of different kinds of meaning. For the German linguist Erdmann (1900), for example, words had *Hauptbedeutung* (core meaning), *Nebensinn* (additional meaning), and *Gefühlswert* (emotive value). Many later linguists have used 'denotation' and 'connotation' for similar distinctions. Lyons (1977), for instance, saw denotation as 'cognitive', 'conceptual' meaning – hence more like Mill's 'connotation'! – and connotation as *Gefühlswert,* emotive meaning. Denotative meanings, he said, are shared by all speakers of the language, while connotations are more subjective and variable. Leech (1974) also saw denotation as basic conceptual meaning, and connotation as something like *Nebensinn*, as additional, 'non-criterial' meaning, stemming from the associations we might have with what a word refers to, and hence, again, subjective and variable.

The most important approach to connotation in semiotics has been that of Roland Barthes, who was a key player in the Paris School structuralist semiotics of the 1960s and 1970s. In defining denotation and connotation Barthes drew on the work of Hjelmslev (1943), who had argued that different ways of expressing the same concept can have different meanings, if only because the same concept can be expressed in different languages, and speakers therefore never only communicate that concept but also their country of origin. Barthes developed his approach to denotation and connotation not in relation to language but in relation to photographic images (1973; 1977), and so established that the term connotation can also be applied to semiotic modes other than language. Images, too, have two layers of meaning – the layer of denotation, that is the layer of 'what, or who, is represented here?' and the layer of connotation, that is the layer of 'what ideas and values are expressed *through* what is represented, and through the way in which it is represented?' Barthes' view is thus, in a sense, closer to that of Mill than to that of the linguists we have just discussed. For Barthes, visual denotation is reference to concrete people, places and things, and visual connotation reference to abstract concepts. He sees these concepts not as individual, subjective associations with the referent but as culturally shared meanings, 'culturally accepted inducers of ideas' (1977: 23).

For Barthes, who was considering only photographic images, denotation was a relatively unproblematic issue. There is, he argued, no 'encoding' into some kind of language-like code which must be learnt before the message can be deciphered. Looking at photographs is similar to looking at reality, because photographs provide a point-by-point correspondence with what was in front of the camera when they were taken, despite the fact that they reduce it in size, flatten it, and, in the case of black and white photography, drain it of colour. Even in the case of paintings and drawings the situation is not essentially different. Although the style of the artist provides a 'supplementary message', the content is still understood on the basis of resemblance to reality. Given this first layer of meaning, a second layer of meaning can, as it were, be superimposed, the connotation. It comes about either through the culturally shared associations which cling to the represented people, places and things, or through specific 'connotators', specific aspects of the *way in which* they are represented, for example, specific photographic techniques. In *Mythologies* (1973) Barthes concentrated on the former. In *Image, Music, Text* (1977) he added the latter. Here is his key example from *Mythologies*:

> I am at the barber's and a copy of *Paris-Match* is offered me. On the cover, a young Negro in a French uniform is saluting, with his eyes uplifted, probably fixed on a fold of the tricolour. All this is the *meaning* of the picture. But, whether naively or not, I see very well what it signifies to me: that France is a great empire, that all her sons, without any colour discrimination, faithfully serve under her flag, and that there is no better answer to the detractors of an alleged colonialism than the zeal shown by this Negro in serving his so-called oppressors. I am therefore again faced with a greater semiological system: there is a signifier, itself already formed with a previous system (a black soldier is giving the French salute), and there is a signified (it is here a purposeful mixture of Frenchness and militariness).
>
> (Barthes, 1973: 116)

This quote clearly describes the two layers of meaning. Denotation is literal and concrete: 'a black soldier is giving the French salute'. Connotation is a more abstract concept, or rather, mixture of concepts – 'Frenchness and militariness' rolled in one. In *Mythologies* (1973) Barthes called such concepts 'myths', and described them, first of all, as very broad and diffuse concepts which condense everything associated with the represented people, places and things into a single entity – Barthes' use of terms like 'Frenchness' and 'militariness' to indicate the meanings of these 'myths' reminds of Mill's 'whiteness' – and second, as ideological meanings, serving to legitimate the status quo and the interests of those whose power is invested in it – in this case French colonialism and military role in Africa (*Mythologies*, though only translated in 1973, dates from 1957).

Two elements of the content of images are singled out as especially important connotators: poses and objects. There is, says Barthes, an unwritten 'dictionary' of poses which is known to everyone who is at all exposed to the mass media, and whose 'entries' again have the kind of broad and ideologically coloured meanings that are so typical of connotation (1977: 22):

> Consider a press photograph of President Kennedy widely distributed at the time of the 1960 election: a half-length profile shot, eyes looking upwards, hands joined together. Here it is the very pose of the subject which prepares the raising of the signifieds of connotation: youthfulness, spirituality, purity. The photograph clearly only signifies because of the existence of a store of stereotyped attitudes which form ready-made elements of signification (eyes raised heavenwards, hands clasped).

Objects are equally significant (1977: 23):

> Special importance must be accorded to what could be called the posing of objects, where the meaning comes from the objects photographed ... The interest lies in the fact that the objects are accepted inducers of ideas (book case = intellectual) or, in a more obscure way, veritable symbols (the door to the gas chamber for Chessman's execution with its references to the funeral gates of ancient mythologies). Such objects constitute excellent elements of signification: on the one hand they are discontinuous and complete in themselves ... while on the other they refer to clear familiar signifieds. They are thus the elements of a veritable lexicon.

Connotation can also come about through the style of the artwork or the techniques of photography, such as 'framing, distance, lighting, focus, speed' (1977: 44). Barthes calls this 'photogenia' (ibid: 23):

> An inventory needs to be made of these techniques, but only insofar as each of them has a corresponding signified of connotation sufficiently constant to allow its incorporation in a cultural lexicon of technical 'effects'.

Like the 'metaphors we live by', connotations are not always innovative. On the contrary, they often communicate well-established dominant ideas, as in the case of Barthes' example. How then can the principle of connotation become a mechanism for invention and innovation? I will try to explain this by means of a short excursion into the semiotics of dress. Peter Bogatyrev (1971 [1937]), a member of the Prague School of semiotics, a group of linguists which, like the Paris School, extended the study of language into other semiotic modes, wrote a monograph describing what dress traditionally communicated in Moravian Slovakia. It could tell you where the wearer came from – there were 28 costume districts, and you could, for instance, recognize a man from Pozlovice because he would wear two velvet bands round his hat and two carmine ribbons with a green one in between, while a man from Biskupice would wear one velvet band and a red ribbon. It could tell you the wearer's occupation – for instance, magistrates wore boots, whereas other people wore the rough leather *krpce*, a kind of moccasin. It could tell you the social class of the wearer – for instance, squires wore bright blue breeches and peasants black or coarse white ones. It could tell you the age and marital status of the wearer – for instance, in the Mutinece-Novorany district unmarried men wore hats with narrow rims and red and white ribbons, while married men would widen the rim and wear a broad gold band. It could even tell you the wearer's religion – for instance, Protestant girls would twist their hair around lacings, while Catholic girls would wear 'horned' head pads.

Such denotative 'languages of dress' no longer exist in Western countries, except in the case of uniforms. There has been a change in what people communicate through dress. In the age of 'lifestyles' (see chapter 7), people use the way they dress to communicate their allegiance to ideas and values, rather than their social class, occupation, and so on. To do so they create 'composites of connotations', sometimes even in uniforms. The cabin crew of one airline I travelled with wore red waistcoats, white shirts and blouses, and red and white dotted scarves and ties – but also blue jeans. Wearing blue jeans in the workplace usually means that you are free to choose what to wear, and if you are not allowed to wear them to work, they tend to be associated with leisure and private time. These cabin crew uniforms, however, introduced them as part of an obligatory uniform and so created a novel 'composite of connotations'. Waistcoats connote the waiter or waitress and therefore the idea of 'service' – rather than, for example, the idea of the 'officer', as would an army style formal uniform. The colour red connotes, in this context, the uniform of the professional entertainer, for example, the musician in a showband – and therefore the idea of 'entertainment'. And while the ties and scarves are relatively formal, this is offset by the informality of the blue jeans, with, as a result, blurred boundaries between the formal and the informal, the private and the public. In short, while the uniform denotes 'airline cabin crew', it *connotes* a complex of abstract concepts and values. It is by means of these concepts that the airline identifies itself as a contemporary company, rather than for example, a 'national airline'. By analogy with 'Frenchness' and 'militariness', we could say that the uniform connotes 'corporateness', a complex of ideas and values characteristic for the corporate age.

The key is, all this is brought about by 'importing' things – types of garments, colours, fabrics, etc. – into the domain of the cabin crew uniform which formerly were not part of it and, in so doing, also importing the ideas and values which, in that domain, are associated with the place from where these garments, colours, fabrics, etc. came – 'service', 'entertainment', informality in public discourse, in short, all those elements which also play such a role in that other form of corporate communication, advertising.

To give a different example of this principle of semiotic 'import', in French music of the late eighteenth century, hurdy-gurdies were imported into the symphony orchestra because these instruments were used in the folk music of the country. Their timbre could therefore connote the idea of the idyllic unspoilt life of country people which played such a role in the dominant aristocratic culture of the time. Needless to say, this 'myth of the idyllic countryside' is not the meaning which the hurdy-gurdy would have in the countryside itself. It is the meaning of the countryside as seen by the 'importers', in this case the French aristocracy.

This kind of 'importing' is an essential characteristic of the semiotic landscape of the era of global culture. Fashion designers, for instance, constantly import ideas from other periods, other cultures, science-fiction costumes in movies, etc., to connote the ideas and values attached to those periods, cultures, and so on in the popular culture, and to provide people with resources for signifying their allegiance to ideas, values, lifestyles, and so on. Some domains do not even have their own form of expression. Advertising music, for instance, will embrace any style of music, so long as it attracts the target audience. In Sydney I lived in a very multicultural district. I once asked my greengrocer for the name of a vegetable I had not seen before. He told me what it was and then explained the different sections of the shop:

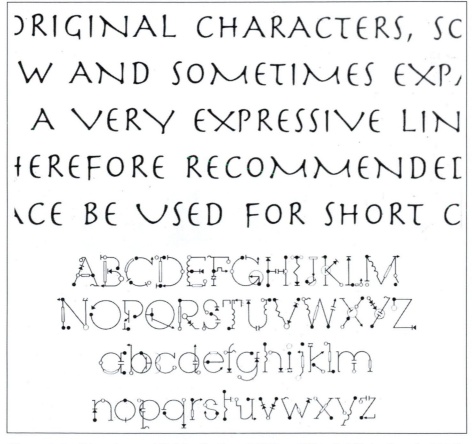

Figure 2.4 'Herculaneum' (Adrian Frutiger, 1988) and 'Circuits' (Peter Grundy, 1982)

'These are the vegetables Greek people buy', 'These are the vegetables Turkish people buy', and so on, and then he finally said, with a mischievous smile, 'And people like you buy everything.' He might have added: 'but you have no section you could call your own.'

To return to typography, letterforms have generally been regarded as denotative – a stem descending below the baseline, with a bowl on the right denotes the sound 'p', for instance. At best they can have a certain elegance and style which can then be savoured like a good glass of wine. But this cannot be said, for instance, of the Herculaneum typeface or the Circuits typeface in figure 2.4. Many of the features of the Herculaneum typeface are imported from Greek and Roman inscriptions and papyri, and therefore carry connotations of 'lasting value'. The Circuits typeface imports the graphic language of electric circuitry into typography and is therefore available for uses in which technical connotations are appropriate. But this typeface does more. It also merges two things which have long been separate: alphabetic writing and imagery – because, however abstract, electric circuit diagrams are also images.

The avant-garde art magazine *Parkett* (figure 2.5) uses a logo with hand-embroidered letters. The logo, which was made by the designer's mother, 'imports' the traditional handcrafted object into the world of logo design. By doing so it rejects conventional styles of corporate logo design as too institutional and too reminiscent of slick advertising and graphic design, and affirms the values of home-made, hand-crafted, traditional forms of expression.

Figure 2.5   Parkett logo (Bice Curiger, 1984)

This example, like the examples in the previous sections, again demonstrates that the new typography is thoroughly multimodal. It communicates not just through the letterforms themselves but also through colour, through texture, through perspective, through framing and through motion. All these are modes which are not unique to typography but part of a multifaceted visual language which it has in common with images, product design, interior decoration, architecture, and more.

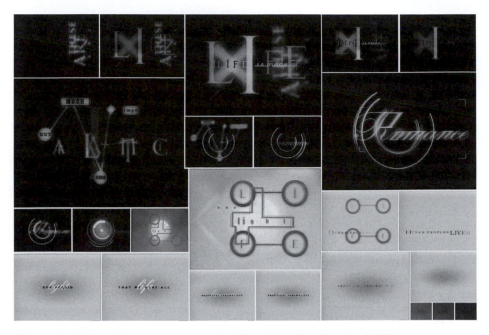

Figure 2.6   True Romance commercial (Jonathan Barnbrook, 1994)

Conclusion

Figure 2.6 shows an example of the typography of Jonathan Barnbrook. Individual words and short phrases are given a separate identity, either typographically, by means of different typefaces, sizes, weight, etc., and/or by means of framing (see chapter 1). These isolated bits of language are then connected again by graphic means, for example, by arrows or lines.

Barnbrook's approach has been very influential. Examples of this kind of typography can now be observed everywhere. It is no exaggeration to say that his work is a form of semiotic research – in typographic form, rather than in the form of, say, an academic essay. Barnbrook sketches the outlines of a whole new form of writing, suitable for the age of computer-mediated communication, where, as I have said before, writing becomes more visual and the image more like writing. Linguists have been doing this kind of thing for some time (see fig. 2.7)

But Barnbrook has turned this kind of analysis of writing into a new writing *practice* and disseminated it to a wider audience. This audience may not understand it in words as I try to do here – and why should they, it is typographic, not verbal communication. But they will certainly be aware of the novelty and relevance of this kind of design, and will respond to it with intuitive understanding.

What can the role of the semiotician be in this process of semiotic innovation? In the first place we should recognize that reflective and innovative practitioners like Barnbrook

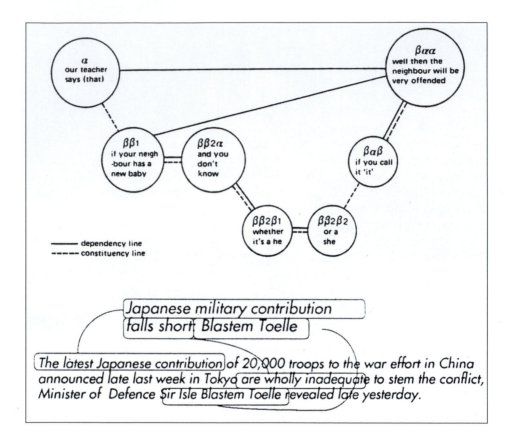

Figure 2.7   Linguistic analyses by M.A.K. Halliday (1985: 201) and one by R. Iedema (1993)

are also semioticians, and do away with the artificial boundary between artistic and intellectual research. I try to do the same thing in the exercises that accompany the chapters in this book – some ask for analysis, some for creative ideas. Luckily the similarities between the work of innovative thinkers and innovative practitioners are now increasingly acknowledged. Both activities are a kind of research, in the sense of defining problems, whether artistic, technical, social, philosophical or otherwise, and searching for their solutions. Increasingly the two kinds of researchers work together in teams. The MIT Medialab is a trailblazer in this regard. In three departments – Information and Entertainment, Perceptual Computing, Learning and Common Sense – faculty staff and research fellows research issues of human communication and human–machine interaction, combining scientific, technological and artistic approaches, and producing not only papers and books, but also operas – for example, Tod Machover's *Brain Opera*, a setting of words by artificial intelligence scientist Marvin Minsky – graphic design innovations – for example, the work of John Maeda – and more.

Semioticians can contribute in a number of other ways as well. In designing new forms of communication it is important to consider as many different models as possible. Often these will come from other domains – for example, not from typography but from electric circuitry – and from other eras and cultures – for example, not from alphabetic writing but from other writing and visual communication traditions, past or present. To be able to elucidate how these work, what they can and cannot do and mean is the essence of semiotic analysis and the core of the semiotician's work.

Semioticians can also help design and implement new uses for semiotic innovations. In many schools children now produce 'concept maps' like the one shown in figure 2.8. Again, isolated units of meaning, separate words or short phrases, are first framed and then connected by graphic means, just as in Barnbrook's work, or in the diagrams of linguists shown in figure 2.7.

Children enjoy this work. They intuitively perceive its relevance and its potential for understanding complex issues. But have we constructed enough explicit understandings of this form of communication to make it possible for teachers to judge such maps in terms of their structure and elegance of expression, or their clarity of thought? Do we know enough to help children develop their skills in making such maps? Should typography be taught in schools as a medium of communication in its own right, a new kind of writing? It is up to semioticians and educationalists to work together towards answering such questions, as was done, for instance by Kress et al. (2000). And there is no reason why designers should not be involved in such enterprises as well. On the contrary.

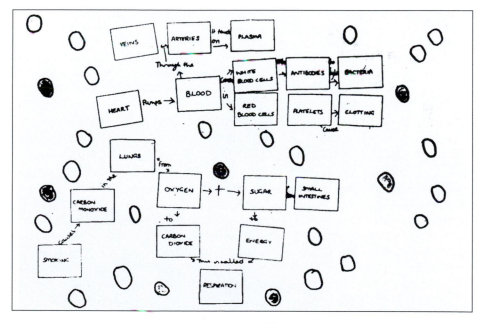

Figure 2.8   Concept map (from Kress et al., 2000)

Exercises

1   Collect some examples of kinetic typography (letterforms that move), for instance from film or television titles or websites. Can you interpret some of the letters' movements as experiential metaphors?

2   Collect some ('structural') political metaphors, either from press reports and editorials or from political cartoons. What do they highlight, and what do they obscure?

3   Collect some front pages from each of two different magazines. What does the typography communicate?

4   Think of a metaphor for the typography of a short text which deals with the detrimental effect of modern food technology (or, if you prefer, its beneficial effects).

5   Use the principle of connotation, as described in this chapter, in designing an outfit for a character in a movie: She is 21, studies anthropology, and likes to be seen as a peaceful and serene person, ready to get actively involved in work that furthers her ideals.

3   Semiotic rules

Semiotic rules

In traditional semiotics the concept of 'rule' plays an important role. The idea is that, just as people can only play a game together once they have mastered its rules, so people can only communicate, only understand one another, once they have mastered the rules of the game of language – and/or other semiotic modes. As a result, the 'rule book' or 'code' became the key to doing semiotics, the key to understanding how people make and communicate meaning. The rules of this 'rule book' were of two kinds. There were first the rules of the 'lexicon', the rules that stipulate what observable forms (signifiers) will be used to signify what meanings (signifieds), and second the rules of 'grammar', the rules that stipulate how signs (signifiers coupled with signifieds) go together to make messages, for example, the rule that in series of adjectives the numeratives come first, so that *the three brown bears* is correct, but *the brown three bears* is not, or the rules of colour harmony, that say that yellow and blue go well together, but magenta and blue less so. De Saussure used the term *langue* for the rule book, and *parole* for its actual use in producing speech. *Langue*, he said, exists:

> ... in the form of a sum of impressions deposited in the brain of each member of a community, almost like a dictionary of which identical copies have been distributed to each individual' so that ' language exists in each individual, yet is common to all, and ... not affected by the will of the depositaries.
>
> (de Saussure, 1974 [1916]: 19)

Again, in Roland Barthes' words:

> [*Langue*] is the social part of language, the individual cannot by himself either create or modify it; it is essentially a collective contract which one must accept in its entirety if one wishes to communicate. Moreover, this social product is autonomous, like a game with its own rules, for it can be handled only after a period of learning.
>
> (Barthes, 1967b: 14)

In this kind of formulation rules rule people, not people rules. Social semiotics sees it a little differently. It suggests that rules, whether written or unwritten, are made by people, and can therefore be changed by people. To represent them as if they can *not* be changed – or not changed at will – is to represent human-made rules as though they are laws of nature. On the other hand, two provisos need to be made. First, not everybody can change

the rules. To be able to change rules you need power, whether it is the power of governments – for example, in legislating spelling reforms, as has recently been done in the
Netherlands and Germany – the symbolic power of influential language users – film and
television script writers, song writers, advertising copy writers, etc. – or the more limited
influence of 'opinion leaders' in groups of friends. Second, there are different kinds of
rules, and different ways of changing things. Think of the way parents might try to instil
rules into their children. They may simply impose them – 'Do it because I say so'. They
may reason with the child – 'What would happen if everybody did that?' Or they may try
to give the right example and hope it will be followed up. The same applies to semiotic
behaviour. In the army, dress is prescribed by explicit rules. There are no such rules for
what university students should wear when they go to lectures, but that does not mean
that anything is possible. There is the influence of role models such as singers and movie
stars, and there may be peer pressure to conform to, or fashion dictates to follow.

   In social semiotics the 'rule book' approach is not entirely rejected. It is a good way
to describe how semiotics works in certain contexts, where explicit and detailed rules
are enforced. But it cannot be applied to each and every situation. Therefore social
semiotics works not only with an inventory of past, present and possible future
semiotic resources, but also with an inventory of different types of rules, taken up in
different ways in different contexts. The major part of this chapter provides a framework for this, a framework for exploring questions like: Who makes how many and
what kind of rules? How are these rules learned? How are they justified, or critiqued?
What happens if you don't follow them? But before I start with this, I need to introduce two further relevant concepts from traditional semiotics.

Arbitrariness

The first type of rules, 'lexicon' rules, stipulates what should be meant by what
signifier. It couples signifiers with signifieds. A key question in semiotics has been the
question of what *motivates* this kind of rule. Why *this* signifier – for example, a
knitted brow, or red – for *this* signified – for example, 'disapproval', or 'danger'? De
Saussure gave a radical answer to this question. There *is* no reason. The rule of the
lexicon is entirely arbitrary. As a result it can only be obeyed, there is no ground for
arguing either its appropriateness or its inappropriateness. The proof is that the same
signifieds are signified entirely differently in different languages (1974 [1916]: 67):

> The idea of 'sister' is not linked by any inner relationship to the succession of
> sounds *s-ō-r* which serves as its signifier in French; that it could be represented
> equally by just any other sequence is proved by differences among languages and
> by the very existence of different languages: the signified 'ox' has as its signifier
> *b-ō-f* on one side of the border and *o-k-s* (*Ochs*) on the other.

He added that this arbitrariness 'protects language from change' (ibid.: 73), allows
it to be based solely on tradition. We use the words we use because 'they have always

been used this way'. And he extends this to other semiotic modes as well. Gestures, for instance, may have 'a certain natural expressiveness' but are ultimately 'fixed by rule' and 'it is this rule and not the intrinsic value of the gestures that obliges one to use them' (ibid.: 68). Onomatopoeia, speech sounds that imitate other sounds (for example, *glug-glug*, or *tick-tock*) may seem to contradict this, but, says de Saussure (ibid.: 69), they are a marginal phenomenon and 'never organic elements of a linguistic system'.

De Saussure does not discuss other semiotic modes in detail, but Saussurean-inspired semioticians who have done this have often added three concepts from C.S Peirce (1965: 156–73): icon, index and symbol. These are three types of sign that differ in the way the link between their signifiers and signifieds is motivated. While in the 'symbol' the relation between signifier and signified is arbitrary, wholly conventional, in the 'icon' there is a relation of partial resemblance – the signifier *looks* in some respect or to some degree like the signified, in the way that a picture of a tree looks like a tree and the steepness of the slope of a graph resembles the rate of growth of some phenomenon, although not, of course, the phenomenon itself. In the 'index', finally, there is a causal relation between signifier and signified, for example, if a footstep signifies the recent presence of a person, it does so because it was actually made by that person. Icons and indices are therefore motivated signs. It is possible to say why their signifiers are appropriate for their signifieds. But that reason is still formulated as objectively existing, built into the system, so to speak, rather than as brought about in the act of sign production or interpretation.

Arbitrary signs ('symbols') do exist, for example, randomly assigned identification numbers, or the colours on a London Underground map, where red stands for the Central Line, black for the Northern Line, and so on. But in most cases we choose signifiers because we see them as apt for our purposes of the moment. While the reasons for such choices are clear to see when we create new signifiers or new uses for existing signifiers, for instance when we give names to our children, or invent new terminology, they are no longer observable for words that were devised so long ago that their origins are lost in history and long forgotten. The same applies to non-linguistic signs. The small slit in the back of jackets, for instance, was once functional, serving to make it easier to mount a horse. Today most people are no longer aware of this. Yet it persists in the design of jackets.

In an essay called 'Against arbitrariness' Kress (1993: 173) argues the social semiotic point of view that meaning is produced in *use*: 'Signs are always motivated by the producer's "interest", and by characteristics of the object.'

One of his key examples is an utterance of a 3½-year-old child who said, while climbing a steep hill, 'This is a heavy hill'. Kress comments:

> Aspects of the child's interest – great expenditure of effort – and aspects of the features of the object to be signified produce a particular signified – perhaps something like 'This activity takes considerable physical effort' – and this expresses aspects of the referent that produced, in part, this signified – the difficulty of climbing the steep hill.
>
> (Kress 1993: 173)

This applies not only to sign production but also to sign interpretation. When, in the previous chapter, I interpreted examples of typography, I did so in a way which:

1   reflected my interests as a social semiotician – I tried to show that letterforms can be meaningful, and that the principle of 'experiential metaphor' can be used in their interpretation; and
2   reflected some selected characteristics of the objects – the letterforms – I was interpreting.

In the case of new semiotic resources and new uses of existing semiotic resources, old rules are cast aside. When very young children make new meanings they do so in a context where they have not yet mastered the rules of the adult world and are experimenting with the semiotic resources at their disposal as part of the learning process. In many other situations our use of semiotic resources is controlled by rules which will vary in detail and strictness. But rules can never control every detail of what we do. In a sense every instance of sign production and interpretation is new. We never just mechanically apply rules. Every instance is different and requires adaptation to the circumstances at hand. What will we wear for *this* particular occasion? What are the best words to persuade *this* particular client or console *this* particular friend in his or her bereavement?

Double articulation

The second type of rule, the rule of 'grammar', stipulates how messages are to be built up from a small number of basic building blocks. In the case of language these building blocks are the speech sounds, the 'phonemes', of which there are, roughly, between 30 and 60 in any given language. These building blocks, which in themselves are meaningless, are then combined to make the more complex building blocks also known as words. Although words already have a meaning potential, they are still only building blocks. We do not speak in single words or interpret text on the basis of isolated words. To get actual instances of communication, words must be strung together to make messages.

Each level has its specific, separate rules of combination. Phonological rules stipulate how words can be constructed from sounds, for example, the rule that, in English, you can have the sequence *b-r* or *b-l*, but not *b-n* or *b-m*. With these rules you can generate all possible English words, those that (already) exist, for example, *brag*, and those that do not (yet) exist, for example, *blan*. Grammatical rules stipulate how messages can be constructed from words, for example, to get a (certain kind of) question you need to put the (finite part of the) verb before the subject – 'Did he make it?' – whereas to get a statement you must put the subject before the verb – 'He made it.' As can be seen, these rules involve coupling a formal structure – for example, a certain word order – with a meaning potential – here a kind of speech act, such as 'making a statement' or 'asking a question'. So the language system is seen as layered, as having two levels of articulation, the level at which words are articulated with sounds, and the level at which messages are articulated with words. Thanks to its doubly articulated structure, it can generate a very large number of messages from a very small number of basic building blocks.

Many semioticians have argued that double articulation is unique to language. Other semiotic modes, they say, have only one layer, only a 'lexicon' of signs. Books with titles such as *Dictionary of Visual Language* (Thompson and Davenport, 1982) provide an alphabetically ordered collection of individual design ideas and symbols, which may have been original when they were invented but have since become clichés – although skilful designers can of course breathe new life into them. But double articulation is *not* unique to language. A toy system like Lego, for instance, also has double articulation. It has basic building blocks, which in themselves are meaningless and do not represent anything, and which are used to construct meaningful objects, for instance buildings and vehicles, by means of the rules of combination that are built into their design – the way blocks fit together. Then, at a second level of articulation, these objects can be used to make 'scenes' or play games or tell stories – the pictures in Lego advertisements and catalogues usually show such larger scenes. Again, most people would see the semiotic mode of smell as having only a single layer. We think of smell as a collection of specific individual smells, perhaps evoking moods or memories, interpreted and evaluated in highly subjective ways. But for the specialists who *produce* smells, for perfumers, scientists, aromatherapists, etc., smell is a *system*, constructed according to the principle of double articulation. Aromatherapists recognize about 50 basic smells that can be combined into a much larger number of complex smells by means of a grammar of 'head', 'body' and 'base', in which a given smell must have particular qualities – for example, a certain amount of volatility – to be able to be used as either head, body or base. The resulting complex smells, in turn, combine to form specific aromas. In other words, what to the consumer of aromatherapies is 'singly articulated', a collection of individual, specific signs, is 'doubly articulated' to their producers.

So it seems that any semiotic mode can either be used according to the principle of 'single articulation' or according to the principle of 'double articulation', either understood and used as a loose 'collection' of ready-made signs, or understood and used as a tightly structured, rule-governed system, with a 'phonology' and a 'grammar'. Not only can smell be thought of, and used, like a language, the opposite is true as well – language can be and is thought of in the way most of us think of smell, as 'singly articulated'. Today's corpus linguists, who work with vast computer databases of real language, see language more and more as a vast storehouse of individual words and 'collocations', strips of words that have a high statistical likelihood of being used together – the computer can extract and quantify such strips automatically from text. Clearly, whether a semiotic resource is singly or doubly articulated is not an intrinsic quality of that resource but follows from the way it is taken up in specific contexts.

The way in which semiotic resources are structured by their use also varies historically. Nowadays many Lego blocks are no longer meaningless bricks but already-meaningful items such as doors, windows, rotors for helicopters, garden furniture, trees, etc., and they are marketed in boxes that allow only one item to be built – only the helicopter, or only the suburban home with its trees and garden furniture. The question then arises, why? Although there is clearly no single cause for developments of this kind, I believe that the *status* of the semiotic mode – and of its users – is an important factor. In the case of Lego, the status of 'engineering' has gone down. In the richest countries recruitment figures show that its appeal as a profession has declined, and many engineers are now recruited from newly developing countries. Meanwhile, the appeal of consumerism and of designing your own 'lifestyle' (see chapter 7) through careful selection and combination of already-meaningful consumer products has gone up. So when Lego moves from double to single articulation, it takes a degree of control away from children, and treats them more as consumers and less as 'engineers', makers, producers. For another example, think of the relation between text and image. Formerly language had the highest status in print media. Images were not essential – illustration, embellishment. As a result images were seen as a 'collection', and language as a 'system'. Today the status of the visual is on the rise. Increasingly the visual gets the lead role in important types of print and electronic texts. As it acquires more status it also becomes more strictly controlled, more prescriptively taught, and more codified. The status of (the traditional form of) written language, on the other hand, is declining and as a result it becomes less strictly controlled and codified. Correct spelling and grammar are taught less vigorously, and gradually people begin to doubt their value, while at the same time very visible and influential uses of language such as advertisements delight in taking liberties with spelling and grammar. Again, smell producers have more power of control over smell messages than smell users, so for them smell is a rule-governed system, while for consumers it is a 'collection' to be used and experienced.

One final aspect needs to be mentioned. Whether 'basic building blocks' are meaningless or not, also depends on context. For the traditional linguist, speech sounds are meaningless, for the poet they are not. The composer Murray Schafer used a range of experiential metaphors to bring out the meaning potential of speech sounds, as can be seen from this extract:

B Has bite. Combustive. Aggressive. The lips bang over it

I Highest vowel. Thin, bright, pinched sound, leaving the smallest cavity in the mouth. Hence useful in words describing smallness: *piccolo, petit, tiny, wee*

L Watery, luscious, languid. Needs juice in the mouth to be spoken properly. Feel it drip around the tongue. Feel the saliva in 'lascivious lecher'.

(Schafer, 1986: 180–1)

Until recently such 'sound symbolism' was a relatively marginal phenomenon. But today it is moving into the foreground, for instance in important fields of corporate

communication like advertising, just as is also the case with the supposedly meaningless letterforms discussed in chapter 2, or the meaningless 'regulation colours' of
buses, trams, trains and planes, which have made way for colour schemes that are
meant to express the values and identities of the companies that run them. In such
circumstances the view that sounds, or letterforms, or colours, are meaningless will
soon seem less and less plausible and more and more outdated to many people.

An inventory of rules

I have argued that the rules of semiotic systems are not objectively there, as a kind of
natural law, or as procedures hardwired into a technology. They are made by people,
they come in different kinds, and they change over time. To explore them we need to
follow the social semiotic method introduced in chapter 1 and first construct an inventory to then investigate how that inventory is taken up in specific social contexts. It is
this I will do in the rest of this chapter, asking five basic questions:

1 How is control exercised, and by whom?
2 How is it justified? Whenever there are rules, the question 'why' can arise. 'Why
   must we do this?' Or: 'Why must we do this in this way?' Hence rules come with
   justifications, and different kinds of rules tend to be justified in different ways.
3 How strict are the rules? How much room do they allow for individuality and
   difference?
4 What happens when people do not follow the rule? What sanctions are attached
   to deviance?
5 Can the rules be changed, and if so, in what way, and for what kinds of reasons?

None of these questions can be asked when semiotic systems are seen as natural
phenomena, as structures that somehow exist and impose themselves on us by the
mere fact of their existence. Below I discuss these questions with respect to five
different 'semiotic regimes', five different types of rule, as they have different answers
in each case.

Personal authority

The first category in our inventory of rules is the rule of personal authority, as exercised by people who (1) are in a position of power, and (2) see no need for justifying
their actions. If we were to ask them why – 'Why does this rule exist?' 'Why must I do
this?' – the answer would be, 'Because I say so'. It is the rule of the 'dictate', and
hence of the dictator, but it can also be found in the family where many children are on
the receiving end of it. The sociologist Bernstein (1971, see also Halliday, 1973)
distinguished between positional and person-centred families. In the former – usually
working-class families – children are told what to do on the basis of direct personal
authority. In the latter – usually middle class families – rules are more indirect and

children are given reasons – 'Playing in that sort of place ruins your clothes'; 'You might get hurt if you do that'. But the rule of personal authority exists elsewhere too, for instance in the workplace.

The rule of personal authority is always ad hoc. You cannot anticipate when rules will be imposed, what they will be, or for how long they will apply. If there is any individual freedom or room for difference, it is a gift or privilege which must be obtained by currying favour with the powerful person. Sanctions, too, depend on whim – 'If you do that again, I'll smack you'. Note that we are looking at these rules from the point of view of those on the receiving end. It may well be that the powerful person operates on the basis of principles rather than on the basis of whims, but those whose actions are being regulated have no way of knowing this, and can neither anticipate what they must do nor whether the rules that apply today will still apply tomorrow.

A semiotic example of personal power is 'the dictate of fashion' (see also chapter 7). Not following fashion has consequences – you will be unfashionable, and hence lose some of your social attractiveness among those who orient themselves towards the rule of fashion. The dictate of fashion never comes with justifications, nor is it grounded on expertise. Experts must demonstrate their right to rule by displaying their qualifications or basing themselves on research results, but fashion designers neither poll people for their preferences, nor cite any other form of research. They simply have the power to unveil, imperatively, what will be in fashion this season. Because this will eventually influence what we can buy in the shops, it has a major impact on the range of semiotic resources available for signifying our identity through the language of dress.

Impersonal authority

There are two forms of impersonal authority, the authority of the written word, and the authority of tradition. I will begin with the written word. In the end, dictatorships do not last and social rules cannot survive unless there is some sense of order and regularity, some sense of 'rule of law', in whatever form – the holy scriptures of a religion, the laws of a nation state, the highway code, an employment contract, the written house style guide of a publisher or publication. In principle, such written codes are explicit and accessible to those who are to follow the rules. Not following them has consequences. After a more or less prescribed number of warnings, and/or an escalating scale of punishments, the eventual sanction is removal from the relevant social group, whether in the form of excommunication, imprisonment, confiscation of the driver's licence, or being fired or demoted.

Documents cannot implement control without help from human agents – priests, the police, the judiciary, employers, etc. In principle such control is exercised according to explicit rules. But because rules can never stipulate everything, there is always room for interpretation – and hence for personal power. The exercise of such power may then either accrue to the written rules – 'case law' – or remain personal and hence arbitrary.

How can laws change? In general, the more detailed they become, the more they need constant updating, and mechanisms for doing so, for example, special councils that have the right to make changes. This will be especially necessary when for one reason or other a majority of people have begun to act in ways that no longer accord with the written law. I will discuss an example of this later in this chapter. If the laws themselves cannot be changed, their interpretation will have to change, and this is of course easier if they are not too precise, if they provide general principles rather than detailed rules that try to foreshadow every possibility.

A new form of writing is the writing of computer programs, and its role in making and enforcing rules is steadily increasing. Many things that were formerly controlled through explicit rule books of the kind we have been discussing can also be controlled by means of the computer programs that build them into the very tools we use to perform the regulated activity. The rules of correct spelling and grammar, for instance, used to be based on explicit authoritative documents, on grammars and dictionaries, endorsed by authoritative centres of learning or national academies, and drummed into people at school. Nowadays, they can be built into the word processor and followed without actually knowing them. Many other forms of semiotic can be automatized, resulting in rules that can be followed automatically, without the need for learning and internalization. The same form of control is currently proposed for traffic rules. The maximum speed of cars, for instance, would then be automatically adjusted in accordance with the prevailing speed limits, instead of drivers having to obey the traffic signs.

In the case of *tradition*, or 'customary law', the situation is different. Nothing is written down, nothing explicitly and systematically codified, at least not in a form that is accessible to those who must uphold the rules, although there will usually be sayings, proverbs and tales to reinforce them. If the question, 'Why do we do this?' were to be asked, people would say, 'Because that's how we have always done it', but the question is rarely asked, because the rules are enforced by everyone, rather than by specific agents. As Bourdieu has put it 'each agent has the means of acting as a judge of others and of himself' (1977: 17). Everyone has a know-how that is experienced not only as having always existed – change does occur, but it tends to elude the participants – but also as not in need of being made explicit, as what, for the most part, 'goes without saying' and is not questioned or in need of justification, other than by reference to the fact of tradition itself. Bourdieu called it 'learned ignorance', to express that, under the rule of tradition, people have on the one hand a great deal of know-how but on the other hand cannot necessarily explicitly formulate what rules they are following. There is often considerable room for difference and individuality, if only because it takes time – and a shift in vision – to actually recognize something as diverging from the tradition rather just forming a variant. Diverging from the tradition, however, will have consequences, as it amounts to a negation of what people hold most sacred and, in the long run, makes it hard to continue as a member of the group. Eventually, offenders will be 'frozen out'.

In many domains of life, tradition is now making way for role modelling and expertise (see below), which allow considerable control without being legalistic and explicit. But not in all. In certain domains tradition continues to be important, for instance in professions where traditions are passed on without explicit instruction by older members of the profession, learnt on the job, 'by osmosis', so that what is in fact a shared habitus is often interpreted as personal experience. I have already described how a view of language as 'tradition' has been a seminal influence on semiotics, through the work of de Saussure.

Conformity

Conformity is not quite the same thing as tradition. Rather than doing what 'we' (our group) 'have always done', it is doing 'what everybody else appears to be doing'. It knows neither explicit codes, nor the know-how that comes from the inculcation of tradition, and requires only one thing, an antenna for 'what everyone is doing'.

The rule of conformity provides little room for difference, because it is based on a fear of being different, of not blending in. It tends to occur in groups which are on the one hand egalitarian, without significant status and power differences, but on the other hand weakly cohesive, without shared traditions – for instance, people randomly thrown together in newly built suburbs, all in their own ways separated from their roots. Going against the rule of conformity has consequences – gossip, innuendo, and ultimately ostracization and social exclusion. Conformity provides little opportunity for change because its inherent egalitarianism creates obstacles to leadership. No one wants to stand up, or upstage others. No one wants to take the lead.

Conformity comes into its own in situations where we have few clues as to how to behave, and of which we have little prior experience. All we then have to go by is what we see others do, and because this does not constitute authentic know-how and experience, it can lead to particularly timid and repetitive forms of behaviour.

Role models

Under the 'rule of the role model', social control is exercised through examples given by high status people, whether in the peer group, the workplace, or the wider community – including the mass media. If we were to ask, 'Why do we have to behave in this way?' the answer would be, 'Because so-and-so does it', where 'so-and-so' is an influential person (but not an 'expert') – it could be an admired friend, someone whose work is recommended as 'best practice', a celebrity admired from afar. Even though it appears to provide much freedom of choice and does not *present* itself as a form of social control, it does give us clues for how to dress, how to talk, how to think about current issues, and much more. Not taking up clues of this kind can be a social handicap and make us appear old-fashioned, out of touch, unable to join in conversations that matter. The rule of the role model not only provides choice, it also allows for rapid and frequent change, for semiotic mobility. As a result it requires constant monitoring of the relevant media, constant comparing notes with friends and colleagues, and constant updating of the consumer goods necessary to signify one's identity and lifestyle.

While former ages had their religious role models (saints), many of today's role models come from global popular culture (stars and celebrities). Some writers on popular culture (for example, Fiske, 1989) deny that popular culture takes part in social control. They see it as raw material, as a resource with which people individually or in groups, and self-reflexively, or even subversively, construct their identities and lifestyles. It may appear so, subjectively, yet, as a result of the 'rule of the role model', we can see large numbers of people across the globe acting in very similar ways and using very similar or identical consumer goods to signify their identity. They only *talk* about it differently. They give it different *meanings*, just as contemporary branding gives different meanings to the different labels of very similar or identical consumer goods. Insofar as it is implemented through the global media, the 'rule of the role model' controls what people *do* and how they do it, not what they think about it, or say about it. It controls and unifies action (globalization), and divides meaning (localization). If attention is focused only on consumption, so that production becomes invisible, if it is focused only on 'local' meaning, and not on the deliberate control strategies of powerful global corporations, then production is treated as a natural phenomenon, which simply is there and would be pointless to criticize.

Expertise

Closely related is the rule of expertise. Here, if we ask, 'Why must I do this?', or, 'Why do this in this way?', the answer is, 'Because so-and-so says so', where 'so-and-so' is someone with specific, accredited professional expertise. Over the last two centuries professional expertise, now increasingly selected and mediated by the mass media and the publishing industry, has replaced religious law and tradition in many fields, including parenting, education, health, food preservation and preparation, and much more. As pointed out by Bunton and Burrows (1995: 208) people are constantly

> ... expected to take note of and act upon the recommendations of a whole range of 'experts' and 'advisers' located in a range of *diffuse* institutional and cultural sites.

As in the case of the role model, it *seems* that there are no explicit rules, only reasoned strategies for attaining certain goals, leading to suggestions, recommendations or guidelines which you can take or leave as you see fit. Yet the message is clear. These are the experts. They know better. Their advice is ignored at your own peril.

A special kind of expertise is that of the scientists who justify forms of social action on the basis of natural law: 'It is right to do this or that because it is natural, because it complies with our true, sociobiological nature, or with the inevitabilities of evolution.' Such rules form a hybrid between the rule of the written word and the rule of expertise, and play an especially important role in the justification of the contemporary neo-capitalist world order.

I will now use the categories I have introduced in this section to discuss two examples, one from a traditional community and one from contemporary Western consumer society.

Dress under the rule of authority

Dress can be regulated through personal authority, as when parents tell children what to wear, or on the basis of explicit, written codes, whether they are highly detailed, as in codes for ceremonial military uniforms or liturgical dress, or relatively open-ended, as in the Biblical admonition that, 'women should adorn themselves modestly and sensibly in seemly apparel' (I Tim 2: 9), or in the *Qur'an* (33: 59), 'O Prophet tell your wives, daughters and believing women to put on their *jilbabs* [long, loose shirtdresses] so that they are recognized and thus not harmed.' But rules of dress can also be based on unwritten traditions, or disseminated by role models of various kinds, for example, fashion models, or the stars of popular music, movies, sports, etc.

The example below relies on anthropological accounts of dress in two traditional Mennonite communities in the USA (Graybill and Arthur, 1999; Hamilton and Hawley, 1999). One is a small Holdeman community in Northern California – about 350 members – the other a much larger Mennonite community in Eastern Pennsylvania. Both are agricultural communities living in relative isolation from others, denying themselves access to modern media – and preserving traditional dress. Nevertheless, they shop in the same shops as non-Mennonites, and so are aware of, and have access to, a large variety of dress styles. They select from these according to the interests and values of their religion, but, as we will see, with some room for personal style, and they also make their own clothes. The prescribed dress for women is a head covering and a modest, long, loose simple dress in a restrained colour, cut in a style prescribed by the church, and worn fairly uniformly by all women. The dress code for men is less precise – they should just dress simply. Most favour jeans and a plaid or plain shirt during the week and wear a dark suit to church with a white long-sleeved shirt buttoned up to the neck and no tie.

This dress code is in the first place controlled through the impersonal authority of the Bible – for example, the quote above – and more specifically written disciplinary statements or Church regulations, *Ordnungen*, as the Amish call them. But these rules leave room for interpretation, so that other forms of control also play a role.

First of all, it is important to realize that, to the members of these communities, following the rules is not experienced as slavishly conforming to rules imposed from outside. The rules are internalized and personalized. To use the modern jargon, people 'own' them. As one woman said:

> I can say that in this kind of dress, I found my role ... For years and years I was looking for something to express that I was a Christian woman ... Once I came here and they gave me some dresses, I thought 'Now I am living how Christ wants me to live.'
>
> (Graybill and Arthur, 1999: 9)

Figure 3.1   Mennonite dress (from Graybill and Arthur, 1999: 15)

Yet there is a great deal of informal social control of the kind that is typical of tradition, where rules are upheld by the talk of the group. 'When you are having trouble with the rules', people say, 'your clothing can show it. This is why everyone watches what everyone else is wearing and how they are wearing it, because clothing shows acceptance of all the rules of the church' (ibid.: 25). Or, in discussing a specific case: 'For quite some time, Leah was in "church trouble", She was ill, spiritually ill. She was expelled for having "foreign spirits". We could all see it in her behaviour and her dress. She was just out of control' (ibid.: 9).

Finally, there is formal social control, with different kinds of sanctions, administered by elders or ministers. 'Marginal members' can get into 'church trouble' and 'set back', denied communion, until they make a public confession of wrongdoing and are accepted again. If that does not happen, expulsion will follow.

How strict are these rules? First of all, they do not apply to everyone in the same way. We have already seen that men have more freedom than women. Young girls also have more freedom and can choose from a wider variety of designs and dress styles. Often they test the limits, for instance by wearing dresses with a tighter fit. The community recognizes that they need to do so to attract a husband, but after marriage women are expected to start dressing 'plain'. Still, even then it is possible for women to be 'marginal' and wear dresses that are considered acceptable even though they deviate somewhat from the norm (see figure 3.2).

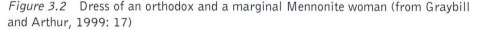

Figure 3.2   Dress of an orthodox and a marginal Mennonite woman (from Graybill and Arthur, 1999: 17)

However strongly the dress rules of these communities are governed by written codes and traditions, there *is* room for change, especially if a high status role model initiates the change, and is then imitated by a sufficient number of others.

> Amish women are supposed to keep their hair covered except at home in the presence of close family members. While the Amish permit unmarried women to use a bandanna to keep their hair covered while in public during the summertime, married women are supposed to wear the black bonnet in public, regardless of weather. Yet many married women were observed in town with only the white bonnet in summertime. One woman noted that as long as the bishop's wife does it, she could also.
>
> (Hamilton and Hawley, 1999: 42)

This can then result in a change in the written rules, the *Ordnung,* if the bishop decides not to do anything about it.

In communities of this kind people regard dress as semiotic and know what it is they express through the way they dress: 'plainness', 'being in this world but not of it' (ibid.: 13); submission to male authority – as one woman said, 'Women wear a black head covering over uncut hair to symbolise a woman's submission to God and her husband', (ibid.: 16) – and group solidarity – 'It expresses that we are one body' (ibid.: 20). But the rules also take account of age and gender and of doctrinal variations, and they do leave some room for individual difference ('marginality'). Finally, however fixed these rules may seem, there are both formal and informal ways in which they can change. I will now compare this traditional semiotic regime with the 'role model' and 'expertise' oriented semiotic regimes that have become dominant in Western consumer society.

Colour and identity under the rule of the role model

In some contexts colours signify aspects of identity on the basis of quite explicit (and quite arbitrary) written rules, as in this extract from the academic dress rules of the University of Newcastle (Australia):

> The academic dress for graduates of the University shall be:
> (a) Doctors of Architecture, Doctors of Education, Doctors of Engineering, Doctors of Letters, Doctors of Medicine, Doctors of Music, Doctors of Nursing, Doctors of Science, Doctors of the University – a festal gown of cardinal; red cloth, with a hood of garnet cloth lined with silk cloth of the appropriate colour, namely
> Doctor of Architecture – deep indian red
> Doctor of Business – turquoise
> Doctor of Education – jade
> Doctor of Engineering – lapis lazuli
> Doctor of Law – waratah
> Doctor of Letters – pearl
> Doctor of Medicine – rhodochrosite
> Doctor of Music – lilac
> Doctor of Nursing – international orange
> Doctor of Science – topaz
> Doctor of the University – silver grey
> and a black velvet bonnet with a gold cord

In other cases colours signify identity through unwritten rules, as in traditional Moravian Slovakian dress (Bogatyrev 1971 [1937]), where gentlemen wore white breeches and peasants blue ones, Pozlovice men carmine and green ribbons and Biskupice men red ones, married men gold hat bands and unmarried men red and white ones, and so on. In such a context colour is used to indicate people's *stable* identities – gender, age, class, provenance – through *conventional* colour signs. Whatever might have once motivated the choice of these particular colours – for example, the price of the dyes – is no longer known. For all practical purposes these colour signs are arbitrary, used the way they are 'because they always have been used that way'.

In contemporary Western consumer society colour also signifies identities, but with a number of significant differences.

1   The identities signified are unstable. They can be made and remade. Like the consumer goods we use to express them, they are disposable and replaceable.

2   The aspects of identity signified are not gender, age, class, etc., but 'personality traits', such as 'adventurous', 'calm', etc.

3   The colour signs used are not arbitrary, but motivated. They are experienced, not as 'always having been there', but as 'always new' and a unique creation of the sign producer.

There are certain accessories that signify change, that identify new territory. Find them, and you've found the fastest, easiest way to transform the look of any garment no matter what its price tag.

(*Australian Vogue*, November 1997: 220)

4   People are not necessarily aware of all the connotations of the colours they wear. They may for instance wear military colours without intending to convey any form of identification with the military. If asked why they wear these colours, they might refer to fashion – 'I wear them because they are "coo" (or "in" or "the latest thing")' – or to taste – 'I wear them because I like them'. Yet the military connotation is objectively there. The military is objectively one of the places – perhaps one of the most important ones – 'where this colour has come from'. Thus appeals to fashion and taste can serve to disavow meaning. They can allow people to take mental distance from the very things they are signifying.

5   Rules are not recognized as rules but as models and 'best practice' or 'trendsetting' examples, or as advice, suggestions, guidelines. In terms of this chapter, the most important types of rule are therefore role modelling, expertise, and the 'fashion dictate'. They are also written, albeit in a style that is very different from that of the Biblical precepts and Church *Ordnungen* discussed in the previous section, because it is predominantly the media which tutor us in the latest dress rules, and they do so in a playful, often almost flippant style, and through a form of 'writing' which is multimodal, involving not only spoken and written words, but also images, layout, typography, movement, etc.

I will now discuss these three kinds of rule in turn. But we should be remember that they often combine, in various admixtures. My main example will be the use of colour in home decoration, but from time to time I will return to the example of dress.

Role models

Home decoration magazines constantly tell their readers how to express their identities and lifestyles through the way they decorate and furnish their homes. The same applies to the television makeover programmes which have now increasingly moved into prime time evening viewing slots, and bring home, night after night, the message that we can remake ourselves and choose our identities and lifestyles. Such texts rely on two kinds of role model:

1   celebrities, for instance authors, actors and other television personalities, of whose exemplary homes we then get a glimpse in the magazine; and
2   ordinary people whose homes are shown as examples of 'best practice'.

Before getting to see the homes, readers are introduced to the role models, as in this feature about the home of actor Michael Melia:

> The kitchen was one of the first things that attracted actor Michael Melia to his Middlesex home. 'We were living in a maisonette at the time. Our kids Charlotte and Tom were growing up and we desperately needed more space. In particular, we wanted a bigger kitchen because my wife Celia had just started a cake-making business,' he says. Michael, whose investigative skills were so much in evidence in the BBC series *Dangerfield*, had also used clever detective work to find the house.
>
> (*House Beautiful*, September 1998: 112)

The same magazine also features ordinary people as role models, for instance Hamish and Vanessa:

> Guessing what Hamish and Vanessa Dows do for a living isn't too difficult – a pair of feet on the house number plate is a dead giveaway for a couple who are both chiropodists, but it's also an indication of the fun they've had in decorating their home.
>
> (*House Beautiful*, September 1998: 20)

In the article itself we learn, amongst other things, that Hamish and Vanessa:

> used nearly the whole spectrum in their house, from mustard yellow and leaf green in the sitting room, to brick red and blue in the dining room. Their bedroom is a soft buttery yellow combined with orange, there's lemon and lime in the breakfast room and cornflower and Wedgwood blues on the stairs. 'I think it's great there are so many bright shades in the house', says Hamish, 'It's a shame people aren't more adventurous with this use of colour. It's when you start being timid that things go wrong'.

In this quote we get both a description of the colours – the fact that they range across the spectrum, and are 'bright' – and the meanings attaching to them – 'adventurous', 'not timid'. There is 'motivation': it is easy to see why these particular signifiers – 'multi-coloured' and 'bright' – should have a potential for meaning 'adventurous' – and why their opposite, a single pale colour, could be said to be more 'timid'. It is also clear that the colours signify 'personality traits' – 'adventurous', 'not timid'. Hamish and Vanessa use their home to signify lifestyle identity, to show what kind of people they are, 'adventurous' people, 'not afraid to use very bright paint shades' and 'always confident about their choices' (ibid.: 20).

Expertise

Colour expertise has a long history. Goethe (1970 [1810]: 328), while recognizing the conventional meanings of colours, was the first to relate colour preferences to 'personality', although only in the case of women:

> The female sex in youth is attached to rose colour and sea green, in age to violet and dark green. The fair-haired prefer violet as opposed to light yellow, the brunettes blues as opposed to yellow-red.

His idea was soon put into practice by artists. The German 'Lucasbund' painters Overbeck and Pforr, for instance, used hair and dress colour to express the 'character' of the women they portrayed. They had colours for 'proud and cool' yet 'cheerful and happy' personalities – black hair with black, blue, white and violet; colours for 'solitariness, modesty, goodheartedness and calm' – blonde hair with blue, grey and crimson; colours for 'happiness and good temper, innocent roguishness, naiveté and cheerfulness' – reddish brown hair with crimson, violet-grey and black – and so on (Gage, 1999: 189). Towards the end of the nineteenth century, these ideas began to be taken up in the then new field of psychology. The early twentieth century psychologist Stefanescu-Goangua, for instance, associated blue with 'peaceful, quiet, serious, cool, calm and dreamy' people (ibid.: 609). Modern colour experts still work in the same tradition, basing themselves on psychological testing, and relating colour to personality traits. Lacy (1996: 36), for instance, applies this kind of expertise to colour in home decoration:

> A yellow entrance hall usually indicates a person who has ideas and a wide field of interests. A home belonging to an academic would probably contain a distinctive shade of yellow as this colour is associated with the intellect, ideas and a searching mind ... A green entrance hall – say, a warm apple green – indicates a home in which children, family and pets are held in high importance ... A blue entrance hall indicates a place in which people have strong opinions – there could be a tendency to appear aloof as they can be absorbed too much in their own world.

Although this kind of expert discourse is descriptive, in magazines and other media, and in the work of the colour consultants who advise companies on their colour schemes, it is used to give expert advice, whether directly – 'Yellow and orange are perfect for a kitchen-cum-dining room because they're bright by day and warm by night' – or by mixing the rule of the role model and the rule of the expert, as in the case of Jane Collins who is introduced as a top interior decorator in an article which shows off her own home:

> Her latest habitat (she moves as regularly and happily as a nomad) is surprisingly spare and elegant, as you might expect from someone with a sense of the aesthetic in her genes. After all, Jane's great aunt was Nancy Lancaster, of

Colefax and Fowler fame, while her brother, Henry Wyndham, is chairman of Sotheby's ...

(*Ideal Home and Lifestyle*, September 1998: 60)

The colours she chooses, incidentally, are quite different from those of Hamish and Vanessa's home (ibid.: 62):

> This room has a tranquil feel due to the soft, calm palette Jane has chosen: biscuit-hued fabric on the walls, off-white silk curtains edged with fine lustrous ivory fringing, faded pink and white striped chairs and blush-rose taffeta cushions on the sofa.

Again, the colours are both described – 'pale pastels', 'biscuit hue', 'off-white', 'faded pink and white', 'blush rose' – and interpreted in terms of personality traits such as 'tranquil', 'soft', and 'calm'.

Fashion

In his book, *The Fashion System* (1983), Roland Barthes analysed the captions of magazine fashion spreads. Three aspects of his analysis relate to our topic:

1 There are two types of fashion meaning, and they can occur either together or separately: (a) the clothes are described as being 'in fashion', 'fashionable', and this is part of their meaning; (b) the clothes are either said to be suitable for certain times, places or activities, and/or linked to 'personality traits' of the kind we have already described: 'frivolous', 'wild', 'feminine', 'liberated', 'sexy', 'happy', 'romantic', 'chic', 'adventurous', 'delicate', 'sophisticated', 'extravagant', and so on.

2 Although the captions present the 'lexical' and 'grammatical' rules of fashion, the rules for how different items and accessories should be combined to create fashionable outfits, the language of the fashion caption is very different from the language of the grammar book. Fashion writing delights in playing with language – in alliteration, rhyme, inversion, metaphor, and so on. It can forever invent new ways of saying that same thing: 'this is "in"'. To give just one example, the caption 'These fresh new cottons preview a delicious turn towards very feminine fashion' has (a) the signifier (cottons), (b) the first kind of fashion meaning ('preview a turns towards ... fashion' tells the reader that cottons are going to be 'in' this season), and (c) personality traits, for example, 'feminine' – and all this is wrapped in language that plays both with sound (alliterations and half-rhymes like 'fresh ... feminine ... fashion') and meaning (metaphors such as 'preview').

3 Fashion captions also provide cultural context for fashion, as when they refer to a dress as 'the dress Manet would have loved to paint'. In this way the provenances of the fashion signs, their connotations, are brought into play. Here we return to

an earlier theme. Are people aware of all the connotations of the clothes they wear? The answer must be both yes and no. Of course we are all aware where military colours come from. But at same the time, this is fashion. We have the option to deny it. We are allowed to say, 'I just wear because it's a cool colour', or 'because I like it'. John Berger (1972: 140), in a discussion of advertising, referred to this kind of knowledge as 'a cultural lesson half-learnt':

What we learn at school of history, mythology, poetry can be used in the manufacturing of glamour. Cigars can be sold in the name of a King, underwear in connection with the Sphinx, a new car by reference to the status of a country house. The fact that these historical or poetic or moral references are imprecise and ultimately meaningless is an advantage: they should not be understandable, they should merely be reminiscent of cultural lessons half-learnt.

The article about Hamish and Vanessa provides us with another example of this last point. The 'personality trait' meanings it gives are quite explicit and attributed to Hamish and Vanessa themselves. In this respect they are represented as knowing what kind of meanings they are making, and as *newly* making these meanings to express who they are and what they value. But a closer look at the colours in the photograph reveals that their colour scheme is not quite as bright as they make out (see figure 3.3).

Although the colours are highly saturated, they are also relatively dark and 'impure', certainly by comparison to modernist, Mondrian-type pure colours. Such colours were very much in fashion in the 1990s, and they had a specific provenance in the historical television series which were then popular. They are, in fact, an exact match of some of the historic colours on the colour chart of a paint manufacturer called Farrow & Ball:

The specialist firm Farrow & Ball whose colours were used to recreate 18th and 19th century England in television adaptations of *Pride and Prejudice* and *Middlemarch*, reports that its sales have constantly risen by 40% each year over the past ten years.

(*Guardian* Weekend Magazine, 19 January 2002: 67)

Perhaps Hamish and Vanessa's interior is not just, or not only, an original and 'motivated' expression of their personalities − it is that as well − but also follows fashion. Hamish and Vanessa not only use the affordances of colour range and brightness to express their personalities, they also draw on cultural connotations, and thereby on the values of the place − or in this case time: the eighteenth and nineteenth centuries − where these colours come from. By decorating their home with these colours, do they symbolically identify with the values of a past era, and with the nostalgia for a 'lost' Englishness that has been so salient with many throughout the 1990s? Perhaps. But neither they, nor the writer of the article says so.

Figure 3.3 Historic colours (*House Beautiful*, September 1998: 21)

Exercises

1   Find a 'how to' book for amateur photographers. Choose a technical section, (for example, 'depth of field') and an 'artistic' section (for example, 'composition'). What kinds of rules are used in each, and why?

2   List the role models and experts in two magazines of your choice – for example, one 'upmarket' and one 'downmarket' magazine, or one magazine for teenage girls and one for middle-aged women. How do the magazines differ?

3   In many European countries there is now an issue about whether girls should be allowed to wear Islamic head coverings in public schools. Collect some relevant newspaper clippings – and/or interview relevant people. How are the two types of dress rule involved represented? What value judgments are attached to each by the parties involved in the debate?

4   Using the internet, look at how companies describe the meanings of the colours of their logos and company colour schemes. What kinds of meanings are signified by what kinds of colours? Are these colour signs motivated?

5   Make a series of photos to bring out (a) differences between things that are apparently uniform and subject to strict rules – for example, Islamic head coverings – and/or (b) similarities between things that are apparently a matter of free choice and individual decision – for example, wearing baseball caps.

4 Semiotic functions

Introduction

The idea of 'functionalism' runs like a red thread through twentieth century thought and practice. Practices previously based on tradition or aesthetics were now thought of as fulfilling pragmatic social functions. Music, for instance, could increase productivity in the workplace, or sales in the supermarket. Films could educate citizens and promote attitudes that suited the social and political climate of the day. Houses were no longer just dwellings but could instil social norms and values in their occupants – I once had an apartment in a building that was originally built as a workers housing project in the 1920s. The windows of the street-side living room were so high that you had to stand up to look out of them. I later learnt that this had been done deliberately to wean the workers away from their habit of hanging out of the window and talking to each other across the street, and to educate them into the values of an inward-looking family life.

Social semiotics, too, has been influenced by functionalism, not least through Halliday's functional theory of language, in which syntax is not a system of formal rules but a resource for social interaction. In this chapter I will compare and contrast how functionalism emerged in three separate fields: the practical field of design – especially architecture – and the theoretical fields of sociology and anthropology on the one hand, and linguistics and semiotics on the other hand. There are two reasons for doing so. First of all, social semiotics is interested not only in multimodal objects of study but also in multimodal (interdisciplinary) theories and methods. Second, my comparison will once again include a look at the history of these theories and methods, in order to show that not only semiotic resources and their uses but also theories and methods arise from the interests and needs of society at a given time, whether researchers are aware of this or not.

Functionalism in architecture

In the nineteenth century, new technologies and new practices began to require new types of buildings – railway stations and factories, for instance. While houses and traditional public buildings were still built in heavily ornamented 'retro' styles – for example, neo-Gothicism – for these buildings new building materials and new construction methods were developed – for example, steel-frame building – and they were built in a functional style, devoid of ornamentation. Eventually this would lead to a new aesthetic, an 'anti-aesthetic': 'If a building provides adequately, completely, and without compromise for its purpose, it is a good building, regardless of appearance' (Hitchcock and Johnson, 1932: 36).

In the USA, this new style was applied to less utilitarian buildings as well, for instance to the skyscrapers which began to be built in New York, and it was a late nineteenth century American architect, Louis Sullivan, who coined the phrase that would become gospel for generations of designers across the world: 'form follows function'. Architects should concentrate on what the building is for, this slogan implies, focus on the activities and objects the building is to house, and on the relations between them, and they should abandon all preconceived ideas of 'correct' style – of what a house, or a school, or an office should *look* like – basing their design purely on the purpose(s) of the building.

Many American architects combined the functional approach with traditional ornamentation. If questioned, they would argue that it is also one of the functions of buildings to please the clients (Hitchcock and Johnson, 1932: 14). In the USA these clients were of course predominantly wealthy individuals and corporations. But in Europe architects increasingly worked for city councils and national governments. Here functional architecture became allied to social engineering. In the late nineteenth and early twentieth century city councils began pulling down their inner city slums, in an attempt to combat anti-social behaviour – a new word at the time. The inhabitants would be re-housed in garden cities of 30,000 to 50,000 people around the cities. The architects used in these projects – and later in post-WWII rebuilding – no longer just designed buildings, they designed whole cities, and whole ways of life. The young Le Corbusier, for instance, envisaged cities with:

> ... three sorts of population: citizens, who will be located in the centre of the city; workers whose life unfolds half of the time in the centre and half in the garden cities; and the labouring masses who will divide their time between suburban factories and the garden cities.
>
> (quoted in Brace Taylor, 1972: 102)

So it was in Europe, in the 1920s, that the key principles of the functionalist programme were most sharply formulated, especially by the artists and designers of the Dutch *De Stijl* movement and the teachers, designers and artists of the German Bauhaus, a short-lived but very influential school of art and design. These principles focused on the following.

Economizing and rationalizing

Like other modern design products, houses should be cheap and affordable, and this was to be achieved by the use of new, often synthetic, materials, and by means of standardization, the use of ready-made parts that could be assembled in various ways.

Functionality

Houses should be functional, 'machines to live in', as Le Corbusier famously put it. Architects should research the activities of the occupants and base their design on this, and this alone. As Van Doesburg said it, in the magazine *De Stijl*: 'The new architecture is functional, that is to say, it develops out of the exact determination of the practical demand' (1924: 78). Here is a characteristic quote from Hannes Meyer, the architect who succeeded Walter Gropius as Director of the Bauhaus in the mid-1920s:

1 sex life	5 personal hygiene	9 cooking
2 sleeping habits	6 weather protection	10 heating
3 pets	7 hygiene in the home	11 exposure to the sun
4 gardening	8 car maintenance	12 service

these are the only motives when building a house. We examine the daily routine of everyone who lives in the house and this gives us the functional diagram – the functional diagram and the economic programme are the determining principles of the building project.

(Meyer, 1928: 117)

But in practice it was, of course, the city councillors and the architects who determined the needs and interests of the future occupants. Indeed, it was often said that with good design people start to *discover* their needs.

Architecture in the service of welfare

In all this it became the mission of architecture to help bring about a harmonious and prosperous 'model' society:

New housing projects are to be the ultimate aim of public welfare and as such an intentionally organised, public-spirited project in which collective and individual energies are merged in public-spiritedness based on an integral, co-operative foundation.

(Meyer, 1928: 118)

This applied not only to housing projects. Architects like Le Corbusier also designed schools, hospitals and other public buildings. Le Corbusier often modelled such buildings on monasteries, with their 'harmony between the individual and the collective life', as he saw it (quoted in Brace Taylor, 1972: 90). In a building commissioned by the Salvation Army and designed to house homeless families he created 'cell' like apartments, concrete blocks with lead padding in between – to create complete silence and isolation – built around communal spaces. In all this, building became 'the deliberate organisation of the processes of life ... nothing but organisation, social, technical, economic, psychological' (Meyer, 1928: 118). Later, however, architectural functionalism would be criticized for causing, rather than solving, social problems, indeed, creating new slums, for example, in post-WWII housing estates.

Avoiding all ornamentation

According to the Czech architect Teige (1929: 40):

> Architecture creates instruments. Aesthetic intervention in utilitarian design inevitably leads to an imperfect object. It obscures the utilitarian aspect and considers practical values such as comfort, warmth, stability, to be necessary sacrifices which people should make for a cultural tradition ... Where the idea of style prevails, form precedes function.

No one has ever been able to follow these principles exactly. Le Corbusier's buildings, for instance, often used modern technology not functionally but symbolically, to express the *idea* of modernity and functionality. He saw the steamship as a key example of a large structure that was entirely functional – and would then use elements of the steamship to make buildings *look* like steamships rather than function like steamships, for example, by making the edge of a building pointed like the bow of a ship, or by using the grey steel of a battleship and the red, yellow and blue colours of semaphore flags:

> Having grasped the nautical associations of the colours, the viewer immediately begins to see formal correspondences between a ramp and a gangplank, a roof and a prow, massive interior columns and smokestacks, exposed kitchen pipes and engine room gadgets.
>
> (Riley, 1994: 212)

Postmodern architecture has rejected functionalism and brought back an emphasis on the visual, at least in the way architecture is talked about and depicted. Not the relation between the elements of the building, its functional parts, but the façade became central, as something that should (a) fit in with its environment – for example, through keeping the façades of older buildings and building new structures behind them – and (b) form a symbolic surface, a surface to read, either because it is covered in messages that may have little or nothing to do with the building itself, or because it connotes styles of building and ornamentation from other times and places, and the values we associate with these.

But the buildings behind these façades are still 'functional'. Where, before, the semiotic aspects of buildings were ignored or disguised as functional, now the opposite occurred. Halliday (1975) has argued that language is both about what we *do* and what we *mean* – and that to mean is in fact just one of the things we do, while the way we do things is itself also meaningful. Similarly buildings are always both symbolic and functional, and this is not just a matter of the difference between (symbolic) façades and (functional) floorplans. It goes deeper. Yes, of course, housing serves the basic functions of shelter, warmth, comfort, stability, and so on, but these are themselves semiotic, as they are inevitably culturally inflected, differently understood and differently practised in different cultures and eras.

Functionalism in sociology and anthropology

Sociological and anthropological functionalism came about in the same period as architectural functionalism, which shows that functionalism was bigger than individual institutions, a way of thinking that ran through society as a whole. The French sociologist Durkheim first defined social institutions such as education and religion as functioning to fulfil the 'general needs', not so much of individuals, as of society as a whole, the 'social organism'. For instance, in *The Elementary Forms of the Religious Life* (1964 [1912]), he described religion, not as a system of meaning, an interpretation of what the world is like and why it is the way it is, but pragmatically, as having a positive function in society, as helping to maintain social cohesion and moral unity.

Under his influence, anthropologists like Malinowski and Radcliffe-Brown, and sociologists like Talcott Parsons and Robert Merton, further developed functionalism. The key idea is to see society as a relation between *parts* – individuals, or smaller groups – and a *whole* – society – in which the activities of the parts function to maintain the unity and cohesion of the whole, while the whole functions to satisfy the basic needs of the parts. In the process, basic human needs are transformed into cultural imperatives which people then 'internalize', so that they become second nature to them and are not seen as impositions. Even basic physiological needs like hunger, said Malinowski, are 'determined by the social milieu':

> Nowhere and never will man, however primitive, feed on the fruits of his environment. He always selects and rejects, produces and prepares. He does not depend on the physiological rhythm of hunger and satiety alone; his digestive processes are timed and trained by the daily routine of his tribe, nation or class. He eats at definite times, and he goes for his food to his table; the table is supplied from the kitchen, the kitchen from the larder. And this again is replenished from the market or from the tribal food-supply system.
>
> (1939: 943)

Clearly Malinowski's anthropological functionalism has much in common with architectural functionalism. But there are also important differences. Apart from the fact that architecture creates the *environment* for the activities of social groups (for example, families) and institutions (for example, schools) while Malinowski discusses the social activities themselves, architectural functionalism saw pragmatic activities such as eating and sleeping as essentially non-cultural, biological. As we have seen, Hannes Meyer called buildings 'biological apparatuses serving the needs of both body and mind' (1928: 117) and Karl Teige (1929: 40) said that culture induces people to 'sacrifice practical values such as comfort, warmth, stability'. For anthropologists, on the other hand, all activities are cultural. Culture both expresses and transforms basic biological needs.

American functionalist sociology sees society as a complex machine in which every part has its function with respect to the whole. Individuals occupy specific positions and fulfil specific roles, and individual personality is seen as nothing more, or less, than the sum, or amalgam, of all the positions an individual has occupied and still occupies, and all the roles he or she has played and still plays. Roles, in turn, that is the things people do, function to maintain order and harmony in society and ensure that the machinery will keep turning. But as especially Robert Merton stressed (quoted in Davis, 1942), people are not always aware of the functions of their actions. Some functions may be 'latent'. Hopi Indians, for instance, perform rain dances which have the manifest function of inducing rain. Of this the Hopi Indians themselves are perfectly aware. But the *latent* function of these dances, according to Merton (ibid.) is to provide an occasion for communal activity and for the reconfirmation of the group's sharing of norms and values. This is of course something the Hopi would not be aware of, and perhaps not even agree with.

The need to interpret every social phenomenon as functional sometimes led to rather extreme points of view. American functionalist sociologists have, for instance, interpreted inequality as functional, arguing that it is society's way of ensuring, through appropriate rewards, that the 'most important' tasks are carried out by the 'most qualified' people (Davis and Moore, 1945), without much regard for the dysfunctional and destabilizing effects inequality can have, or the fact that the highest rewards are not always given on these basis of qualifications and experience, but also on the basis of birth and privilege. Other functional sociologists do build in the possibility of 'dysfunction' and 'deviance', often in terms of health metaphors, as a kind of 'pathology' of the 'social organism'.

During the 1960s functionalist sociology increasingly came under fire. It was seen as insufficiently critical of society, a thinly disguised ideological legitimation of American society in which there was no place for the different and often conflicting interests of different groups, and in which individuals were seen as cogs in society's machinery – fulfilling predetermined roles with greater or lesser efficiency, and unable to offer resistance, or induce change. In short, there was no place for any form of social agency (Giddens, 1976). Approaches like ethnomethodology and conversation analysis brought a new kind of sociology, which focused not on the 'macro', on society as a whole, but on the 'micro', on individuals interacting in specific, local situations. This new sociology argued that people do not fulfil predetermined roles but improvise and adjust how they act and interact, for instance on the basis of unexpected forms of feedback.

So it was not only in architecture but also in sociology that the pendulum swung in the 1960s and 1970s. There was now, on the one hand, a somewhat discredited sociology that looked at the broader picture, but without paying sufficient attention to agency and the possibility of resistance and change that follows from it, and, on the other hand, a sociology of local actions described in an institutional vacuum. It became an increasingly ritualized intellectual debate between the view that social actors are structurally determined and the view that they are active, empowered agents. Too often it was forgotten that this is not an either–or issue, that not all people are equally determined or empowered, and that different situations are structurally determined to different degrees. Take the example of family apartments or houses. How actively and fully we can change the places we live in depends on whether we rent or own, on the amount of money we can spend, and on quite a few other factors. But we can, in principle, change them, while we cannot change the television programmes we watch, despite the recent tendency in media studies to speak of television audiences as 'active audiences', and to discuss TV programmes as if there were no institutional interests behind their production and distribution.

Functionalism in linguistics and semiotics

Functionalism has also played a role in linguistics and semiotics, most recently under the influence of Michael Halliday,[1] who distinguishes two related kinds of function: (1) 'function in structure', and (2) 'function in society' (or 'use of language'). The term 'structure' in 'function in structure' refers to syntactic structure, which in mainstream twentieth century linguistics had usually been a matter of formal rules of 'well-formedness' or 'correctness'. Linguists like Halliday reinterpreted them in functional terms. So here, the 'whole' was not 'society' but the 'clause', or the 'text', and the 'parts' were not 'individuals' or 'groups' within society but the elements of clause or text structure. Here is an example:

> [Nguyen Ngoc Loan]   [shot]   [the Vietcong suspect]

Each of the parts of this clause – as indicated by the brackets– not only has a particular position in the clause (initial, medial, final) but also a functional role with respect to the whole. The verb form 'shot' functions as the process, as that what is done or happens. The role of the nominal group 'Nguyen Ngoc Loan' is that of 'actor', or 'doer' of the action, and the role of the nominal group 'the Vietcong suspect' is that of the 'goal', the 'entity to which the action is done'. Each part contributes to the construction of the whole, the represented action, just as, in sociological functionalism, each part of society contributes to the 'social organism'. As Halliday put it:

> [grammar] construes all the bits of a language – its clauses, phrases and so on –
> as organic configurations of functions. In other words, each part is interpreted as
> functional with respect to the whole.
>
> (1985: xiii)

The idea of the 'function in structure' has carried over into social semiotics, for instance in Kress and Van Leeuwen's systemic-functional grammar of visual design

Figure 4.1   Vietnam Execution (Eddie Adams, 1968)

(1996). In figure 4.1 the *vector* formed by Loan's outstretched arm and gun functions as 'process', and the two main *volumes*, Loan and the Vietcong suspect, have the roles of actor and goal, respectively. In other words, different semiotic modes can realize the *same* roles by different means, through different observable forms.

The other aspect of Halliday's linguistic functionalism, 'function in society', relates to the function of the whole for the parts. Like functionalist sociology, Halliday's account of the function of language in society stresses that the basic needs of individuals are fulfilled by the 'whole' that unites individuals, in this case language: 'Language has evolved to satisfy human needs, and the way it is organised is functional with respect to those needs' (1985: xiii). The relation between 'function in structure' and 'function in society' is most clearly articulated in Halliday's account of child language acquisition (op. cit.), which I will therefore describe in a little more detail.

Between the age of 6 and 18 months approximately, says Halliday, children may not yet be learning language but they *are* already learning the *functions* of language, using their vocal resources to explore what you can *do* with language, and discovering, in this order, and always in the context of actual interactions with the mother or other carers:

1 The *instrumental* function of language, the fact that you can use language to express what you want.
2 The *regulative* function of language, the fact that you can use it to get people to do things for you.

3   The *interactive* function of language, the fact that you can use it to interact, for example, to greet or express your pleasure at seeing someone.

4   The *personal* function of language, the fact that you can use it to express your feelings, for example, your pleasure or disgust at something.

5   The *heuristic* function of language, the fact that you can use it to find out about things.

6   The *imaginative* use of language, the fact that you can use it to pretend, and

7   The *informative* use of language, the fact that you can use it to impart information.

To explore these functions children develop a repertoire of some 50-odd vocal noises which may be inventions or imitations of words they have heard, for example, *nanananana* for 'I want that thing now'. Only the mother and perhaps one or two others will understand this 'protolanguage', but it does serve its purpose of communication and it does demonstrate to the child not only that you can, for instance, regulate other people's behaviour but also that you can use language to do it.

At about 18 months, the child gradually begins to understand that these communicative functions coincide with the functions of the elements of language – for instance the regulative function with the imperative mood. This signals the beginning of its 'move into the adult language'. As in architectural functionalism, 'form follows function' – language is only adopted once the child has come to understand the needs it fulfils and the functions it can serve.

Later the child generalizes the seven 'protofunctions' into two 'metafunctions': '(1) to understand the environment (the *ideational* function), and (2) to act on the others in it (the *interpersonal* function)' (Halliday, 1985: xiii). To these a third metafunctional component will be added, the 'textual', 'which breathes relevance into the other two', and marshals combined representations-cum-interactions into the kind of coherent wholes that we recognize as specific kinds of texts or communicative events (ibid.). Halliday stresses that language always fulfils these three functions simultaneously, and that there is no particular hierarchy among them – all three are equally important. The metafunctions have also played a key role in the development of social semiotic extensions of Halliday's linguistic theory. In developing their grammar of visual design, for instance, Kress and Van Leeuwen (1996) began their research by assuming that all semiotic systems will be able to fulfil all three of Halliday's metafunctions, and by asking how the ideational, the interpersonal and the textual function are fulfilled in visual communication.

Roman Jakobson's account of the functions of language (1960) has been even more widely used in semiotics. Jakobson recognized six functions, and related them to the elements of communication: (1) the *referential function* is oriented towards the *context* referred to in the act of communication, to what the message is about, (2) the *emotive function* is oriented towards the *addresser*, and 'aims at a direct expression of the speaker's attitude toward what he is speaking about' (1960: 354), and (3) the *conative function* is oriented towards the *addressee*, and similar to Halliday's 'regulative' protofunction: language in its function of *doing* things to, for or with the addressee. These first three functions correspond to those of Bühler (1934), who related them to the system of 'person', the emotive function to 'I', the first person, the conative function to 'you', the second person, and the referential function to 'he, she, it, they', the third person.

But Jakobson added three further functions: (4) the *phatic function* –this term came from Malinowski – which is oriented towards the *channel*, or, more precisely, towards 'keeping the channel open', and 'displayed by a profuse exchange of ritualised formulas, or by entire dialogues with the mere purport of prolonging communication'. In other words, it is communication for the sake of communication, communication to avoid awkward silences (1960: 355); (5) the *metalingual function*, oriented towards the *code,* and coming to the fore 'whenever the addresser and/or the addressee need to check up whether they use the same code', whether, for instance they mean the same thing by a given word, as in 'Do you know what I mean?' or 'I don't quite follow you', and (6) the *poetic function*, which focuses on the *message* itself, and brings in an aesthetic element, not just in poetry but also in everyday language:

> 'Why do you always say *Joan and Margery*, yet never *Margery and Joan*? Do you prefer Joan to her twin sister?' 'Not at all, it just sounds smoother.'...A girl used to talk about 'the horrible Harry'. 'Why horrible?', 'Because I hate him'. 'But why not *dreadful, terrible, frightful, disgusting*?' 'I don't know, but *horrible* fits him better.' Without realizing it, she clung to the poetic device of paronomasia.
>
> (Jakobson, 1960: 356–7)

Two of the differences between these two accounts are worth looking at more closely.

The balance between the social and the individual

Halliday recognizes neither an 'emotive', nor a 'poetic' function, even though something like the former does exist in the child's protolanguage – the 'personal' function. His arguments for this are linguistic: these functions 'are not distinguished in the linguistic system' (quoted in Parret, 1974: 95). But Jakobson *also* motivates his functions by relating them to specific linguistic expressions, it is just that he draws the line between what does and what does not belong to the linguistic system a little differently and more inclusively. For Jakobson, the emotive function is expressed by overall or 'prosodic' features that cannot be tied to specific elements, for instance by features of voice quality or of attitudinal style, in short by the features that 'flavour all our utterances, on their phonic, grammatical and lexical level' (1960: 354). And the poetic function is expressed by poetic systems such as rhyme, alliteration and metric structure. The net result is, of course, that there *is* more space for expressiveness and aesthetic pleasure in Jakobson's version of linguistic functionalism.

Hierarchical and non-hierarchical relations between functions

Both Halliday and Jakobson see all their functions as always all present in every utterance. But while Halliday says that all three functions are always equally important (1978: 50), Jakobson says that any given function can dominate the others in specific contexts. The poetic function for instance 'is not the sole function of verbal art but only its dominant, determining function, whereas in all other verbal activities it acts as a subsidiary, accessory constituent' (1960: 356). This principle can be extended to other functions. In an advertisement, for instance, the 'conative' function will be in the foreground, in a news report the 'referential' function, at least on the level of 'manifest' functions.

Halliday's functional linguistics, and the functional approaches to semiotics it has inspired, have been widely used as research and development tools in pragmatic enterprises such as the teaching of writing and the design of documents, and they have also been influential in critical linguistics and critical discourse analysis, because they are useful for bringing out the functions of socially important texts, such as political speeches, media texts, etc. But they have also been critiqued for being too producer-oriented and assuming that the act of interpretation is structurally determined, and for not allowing space for expressiveness and creativity. Such critiques have not always been fully acknowledged or convincingly countered. Some functional linguists and semioticians have just ignored them or rejected them flat out, others have dressed up functional social semiotics in postmodern wrappings without essentially changing the theory, much as architects have hidden functional structures behind postmodern façades, and postmodern social theorists have allowed functionalism in by the backdoor (see for example, Mouzelis' (1995) critique of Giddens).

Here I want to explore these issues by looking at specific examples of designed objects, and investigate three issues, (1) 'function in structure', inbuilt functionality, (2) 'function in society', and (3) the degree to which users are either structurally determined by the way the object is designed and the rules of use that surround it, or free to use it as they want. While I will not pretend that I can solve issues that have been debated throughout the twentieth century with a single example, I do hope my example will help make the issues a little clearer and the theory a little less abstract. The example will also serve as a recapitulation of the themes of the previous chapters, as I first construct the inventory of a semiotic resource, then investigate the discourses that regulate it, and finally look at the way this resource is actually used.

Functional analysis of the pram rattle

My example will be a particular kind of toy, the pram rattle. Hung across the pram or cot, pram rattles consist of eye-catching shapes strung together on an elastic string or plastic rod, that move when the baby swipes or kicks at them. The movement causes a play of light on the shiny plastic and a 'rattle' noise. Pram rattles are therefore a tool with a pragmatic function. They are designed to help babies develop their eye to limb

Figure 4.2   The rabbit pram rattle (Mothercare)

co-ordination. But the eye-catching shapes are also the child's first 'movie show'. Like buildings, pram rattles are at the same time pragmatic, functional objects, and symbolic objects.

The 'rabbit pram rattle' (figure 4.2) has four near-identical rabbits, made of shiny, rigid and quite thick plastic, strung on an elastic string which can be attached to the sides of the pram or cot with plastic hooks. They are white and wear jackets in various pale pastels – yellow, green, pink and blue. When the string is stretched, the rabbits can rotate. In addition the whole elastic string, rabbits and all, can be moved – and

Figure 4.3   The rainbow galaxy pram rattle (Early Learning Centre)

then of course bounces back. Pellets inside the rabbits will cause a soft, tinkling rattle when the string is pulled and/or the rabbits rotated.

The 'rainbow galaxy pram rattle' has a completely different construction. The separating elements (gold stars) are sewn onto the (soft toy) 'aliens', and the 'aliens' themselves are connected to each other with velcro fasteners. This means that they cannot rotate, and that the whole thing can be taken apart. A ring is fastened to each end, also with velcro, and connects to an elastic band which can loop around the sides of the pram or cot. Pulling at this ring, or swiping at the rattle, will create some movement, and hence some noise, because there is a box with beads inside the leftmost alien, but not as much as in the rabbit pram rattle. The three aliens are made of fleecy fabric, in relatively dark, mixed colours – anaemic greens and blues, orange, purple – except for the shiny silver and gold fabric on the soles of their feet. Each one produces a different sound – the squeak of the middle one is produced by squeezing, the scrunchy noise of the one on the right by rubbing his belly between one's fingers.

I will now first look at what Halliday would call 'function in structure', at what these toys have been designed to be able to *mean* and *do*, or, more technically, at their ideational and interpersonal meaning potential.

Ideational meaning potential of the pram rattle

The key to the ideational meaning potential of these rabbits must lie in the simple fact that they combine human and animal elements. The field of possible meanings is therefore formed by everything that has been said or can be said about the ways in which humans can be like rabbits, or rabbits like humans. That is a wide field, yet there are some dominant cultural patterns which many mothers will be familiar with. Peter Rabbit stories, for instance, depict rabbits as living a human-like, cosy nuclear family life in their burrows, sheltered from the dangers lurking outside, and this discourse also characterizes many TV nature programmes about small burrowing animals. Another key characteristic is their lack of trousers, and the lack of genitals which this reveals. In this, as in other aspects, the rabbits symbolize children as being in a state of sexless innocence, and as being in part still animal-like, instinct driven and without responsibility, in part already human. Note also the colours of the rabbits. The dominant colour, white, has a well-established meaning potential as the colour of purity, innocence and virginity. Pastel colours lack saturation, which, depending on the context, could be interpreted as weak and lacking vigour, or as tender, calm and peaceful. We know that pastels are worn by babies – where they are a traditional signifier of gender difference – and by women who seek to express a soft and yielding type of female identity. In art they appear in watercolours of peaceful rural landscapes and in idyllic imaginations.

The iconography of the rainbow galaxy pram rattle draws on quite different sources. The insect-like eyes on stilts and stegosaur-like bony back plates of 'Krypton', the dragon's mane of 'Neon' and the lizard-like tail and silver horns of 'Xenon' – these are the names of the three characters, as disclosed on the box – are all symbols of dread which have been, and still are, widely exploited in popular culture and before that in various kinds of demonic iconography – for example, Bosch. In contemporary toys and media for children such creatures of dread are made to look human, friendly and comical, but we could also turn the proposition around and wonder whether fellow human beings are represented here as threatening and dangerous, as 'risks', albeit in a humorous vein. As for the colours, in a study of toys and gender (Caldas-Coulthard and Van Leeuwen, 2002) we looked at the use of pink, lilac and purple in toy cata-logues and found that dark pinks and purples permeated the background of pictures showing romantic medieval castles, enchanted forests, wild storms, etc. Although the rainbow galaxy pram rattle is, overall, bright enough for the 'fun' element to domi-nate, there is also an undertone of menace and brooding mystery.

It can of course be argued that such meanings are not yet understood by very young babies. But just as caring parents will take their babies to play in the pool long before they are ready to swim, and talk to them long before they are ready to speak, so they will surround them with cultural artefacts long before they are ready to recognize what these artefacts represent or grasp their full significance.

Interactional meaning potential of the pram rattle

What can be done with these toys? This is constrained to some degree by the materials they are made of, and by their kinetic design, the way they move or can be made to move. The rabbits, for instance, are made of hard plastic, while the aliens are made of soft fabrics. So the rabbits lend themselves less easily to tactile experience. They do not yield to touch, or respond to stroking as soft toys do, nor can they be squeezed, bent or folded in any way. The 'aliens' on the other hand can. They are soft toys, hence potentially cuddly, and, like 'Muppet' style soft glove puppets they can be made to assume many different postures and expressions – Xenon's tail can be made to wag or wobble, for instance, and Krypton's eyes-on-stilts can be made to move, so as to make him look in different directions. They therefore have more potential for expressing emotive meaning, and leave more room for creativity in the way they can be moved. This is enhanced by the fact that they are individual 'characters' – detachable, each with his own unique appearance and sound.

On the other hand, the rabbits more easily accommodate the child's as yet unco-ordinated actions. Kicking against them will produce real results, a sound, and a twin-kling of lights as the rabbits bounce and tumble around their axis on the string. The same cannot be said of the aliens. Kicking them produces no twinkle and hardly any noise. It might even make them come apart. From the point of view of responding to baby's early actions their potential is very limited.

So what these toys allow parents to present to their children is, ideationally, either an idyllic, almost Victorian conception of childhood in which children are protected from anything that might shock or upset their tender sensitivities, or a world which is already more adult, more ambivalent and more dangerous. Interactively, there is either a tool to help baby develop eye-to-limb co-ordination or a kind of puppet show which, however, leaves more space for emotive communication. Both these pram rattles have a symbolic as well as a pragmatic aspect. But in the rabbit pram rattle the pragmatic function dominates over the symbolic one, just as was the case in modernist architecture, while in the rainbow galaxy pram rattle the symbolic overrides the pragmatic, just as is the case in postmodern architecture.

Rules of use

Just as the interpretation of texts is structured not only by 'what the text says', but also by contextually specific rules of interpretation, so the use of toys, too, is not only structured by their design but also by contextually specific rules of use. This can be studied by looking at the discourses that surround the toys and regulate their use in various ways. Such discourses can be found, for instance, in parenting books and magazines, or in the texts on the packaging of the toys.

The dominant 'pram rattle' discourse is an expert discourse. Rules for how to use toys are justified by a lay version of developmental psychology. Without going into details, the key elements are:

1 a good toy is beneficial to the child's development
2 a good toy facilitates specific developmental work for children in specific age brackets
3 although parents can provide the necessary environment, materials and encouragement, the toy is there for the child to develop spontaneously, on its own.

To this, another element may be added – developmental 'work' is also fun, and playing with babies helps the parent–child bonding. Here is a typical example, from the magazine *New Baby* (May, 2000):

> Cot mobiles and baby gyms are great fun for very small babies because they give them something to look at, particularly if they have toys that move round when the mechanism is wound up, or have twinkling lights. They're great for teaching hand-eye co-ordination and cause and effect – if your baby bats the hanging toys with his hands or feet, they'll move and maybe make a noise. Show your baby how to swipe things, then let him explore.

Regulatory texts of this kind will generally single out only certain aspects of the toy's design. The example above, for instance, makes no mention of the fact that pram rattles and baby gyms are also symbolic representations and treats them as purely instrumental, as serving only to fulfil the baby's needs for physical and perceptual development. On the packaging of the rabbit pram rattle the word 'rabbit' is not even mentioned, and the rabbits are referred to as 'fun shapes'. The packaging of the rainbow galaxy pram rattle, on the other hand, merely reinforces the 'fun' element and leaves out the developmental discourse that is so common elsewhere:

Three funny activity aliens with scrunchy stars – squeak ... rattle ...scrunch ...

In advertisements, too, babies are seen as 'already in culture', and not just as developing bodies. Fisher-Price produce a 'kick 'n' play' piano – a kind of pillow with five large 'piano' keys that make a sound when kicked or hit. The toy is advertised with a photo of a smiling baby using the piano, and the text addresses the baby rather than the mother:

> Get down to some foot-tapping music, animal sounds and twinkly lights at the bottom of your cot ... then when you can get your hands on that keyboard take the floor and play.

There are many other indications that babies are increasingly treated as 'already in culture', as miniature adults, rather than as not-yet-quite-human creatures inhabiting the categorically different world of early childhood. Instead of dressing babies in pink and blue woollies, we see babies dressed in leather jackets and jeans, or fashionable dresses. Instead of rabbit families in pale pastel jackets, we see miniature versions of Star Wars characters, work stations with computers and telephones, and so on.

Using the pram rattle

Today's toys are produced and distributed by global corporations, and that means that babies are, almost from birth, part of global culture. But the toys are used in the 'micro' situation of mother–child interaction – or interaction with other carers, or siblings. To what extent are these interactions structured by the design of the toys, and by the discourses of social institutions such as the health care system, 'Dr Spock' type parenting books, *New Baby* type magazines, advertisements, etc? To what extent do people follow the 'rules'? Let us have a look at (part of) such a mother–child interaction, recorded by the father as part of a research project on 'toys as communication':[2]

> A baby – 12 weeks and 4 days old – lies in a bassinet. Her mother kneels next to her, leans over to pick up the box with the 'rabbit pram rattle', and then shakes the box.
>
> *Mother.* Right ... Annabel ...
>
> She shakes the box again.
>
> *Mother.* What's that? ... (excited high-pitched voice) What's thaaaat?
>
> The baby looks intently at her
>
> *Mother.* Oh, she's excited about this ... Weeeell ...

She opens the box and takes out the rattle, holds it up.

Mother: Bunny rabbits! You've got a rattle like that, haven't you?
Look ... Bunny rabbits ...

She holds the rattle in position and shakes it.

Mother: (excited, high-pitched voice) Ooooh! Ooooh! Loook!

The baby's legs move

Mother: Oh look, put 'em by your feet.

She holds up the rattle in front of the baby's feet and shakes it.

Mother: Ooooh! Kick, kick, kick ... Ooh, you've had a busy morning today.

The baby's feet now actually kick the rattle.

Mother: Look ... oooh ... they are lovely ... you like those ... you like those...

[The interaction continues, with the mother now holding the rattle near the baby's hands. Eventually she puts the rabbit pram rattle away, picks up the box with the rainbow galaxy pram rattle and holds it up in front of her baby.]

Mother: What about this one?

She starts to unpack the rattle.

Mother: What do you think? What's in here? What's in here? ... What's in there? ... That's exciting ...You've got a lot of new presents this morning ...

She holds up the rattle and shakes it.

Mother: Who are *they*? What are *they*? They are funny ones.

She brings the rattle close to her ear, as if to check why it isn't producing more noise.

Mother: One of them makes a noise ...

She holds the rattle up again and shakes it.

Mother. Well ... What do you think about those?

The baby makes a little noise and moves her arms and legs vigorously.

Mother. What do you think about those hey? They are funny ones.

They're monsters.

She shakes the rattle.

Mother. Now this one is nice ...

She moves the rattle close to her ear again, shaking one of the characters and listening to it.

Mother. This is a nice one ...

One of the velcro fasteners suddenly comes unstuck.

Mother. (lowering her voice, away from the 'baby talk' pitch level) Oh, they come off.

She shakes the 'alien' and discovers that pinching it makes it squeak.

Mother. (back to 'baby' pitch) Oooh! This is a squeaky one!

She squeaks him again. The baby shakes her arms and legs vigorously and looks on intently.

Mother. Oooh ... (creating a voice for the alien) Ho-ho-ho ... It's like a dragon.

[She continues, using the 'aliens' as puppets, creating sounds for them, making them wiggle, 'walk' across the baby's tummy, caress the baby's cheek, and so on.]

Clearly this mother knows what she is supposed to do with a pram rattle. She follows almost exactly the *New Baby* magazine 'rules', and with the rabbit pram rattle this is successful. Note, however, that she also treats the rabbits as symbolic representations – she tells her daughter that they are 'bunny rabbits'.

When she tries to use the 'aliens' pram rattle in the same way, she more or less accidentally discovers that the characters can be detached, and how the sounds are produced, and then changes to a kind of puppet show, emphasizing not the baby's own action but the funny 'characters' of the three aliens and making *them* do things rather than the baby, who thereby becomes a 'spectator', rather than a 'producer' of movement. In the end the mother turns to her husband, who has been filming the episode, and says: 'Well, she likes them. I'm surprised about that because they look a bit odd.'

There is nothing wrong with this. An 'interactive' puppet show of this kind is a pleasurable thing for a mother and her baby to do. My point is that this is not acknowledged in the 'parenting' literature', not part of what mothers are encouraged to do with their babies at this age, not part of 'serious developmental work'. On the other hand it is, as I have tried to show in some detail, encouraged by the *design* of the rainbow galaxy pram rattle, part of the meaning potential of this semiotic resource.

The 10 mothers who recorded themselves for our project certainly did not all do exactly the same thing. Some held up the rattles vertically and moved them about trying to make their babies follow them with their eyes. Others tried to make their babies hold the hook with their hands or grab the rattle. But all these actions were geared towards making the *baby* do things, making him or her the active agent. When they then moved to the rainbow galaxy pram rattle, they changed their approach, treating the 'aliens' as characters, giving them funny voices, making them talk, referring to them as 'he' or even giving them names, none of which happened with the rabbit pram rattle. Clearly these mothers were not totally determined in the way they used these toys. But they were not totally free either. There were constraints, partially 'built in', and partially resulting from their awareness of the developmental discourses of childhood experts, and of today's popular childhood culture, with its many aliens, dragons, prehistoric monsters, and so on.

Clearly, each of these two toys has its upside and its downside. The rabbit pram rattle works well at the 'conative' level, but is a little old-fashioned and suppresses the referential and the emotive. The rainbow galaxy pram rattle works well at the emotive and referential level, but at the cost of its conative functionality. Would it not be better to have the two sides in balance, to develop a semiotic approach to the production and interpretation of designed objects which integrates the symbolic and the practical side of social interaction?

Exercises

1   In *Reading Images* (1996: 121–30) Kress and Van Leeuwen give a functional interpretation of the gaze in pictures. If someone looks at the viewer, they say, this expresses a symbolic 'demand' on the viewer. The person in the picture is represented as doing something to or for the viewer. Just what s/he is doing then depends on facial expressions, gestures, or what kind of person it is, and so on. For instance, an African person with a pleading look and an outstretched hand will be read as begging for a donation to an aid agency, a heavily made-up woman's seductive smile and cocked head will be read as a sexual invitation, and so on. When there is no such look at the viewer, there is an 'offer', as Kress and Van Leeuwen call it, following Halliday (1985). The viewer is simply offered information, a scene to contemplate. S/he is in the position of a 'voyeur'.

Collect pictures of 'locals' from tourist brochures and/or travel features in magazines or newspapers. What kind(s) of people are depicted as 'demanding' what,
and how? What kind(s) of people are depicted as not making a 'demand'?

2   Identify the functions of text and image in a magazine advertisement using both
     Halliday's and Jakobson's theories. To do this, simply ask: which aspects of the
     text and the visuals have an ideational function, which an interpersonal function,
     and so on.

     Which of the two theories brings out best what the ad is trying to do, and why?

3   Take a modern, designed object, for example, the famous lemon squeezer
     designed by Philippe Starck (figure 4.4). Describe its ideational and its interper-
     sonal meaning potential.

     Ask people to actually use the object, and then find out what they think about its
     functionality. Also ask them where they would put it if they had one. Conclusions?

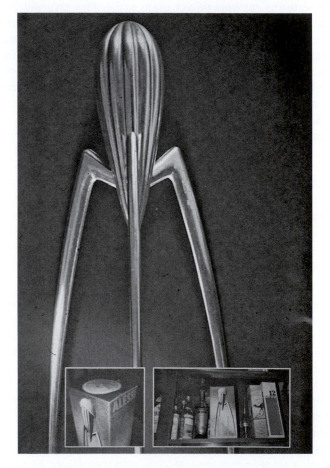

Figure 4.4   Juicy Salif lemon squeezer (Philippe Starck, 1990)

4   Find a picture of someone dressed in fashionable clothes that have military connotations – or other connotations, according to your interest. Ask one group of people to describe what kind of people would dress like that. What are they like? What kind of things would they do? What would they think about war – or whichever field of connotations you are focussing on? Then ask another very similar group of people: 'What do these clothes mean?'
Do you get the same answers? If not, why do you think this is?

5   Make two series of photographs of the façades of buildings (a) predominantly functional façades, and (b) predominantly symbolical façades. What were your criteria for choosing the buildings?

Notes

1   Halliday was inspired by the earlier functionalist accounts of language of Bühler (1934), Mathesius (see, for example, Vachek, 1966) and Daneš (1964), as well as by Malinowski.

2   The project, *Toys as Communication,* was funded by a grant from the Royal Bank of Sweden and directed by Professor Staffan Selander of the Institute of Education, Stockholm University. The work discussed here was done in collaboration with Dr Carmen Rosa Caldas-Coulthard, of the University of Birmingham. Video recordings of mother–baby interactions were arranged and transcribed by Caroline Warren.

PART II

Dimensions of semiotic analysis

In this part of the book I introduce the key dimensions of social semiotic analysis:

- *Discourse*
  The concept of 'discourse' is the key to studying how semiotic resources are used to construct representations of what is going on in the world.
- *Genre*
  The concept of 'genre' is the key to studying how semiotic resources are used to enact communicative interactions – interactions that involve representation – whether face to face, as for instance in conversations, or at a remove of time and/ or place, as for instance through the means of books and other media.
- *Style*
  The concept of 'style' is the key to studying how people use semiotic resources to 'perform' genres, and to express their identities and values in doing so.
- *Modality*
  The concept of 'modality' is the key to studying how people use semiotic resources to create the truth or reality values of their representations, to communicate, for instance, whether they are to be taken as fact or fiction, proven truth or conjecture, etc.

Although I discuss these four dimensions one by one, they never occur in isolation and are always all part of every communicative event and every semiotic artefact. Only looking at them together will give a complete, multidimensional picture.

5 Discourse

As we have seen in part I, social semiotics explores two closely related issues: the material resources of communication and the way their uses are socially regulated.

The material resources of communication may be physiological or technical. Physiological resources include our vocal apparatus and the muscles we use to create the facial expressions, gestures and other physical actions that realize 'non-verbal' communication. Their use is always socially regulated. The voice, for instance, can produce a wide range of sounds. But in most situations it is called on to produce only speech sounds, and only such speech sounds as are appropriate to the given situation, and to the age, gender, class and social role of the speakers involved. The same applies to 'non-verbal' communication. From an early age we observe and imitate the socially permitted or desirable forms of non-verbal communication, and are often explicitly instructed in them – 'Look at me while you speak', 'Don't put your hands in your pockets', 'Sit straight', etc. This is not to say that there is no room for freedom, for an element of individual style in the way we communicate. There is, though more so in some situations than in others. But communication always takes place within – or sometimes in opposition to – the socially defined boundaries of specific situations. If we stray outside them, eyebrows will be raised, and if we persist, there may be other, more serious consequences: we will no longer 'fit' into this particular situation.

Technical resources extend the potential of our physiological resources. We can communicate not only with our voice but also with musical instruments; not only with facial expressions and gestures but also through the clothes we wear and the way we groom our bodies. This even includes communication through sensory modalities over which we have no conscious articulatory control, such as when we use fragrances to communicate something about ourselves or about particular spaces. Finally, we have developed technologies to preserve our communicative acts – for instance, writing and recording – and to relay or distribute them across distances – for instance, telephony and broadcasting. The use of these resources is also socially regulated, for instance through the question of who is given access to them and in what roles – as producer, consumer, or, with today's more interactive media, something in between – and through the 'languages' people have developed to regulate their use, or which, in the case of new media such as email, we can see developing in front of our eyes.

The subject of social semiotics, therefore, is the coming together of these two aspects of semiotic resources, their physical or technical nature – and the semiotic potentialities this affords – and the social regulation of their use – together with its history. This means that social semiotics is by and large about the *how* of communication. How do we use material resources to produce meaning? But there can be no 'how' without a 'what'. We need to look at 'meaning' itself as well. This I will do through an account of 'discourse'.

The term 'discourse' is often used to denote an extended stretch of connected speech or writing, a 'text'. 'Discourse analysis' then means 'the analysis of an extended text, or type of text'. Here I use it in a different sense, building on the work of Michel Foucault (for example, 1977) and defining discourses – note the plural – as *socially constructed knowledges of some aspect of reality*. By 'socially constructed' I mean that these knowledges have been developed in specific social contexts, and in ways which are appropriate to the interests of social actors in these contexts, whether they are large contexts – multinational corporations – or small ones – a particular family – strongly institutionalised contexts – the press – or relatively informal ones – dinner table conversations, etc. For instance, a 'special operations' discourse of war may be drawn on by Western journalists when reporting US and 'coalition' military interventions, but it may also be used in certain kinds of conversation, or in airport thrillers, Hollywood movies and computer games. Such a discourse serves the interest of the country or countries in which the relevant texts are produced, and hence usually leaves out or backgrounds such things as aerial bombardments and civilian casualties, concentrating instead on:

1   the elite ground forces involved in special operations – high combat skills, superior technology and team work, stress on the speed of the operation and the quick and efficient 'insertion' and 'extraction' of the force;
2   the enemy – represented as a despotic warlord, tyrant or super-terrorist, leading ill-disciplined and ill-equipped men; and
3   the weak and inefficient victims of this enemy – local populations, or the UN peace keepers and food relief agencies who, according to this discourse, cannot operate without the protection of the elite forces.

Historically this discourse goes back to Reagan's doctrine of the quick, effective operation and his creation of 'Delta Force'. The point is, it is not the only discourse of war. There are others, for instance the 'ethnic conflict' discourse, or discourses in which 'economics' or 'ideology' feature as explanatory categories, or 'themes' to use Foucault's term – see, for example, Joas' (2003) account of the way philosophers and sociologists have constructed war over the last few centuries.

A key issue here is the plurality of discourse: there can be and are several different ways of knowing – and hence also of representing – the same 'object' of knowledge. That object exists of course. There *are* wars and they *do* cause enormous suffering. But our *knowledge* of them is necessarily constructed in and through discourse, and is socially specific. This also means that the same individual can have different knowledges of the same object, and may well be able to talk about the same war in several different ways, depending on the situation as well as on his or her own individual interests and purposes.

To summarize the main points:

- Discourses are resources for representation, knowledges about some aspect of reality, which can be drawn upon when that aspect of reality has to be represented. They do not determine what we can say about a given aspect of reality, yet we cannot represent anything without them. We need them as frameworks for making sense of things.
- Discourses are plural. There can be different discourses, different ways of making sense of the same aspect of reality, which include and exclude different things, and serve different interests.
- Evidence for the existence of a given discourse comes from texts, from what has been said or written – and/or expressed by means of other semiotic modes. More specifically it comes from the similarity between the things that are said and written in *different* texts about the *same* aspect of reality. It is on the basis of such similar statements, repeated or paraphrased in different texts and dispersed among these texts in different ways, that we can reconstruct the knowledge which they represent.

The plurality of discourses

By way of example, I will sketch two discourses of the heart.

1   The 'heart as pump'

Here the heart is primarily conceived of as a mechanism, a pump. Knowing about the heart means knowing which parts it consists of and how it works. Here is an example from a textbook of over 1,000 pages called *Principles of Anatomy and Physiology*:

> The heart is magnificently designed for its task of propelling blood through an estimated 100,000 km of blood vessels. Even while you are sleeping, your heart pumps 30 times its own weight each minute, about 5 liters to the lungs and the same volume to the rest of the body.
>
> (Tortora and Grabowski, 1996: 579)

The same discourse can also be found in a Knowledge Adventure CD-ROM for children titled '3D Body Adventure' (1995):

> The heart is a very well designed pump indeed. It is more reliable and energy-efficient than any pump ever created by man.

And just as mechanical technologies such as cars now also incorporate some digital technology, so does the heart, in this CD-ROM:

> The AV-node is smart and delays its signal just long enough to allow the atria to finish contracting.

It is clear that this discourse, this way of knowing about the heart, underlies many instances of text and talk, sometimes in detail, sometimes in sketchy outline. It can even be fictionalized, as in this excerpt from a piece of school homework, produced when a high school teacher had asked his students to write a story describing the life of a red blood cell in its journey about the body:

> Dear Diary,
> I have just left the heart. I had to come from the top right chamber of the heart (right atrium) and squeeze my way through to the right ventricle ...
> (Kress et al., 2000)

The 'heart as pump' discourse originated in William Harvey's *Exercitatio* of 1628. In its time it was heavily criticized by key medical authorities. As I will discuss in some detail below, it is typical of the scientific rationality which has, for centuries now, served the interest of economic and technological progress so well, even though in this case the surgical applications it makes possible had to wait until 1925.

2   *The heart as risk factor*

Here the heart is conceived of primarily as a risk factor, and knowing about the heart is in the first place knowing which foods to eat and which to steer clear of, which activities to engage in and which to avoid, so as to minimize the risk of heart disease. The following quote is from an American book called *Mind, Body and Sport*:

> In October 1992, the American Heart Association (AHA) added physical inactivity to its list of major risk factors for heart disease. This placed lack of exercise in the same category as smoking, high blood pressure and high cholesterol levels. 'We are not born with this disease', said Dr Gerald Fletcher, chairman of the AHA committee that wrote the position statement. 'We really develop this disease because of our lifestyle'.
> (Douillard, 1994: 45)

The children's CD-ROM I have already quoted from above also uses this discourse, with slight variations:

> The risk factors for having a heart attack are well known. These risk factors include a diet high in fat and cholesterol, smoking, obesity, physical inactivity, high blood pressure, diabetes and a family history of heart attacks. It is thus possible for persons to lower their risk of a heart attack if they choose to. Of note, the incidence of heart attacks is four times lower in Japan than in the United States. This is because the major risk factors are much less common in that country.

This discourse is of more recent date. Over the past few decades it has become apparent that our increased rate of consuming natural resources and our highly developed technologies in fields such as nutrition and medicine have brought about risks which are both invisible – and hence for practical purposes exist only in discourse, in our beliefs – and probably irreversible, at least in the short term. As Beck (1994) has pointed out, this signals the end of the monopoly of scientific rationality, and the emergence of a new kind of social rationality or ethics which will have to work together with scientific rationality. Discourses such as the 'heart as risk factor' are in the mainstream interest as they suggest that the solution lies with individuals and leave out the role of industry. That this can only be done by people with the money, time and expertise to turn their lifestyle into a science is usually also excluded from these discourses.

These two examples do not exhaust the discourses of the heart. Others relate to heart disease and construct knowledge of the symptoms and complaints of patients and of relevant treatments. They can operate at different levels, from first aid to open heart surgery. And then we have not even mentioned other kinds of discourses of the heart, for instance the discourse of the heart as the site of love. As Roland Barthes analyses it, in *A Lover's Discourse: Fragments*:

> The heart is the organ of desire (the heart swells, weakens, etc., like the sexual organs), as it is held, enchanted, within the domain of the Image-repertoire. What will the world, what will the other do with my desire? That is the anxiety in which are gathered all the heart's movements, all the heart's problems.
>
> (1978: 52)

I will return to this kind of discourse below. For the moment, let me summarize the key points that emerge from these examples.

Discourses are finite

As Foucault has formulated it, discourses contain a limited number of 'statements'. Below I will discuss in more detail what kind of statements – or more generally, 'elements' – discourses contain, but I hope the quotes above do establish that certain bits of knowledge such as that of 'the heart as pump' are shared between many people, and recur time and time again in a wide range of different types of texts and communicative events, even if they are not always formulated in the same way, and not always complete. But then, once I know a discourse, for example, the 'heart as risk factor' discourse, a single part of it can trigger the rest. Hearing only the phrase 'risk of heart failure', can immediately bring other elements of the discourse to mind, for example, smoking, obesity, lack of exercise, etc.

Discourses have a history

This is another one of Foucault's key contributions to the theory of discourse. As with any other discourse, it is possible – and enlightening – to study how and why the 'heart as pump' discourse came about, as well as how it eventually became common sense, repeated everywhere, taught in schools, etc., until it finally became contested once again, as is now, gradually and tentatively, happening as a result of the emergence of competing discourses, such as the 'heart as risk factor' discourse. This is why I pay particular attention to discourse history in this chapter.

Discourses have a social distribution

We are not likely to encounter the 'heart as pump' discourse in 'lonely hearts' advertisements, or in fitness magazines, or in books with titles like *Mind, Body and Sport.* Nevertheless, all the various 'health'-related discourses of the heart, despite their differences and conflicting aspects, do belong to one and the same 'discursive formation', to use Foucault's term. They rest in the end on the same kind of social authority, the medical authority (see the reference to the American Heart Association in the quote above) are continuously reported and supported by the same types of media, and emanate from the same sources of professional and institutional power – hospitals, laboratories, etc. As a result they can happily appear together in the encyclopaedia, that authoritative compendium of knowledge – in which, however, you will not find the 'lover's discourse', at least not under the heading of 'heart'.

Discourses can be realized in different ways

A given discourse can be realized in many ways. The discourse of 'the heart as risk factor', for instance, can be realized through action, through the actual enactment of a certain healthy lifestyle, or through *representations* of such a way of life – which is not to say that there cannot be contradictions between the way people act and the way they represent their actions. These representations again can take many forms – conversations, textbooks, school 'lessons', school 'homework', encyclopaedia entries, media reports, television programmes, advertisements, magazine advice columns, books on healthy lifestyles and natural medicine, etc. And they can be realized not only through speech and writing but also through sound and pictures, for instance in advertisements, which may either show the unhealthy food or the unhealthy lifestyle as particularly unappetizing, or their healthy counterparts as particularly attractive.

Discourse history

Discourses like the 'heart as pump' discourse have become so commonplace that we can hardly imagine an alternative. We have to go back in time to make ourselves realize that they did not always seem self-evident and that their emergence as new

Figure 5.1   'Interrupting is bad for your heart' (*Men's Health*, July/August 2001: 38)

ways of thinking related to new interests, new social practices and new social relations. For this reason discourse history is an important part of the social semiotic
approach to discourse. In the following account of the history of the 'heart as pump'
discourse I rely for the most part on a two-volume history of the body by the Dutch
neurologist and cultural historian Van den Berg (1961).

Before William Harvey described the heart as a pump, the prevailing theory was that
of Galenus, a doctor who lived and worked in Rome in the second century AD. According
to Galenus the heart was a kind of furnace which fused liquid, warmth, air and spirit
together to distil blood. Harvey's contemporaries could have known better, because
they had been able to see the heart – Vesalius had already introduced modern anatomy

in the sixteenth century. But they did not, and they strongly criticized Harvey's innovative discourse, so much so that it had an adverse effect on his practice as a doctor. Two aspects were particularly controversial. The first was the issue of the heart valves, which, for the medical authorities of Harvey's time had to be porous, because they had to be able to let in air. The second was the issue of the audible heartbeat. Strangely enough no medical treatise before Harvey had ever described the heartbeat as audible, and Harvey was ridiculed for his description of the audible heartbeat, even though in other discourses of the period – used, for instance, in poetry – the sound of the heart was often mentioned. Clearly, for these critics, the heart could not and should not be thought of as a hollow muscle, a pump. It could not be thought of in a way that was so completely incompatible with the authoritative knowledge of the time.

On the other hand, Harvey's discourse did not come from nowhere, and did not rest solely on scientific observation. The idea of the 'mechanism' as a major explanatory paradigm was available in the discourses of this time. The philosopher Descartes, a contemporary of Harvey who supported him strongly even though he himself viewed the heart as a kind of combustion engine rather than as a pump, had come to think of the body as a machine.

> The action of the body apart from guidance of the will, does not at all appear strange to those who are acquainted with the variety of movements performed by the different automata, or moving machines fabricated by human industry.
>
> (Descartes, 1972 [1649]: 339)

This discourse of 'bodily action as a mechanism' was not only realized in philosophical treatises but also in all kinds of cultural artefacts and practices. The gardens of the French royal palace were decorated with statues that moved by means of concealed hydraulic mechanisms, and mechanical toys were popular with the well-to-do merchant class – walking dolls, carriages moving by means of a clockwork, birds twitting their tails in time to the tinkling of a music box.

Why this fascination with mechanisms? Whose interests were involved? In the first place those of the new merchant class. They not only collected mechanical toys, they also had become quite active in scientific research. As Mumford described it:

> Was it an accident that the founders and patrons of the Royal Society in London were merchants from the City? ... King Charles II might laugh uncontrollably when he heard that these gentlemen had spent their time weighing air; but their instincts were justified: the method itself belonged to their tradition, and there was money in it. The power that was science and the power that was money were, in the final analysis, the same kind of power: the power of abstraction, measurement, quantification.
>
> (Mumford, 1934: 25)

It was these merchants who would eventually apply the idea of human beings as mechanical devices to the cost of labour in the production of goods, first by controlling and disciplining them, by slaving them to the machinery of the factory, and then by completely replacing them with machinery, a process which is still continuing. To quote Mumford again (1934: 364): 'The Western European conceived the machine because ... he wished to reduce the movements of his fellows as well as the behaviour of the environment to a more definite, calculable basis'. Without the discursive theme of humans as mechanical devices, of which the 'heart as pump' discourse forms part, this would not have been possible.

There is one further aspect to the history of the 'heart as pump' discourse. Around the same time that Harvey published his treatise on the circulation of blood, a priest by the name of Jean Eudes started the cult of the sacred heart. In the process he elaborated a quite different discourse of the heart. Here the heart became an object of devotion. People prayed to the heart of Christ, which had loved all humankind and died on the cross for their sins, and the heart of Mary. Like Harvey's heart, it was a very visible heart (see figure 5.2), but it stood for the quite different values and quite different interests of another institution, religion. In many ways the contradictions involved still exist today. Even now we have, side by side, two incompatible discourses of the heart – a subjective discourse of the 'heart as the site of love', with clear roots in religion, and an objective, scientific discourse of the 'heart as pump'.

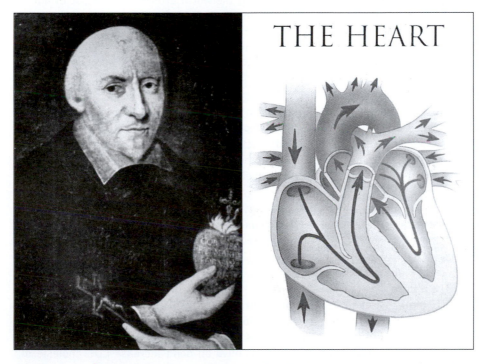

Figure 5.2   The Sacred Heart of the Loving Christ (early seventeenth century engraving) and The heart as pump (from Tortora and Grabowski, 1996)

Although it is too early to say, it is possible that the discourse of the 'heart as pump' is losing its dominant place, now that competing discourses such as that of the 'heart as risk factor' are on the rise. Even medical authors must now acknowledge them and take up position in regard to them. Much work will need to be done before this discourse can become as well developed and common sense as the 'heart as pump' discourse. But the increasing crisis of the medical profession and its institutions does provide the soil in which such a discourse can grow, and pioneering theoreticians of our 'risk society' such as Ulrich Beck (1994) have begun to formulate how it will have to combine two ways of thinking which until recently have been considered separate domains, scientific rationality and social rationality. Once that has been achieved – if it can be – we may well come to view the 'heart as pump' discourse as somewhat antiquated, as belonging to the era of the 'quick technological fix' approach to solving problems, rather than to an 'environmentally and socially responsible ways of life' approach.

Discourse as the realization of social practice

As already discussed in relation to the idea of experiential metaphor (chapter 2), our discourses, our knowledges about the world, ultimately derive from what we do. Our actions give us the tools for understanding the world around us. The use of human technologies as models for understanding nature, as in Descartes – or modern genetics – is just one example. This insight is common in anthropology and sociology. Durkheim, for instance, stressed that myths are modelled after rites, conceptual categories after social life, and classifications after social organization:

> The first logical categories were social categories. It was because men were grouped, and thought of themselves in the form of groups, that in their ideas they grasped other things, and in the beginning the two modes of groupings were merged to the point of being indistinct. Moieties were the first genera, clans the first species. Things were thought to be integral parts of society, and it was their place in society which determined their place in nature.
>
> (Durkheim and Mauss, 1963: 82–3)

In some cases it is easy to see the link between discourse and social practice. Here, for instance, is an extract from an article about coronary diseases in a men's health magazine:

> The natural fix:
> It's the same exercise and low-saturated-fat diet strategy you'd use to lower blood pressure: exercise aerobically for at least 30 minutes three or four times a week, cut your saturated-fat intake as low as possible, and – crucially – eat more fibre. 'Monounsaturated fats such as olive oil don't increase LDL cholesterol,' says cardiologist Chris Rembold.
>
> (*Men's Health,* July/August 2001: 80)

Clearly this discourse, the knowledge that underlies this passage, centres on *practices*, practices of dieting and exercising, although there is a medical discourse as well, used to lend authority to the 'heart as risk factor' diet.

In fictional representations it may be a harder to see the link between discourses and real life social actors and social practices. After all, story tellers are allowed to take liberties with reality, to invent, disguise and transform. Still, even non-naturalistic stories such as fairy tales ultimately refer to real social actions and social actors, but they *transform* these actors and practices by locating them in a mythical or distant past (or future) so as to allow them to represent more than one (set of) social actor(s) and social practice(s) at the same time. Will Wright's study of Westerns (1975) provides a good example. He showed first of all how the actors and actions of Westerns changed in the early 1960s, towards a pattern he called the 'professional plot'. Characteristic of this kind of plot is the replacement of the individual hero – the lone hero riding into town – by a collective of heroes, a team of fiercely independent men who work for money rather than love, justice or honour, are technically highly competent and organized and form a tight elite with a strong code of solidarity in the group. Wright then showed how this kind of change also occurred in the real world, where research teams replaced individual scientific geniuses, corporate management teams individual business entrepreneurs, and so on. By being located in a mythical time, Westerns can represent all these spheres of social life at once and concentrate on the themes and values they have in common. Bruno Bettelheim (1978) has mapped the actors and actions of fairy tales onto contemporary and actual social practices – especially those of the family – in a similar way.

What happens when a text is not a story, when it does not describe human actors and actions, but, for instance, the anatomy and function of the heart? Here, too, understanding is ultimately based on *doing*. The practices that underlie such texts are scientific practices, for instance the practice of anatomy. As the anthropologist Malinowski has written (1935: 58):

> Even in the most abstract and theoretical aspects of human thought and verbal usage, the real understanding of words ultimately derives from active experience of those aspects of reality to which the words belong. The chemist or physicist understands the meaning of his most abstract concepts ultimately on the basis of his acquaintance with chemical and physical processes in the laboratory. Even the pure mathematician, dealing with that most useless and arrogant branch of his learning, the theory of numbers, has probably had some experience of counting his pennies and shillings or his boots and buns. In short, there is no science whose conceptual, hence verbal, outfit is not ultimately derived from the practical handling of matter.

The 'heart as pump' discourse is clearly modelled on the technological practices and interests of William Harvey's time. But medical discourses may also be based on other kinds of social practices, for example, on practices of colonization and military conquest, as Susan Sontag has shown in *Illness as Metaphor*, which I quoted in chapter 2:

> Cancer cells do not simply multiply, they are 'invasive' (malignant tumors invade even when they grow very slowly', as one textbook puts it). Cancer cells 'colonise' from the original tumor to far sites in the body, first setting up tiny outposts ('micrometastases' whose presence is assumed, though they cannot be detected). Rarely are the body's 'defences' vigorous enough to obliterate a tumor that has established its own blood supplies and consists of billions of destructive cells. However 'radical' the surgical intervention, however many 'scans' are taken of the body landscape, most remissions are temporary, the prospect is that the 'tumor invasion' will continue or that 'rogue cells' will eventually regroup and mount a new assault on the organism.
>
> (1979: 64–5)

In short, I believe that all discourses are modelled on social practices and that our understandings always derive from our doings. But discourses *transform* these practices in ways which safeguard the interests at stake in a given social context. Representations of scientific practices, for instance, especially when aimed at the general public rather than written for the eyes of peers, must establish their authority by presenting themselves as the objective truth, and will therefore prefer the language of 'being' – 'Dinosaur nostrils *are* located high on the forehead' – above the language of 'doing', above a discourse which makes it obvious that these facts have been distilled from scientific doings (perceptions, reasonings and actions) – 'Nineteenth century scientists *found* an intact Diplodocus skull, *observed* a large hole at the top of the head and because they *assumed* that all dinosaurs were aquatic, *guessed* that all dinosaur nostrils were located high on the forehead'. The two statements about dinosaurs do not mean the same thing of course, but they are based on the same discourse, the same understanding of the physiology of dinosaurs. The difference is that the first example omits the scientists' actions, while the second does not.

The anatomy of discourse

A discourse such as the 'health diet' discourse of eating is a knowledge of a particular social practice. The indefinite article is important. It is *a* knowledge. There are alternatives, other versions. Eating can be represented as primarily about health, or primarily about pleasure, for instance, and there can also be religious discourses of eating, to mention just some possibilities. This suggests that discourses are never only about what we do, but always also about why we do it. The discourses we use in representing social practices such as eating are versions of those practices *plus* the ideas and attitudes that attach to them in the contexts in which we use them. These ideas and attitudes are of three kinds:

1   *evaluations,* for instance evaluations of the food involved – is it tasty, filling, nicely presented, etc. – or the manner of eating it – is it too slow or too fast, are utensils used properly – or some other aspect of the practice;

2   *purposes,* for instance, curing or preventing heart disease, or celebrating a particular occasion – different discourses can attach different purposes to the same practice; and
3   *legitimations,* reasons why particular things should be done in particular ways, by particular people, etc., as when it is said that a particular kind of food should be eaten *because* an expert cardiologist recommends it.

Close reading of texts, for instance the 'natural fix' text we have already quoted, soon reveals these aspects of discourse:

> The natural fix:
> It's the same exercise and low-saturated-fat diet strategy you'd use to lower blood pressure: exercise aerobically for at least 30 minutes three or four times a week, cut your saturated-fat intake as low as possible, and – crucially – eat more fibre. 'Monounsaturated fats such as olive oil don't increase LDL cholesterol,' said cardiologist Chris Rembold.

This extract contains at least two purposes. The 'fix' of the title suggests that we exercise not to have a beautiful body, as for example in body-building, or for pleasure, but to 'fix' a health problem. Similarly we eat not to satisfy our appetites, but, again, to 'fix' a health problem. The term 'strategy' in 'the strategy you'd use … to lower blood pressure' represents exercising and eating as carefully planned strategies for attaining a specific goal, the lowering of blood pressure. The cardiologist's expert statement, finally, serves as legitimation, as the answer to an implicit question: 'Why should we lower our blood pressure in this way?' And the word 'natural' also has a legitimatory function, because it refers us to the view that, in matters of food, 'natural' is good, and 'artificial' bad. This view is so widely accepted that the word 'natural' by itself is sufficient to trigger it. If it is 'natural' then it is good.

Evaluations and legitimations can also be realized visually. Figure 5.3 shows a Japanese couple being photographed as part of their Western style wedding. But the photographer has included a stylist who is making some last minute adjustments to the bride's dress. This is probably not the kind of photo the couple would like to include in their own photo album. Yet the photographer has selected it for inclusion in an exhibition and a book. And I think what he suggests in this way amounts to a negative evaluation. This wedding is 'fake'. They are 'only posing'. It is 'style over substance'. In figure 5.4 the same photographer has included two elderly passers-by in a photograph of a newly-married French couple standing on the front steps of a church. Again it is not a standard wedding shot, not the kind of shot the couple would want in their album. But here the evaluation is positive. The photo establishes a kind of kinship between the young and the old couple, and in this way suggests that marriage is for life, that it forms the meaning and fulfilment of life. In both cases the photo represents the practice of wedding *plus* something else, and that something else brings in the value judgment, and functions as legitimation, or, in the case of figure 5.3, de-legitimation, critique.

Figure 5.3   Wedding (Elliott Erwitt, 1978)

I have established that discourses consist of a version of a social practice *plus* ideas about it and attitudes to it, and I have discussed these ideas and attitudes. What about the 'versions' themselves? How does discourse transform reality into a version of that reality? This I need to explain in two steps. First I need to inventorize the elements of social practices, and then I need to look at how they are transformed into discourse.

I list below the elements that must necessarily be part of any social practice *as it is actually enacted*. Note that this does not include evaluations, purposes and legitimations because these are added in discourse. Note also that a discourse about a given practice need not include all the elements of that practice. Knowledge is selective. For instance, a 'health diet' discourse of eating excludes place and manner of eating. It has no interest in where the food is eaten and how. It is concerned only with the food itself and the times when it is eaten. In a 'dinner party' discourse, on the other hand, the place where the food is eaten and the way the table is laid are important and do form part of the discourse.

Actions

By actions, I mean the things people do, the activities that make up the social practice, and their chronological order. In the case of exercising, for instance, the actions are the actual physical movements, performed in a specific order. But that order need

Figure 5.4   Wedding (Elliott Erwitt, 1953)

not be part of a given discourse about exercising. It may be edited out. Some discourses contain a great deal of detail about the actual actions of the practice, for instance the participant-oriented discourses used in instruction sessions, specialist magazines and books, etc. Other discourses contain only a vague, general knowledge of the actions involved in the practice, and concentrate on evaluations and/or purposes and legitimations.

The 'natural fix' text gives us next to no detail about exercising. Exercising is only referred to by the general term 'exercise aerobically'. This text is about the purposes of exercising and about its medical justification, not about the exercises themselves.

Manner

'Manner' refers to the *way in which* (some or all of) the actions are performed, for instance 'graciously', 'efficiently', 'slowly', 'energetically', etc. Clearly in some practices this matters a lot – for example, playing music, dancing – while in other cases only the result matters, not the way in which it is achieved.

Actors

The actors are the people – sometimes also animals – involved in the practice, and the different roles in which they are involved, for instance active and passive roles. Again, a discourse about a given social practice may not include all the actors who must of necessity take part in it. Aerobic exercises, for instance, are usually done in groups, and include an instructor. But this is not included in the 'natural fix' text, because it is not relevant to the interests of the men's health magazine from which the piece is taken. What the magazine is primarily interested in here is not the exercises them- selves, but their effect on health. It uses the discourse of the doctor, not of the aerobics instructor, or the cook preparing the healthy food.

Presentation

Presentation is the way in which actors are dressed and groomed. All social practices have their rules of presentation, although they differ in kind and degree of strictness (see chapter 3). But, even though aerobics classes do have their 'dress code', this is filtered out from the 'natural fix' text.

Resources

By 'resources' I mean the tools and materials needed to enact a social practice. Certain things are needed to 'eat fibre' – for instance the food itself, perhaps also a plate, a knife and fork, etc. The 'natural fix' text does mention the food, but in an abstract way. It refers not to the concrete food itself but to its ingredients and quali- ties. A 'health diet' discourse of eating of this kind is not concerned with what you eat or how it tastes, so long as it contains the right ingredients and has the right qualities.

Times

Inevitably social practices are timed – they take place at certain times, and they last for certain amounts of time. This aspect of the practice of exercising *is* included in the 'natural fix' text, although still in a relatively vague and open-ended way: 'for at least 30 minutes three or four times a week.' Amounts are crucial in any form of health prescription. Just as amounts of food are important in 'health diet' discourses – 'cut your saturated-fat intake as low as possible' – so amounts of exercise are important in 'health exercise' discourses.

Spaces

The final concrete element of the social practice is the space(s) where the action takes place, including the way they should be arranged to make the practice possible. Although aerobic exercises need certain types of space, this aspect is left out in the 'natural fix' text.

In reality all these elements must necessarily be part of the way a social practice is actually enacted. But, as I have stressed already, specific texts may include only some of them, and so do the discourses on which these texts draw for their content. Knowledge is selective, and what it selects depends on the interests and purposes of the institutions that have fostered the knowledge. It is possible to know everything you need to know about film in order to pass exams in film studies at university, and yet not be able to load film into a magazine. It is also possible to know everything you need to know to be a first-class camera operator and yet be unable to pass an exam in film studies. The social practice is the same in both cases – film making. But the knowledges, informed by the very different interests and purposes of the film industry and university film studies, differ.

Figure 5.5 shows that part of the 'health diet' discourse that has been used in the 'natural fix' text. These are the kind of 'statements' that make up a discourse – statements that string together some or all of the elements listed above. Sometimes the statements can be ordered chronologically, and this can then be indicated in the scenario by means of a flowchart type arrow. At other times there is nothing to suggest chronological order. The discourse is de-temporalized and does not include the order of the actions. This is then indicated in the 'scenario' with a '~' sign.

The 'natural fix' text represents the social practices of 'health dieting' and 'health exercising'. But it is itself also a social practice, the practice of prescribing a remedy for chest pains, as enacted by the men's health magazine. In chapter 6 we will call this kind of practice a genre. A genre is a social practice that recontextualizes one or more other social practices, that imports these social practices from their own context – actually doing exercises – into another context – that of the magazine – for the purposes of representing them to the participants of that other context, and in the light of the interests and purposes of that other context. Needless to say, the represented practice may itself also be a genre.

actor	action	resources	purpose	legitimation
(reader)	eats	small amounts of saturated fat	to fix chest pains	because it's natural
~				
(reader)	eats	unsaturated fat	to fix chest pains	because it's natural and approved by the cardiologist
~				
(reader)	eats	larger amount of fibre	to fix chest pains	because it's natural

Figure 5.5 'Health diet' scenario

actor	action	resource
(writer)	identifies recommended practice (exercise and low-saturated-fat diet strategy)	magazine
	↓	
(writer)	suggests aerobic exercise	magazine
	↓	
(writer)	suggests low saturated-fat intake	magazine
	↓	
(writer)	suggests eating more fibre	magazine
	↓	
(writer)	adduces expert opinion to lend weight to suggestions	magazine

Figure 5.6   Magazine 'health prescription' scenario

When we look at a text as an instance of social practice, we look at it as a sequence of actions – in this case speech acts, the kinds of things we do with words. As shown in figure 5.6, the 'natural fix' text first *identifies* the recommended 'fix', then *makes three suggestions*, and finally *gives authority* to these suggestions by means of an expert opinion, a kind of doctor's signature. Note that written texts include only two elements of the social practice, the actions and the medium through which they are realized – the magazine. *Not* represented are the writer and the reader, and the circumstances of writing and reading – time, place, dress and grooming, etc. For a full understanding of the social practice, of what men's health magazines *do* to or for their readers, these elements are also important.

We can now move to the second step of the argument. How is reality changed into discourse? I will answer this question in terms of four basic types of transformation, all of which we have in fact already touched on in the discussion above.

Exclusion

Discourses can exclude elements of the social practice, for instance certain kinds of actors. This can have a very distorting effect, for instance in discourses of war that exclude the victims.

Rearrangement

Discourses can rearrange the elements of social practices, for instances when it 'de-temporalizes' elements which in reality have a specific order, or when it imposes a specific order on actions which in reality do not need to take place in any specific order.

Addition

Discourses can add elements to the representation – most notably evaluations, purposes and legitimations.

Substitution

The term 'substitution' refers to the fact that discourses substitute *concepts* for the concrete elements of actual social practices. In the process the concrete can be transformed into the abstract, the specific into the general, and 'doing' into 'being'.

I have already given an example of the way in which the concrete can transform into the abstract when I described how the 'health diet' discourse substitutes a quality of food – 'low-saturated-fat' – for the food itself. The potential for abstracting qualities from people, places and things is endless. Which qualities will be abstracted depends on the interests and purposes of the social context that has developed or adopted the discourse. 'Health diet' discourses will abstract chemical qualities, other discourses may abstract qualities of colour, taste or texture, or still other qualities such as 'hearty', 'filling', 'crunchy', etc.

I have also discussed an example of generalization, when I indicated how the 'natural fix' text substitutes the general term 'aerobic exercises' for a wide range of specific physical movements. This substitution is typical of the kind of 'general knowledge' we find in contexts where social practices are represented to outsiders, rather than to those who are actually involved in them, whether in the media or in education. Generalization can also be realized visually, through a reduction of detail in representation, or through visual stereotypes. This will be discussed in more detail in chapter 8.

Another substitution is objectification, 'representing actions and events, and also qualities, as if they were objects' (Halliday and Martin: 1993: 52), as when the term 'aerobic exercise' substitutes for the actions of exercising. Benjamin Whorf (1956) showed how this transformation, which is possible in many European languages, was not possible in some of the native American languages he was studying. For instance, in Hopi one cannot say 'This is a wave'. 'Wave' must be a verb. As Whorf says:

> Without the projection of language no one ever saw a single wave. Some languages cannot say 'a wave'. They are closer to reality in that respect.
>
> (Whorf, 1956: 262)

But similar differences can exist within a language. Objectification has played a key role in the development of scientific discourses, in English as well as in other languages. 'Things' can be counted, measured – and described in terms of static, permanent qualities. They are more easily manipulated – in practice as well as in discourse. Processes, on the other hand, are fluid and ever-changing and less easy to grasp and control.

These are only some of the possible substitution transformations. The selected readings section in the back of this book refers to some relevant further reading.

The 'special operations' discourse of war

For a final example I return to the 'special operations' discourse of war, using the computer war game Delta Force® – *Black Hawk Down*®. This game was released in March 2003 by NovaLogic, not long after Ridley Scott's film of the same title. Its setting is the American intervention in Somalia in 1993. It uses actual documentary footage as an introduction to the game, and also features a list of the American soldiers who died in Mogadishu. At the time of writing, May 2003, it has already sold half a million copies worldwide. The company that produced it specializes in 'special operations' titles such as the Delta Force series, and has a subsidiary (NovaLogic Systems) which works in the area of military simulation, collaborating with the US Army's Training and Doctrine Command Analysis Center on the high profile Land Warrior System, a system which allows training in reconnaissance, the use of advanced electronic satellite communications and location equipment. The company also has links with Lockheed Martin Aeronautical Systems, producing flight simulations for its military aircraft. There is thus a link between war games and real wars, both in the game itself, and in the activities of the company which has produced it.

I will compare the scenarios of a section of the documentary introduction and a 'mission briefing' from the game. Here is a transcript of part of the documentary introduction:

1 CS Aidid addressing crowd. Super title: 5 June 1993	Voice over: Mohamed Farrah Aidid, militia leader of the Habr Gadir clan orders an attack ...
2 VLS High angle. Somali people running for cover. Zoom in	... on a UN relief shipment, killing ...
3 MLS Masked militia man with gun sitting atop a pile of bags of rice	... 24 Pakistani soldiers
4 MS Militia man swivelling rocket launcher around	In response to the ...

5	LS Militia man with gun	... continued Habr Gadir threat ...
6	MlS Militia man with rifle mounted on pickup truck	... task force rangers ...
7	MLS Militia man on pickup truck with rifle	... enter Mogadishu ...
8	MS Militia man on pickup truck	... with the sole purpose of capturing Aidid
9	VLS Black Hawk helicopters flying over desert. Super title: 26 August 1993	(music)
10	MLS Two US soldiers about to crash in door	(music)
11	LS Two US soldiers crouched on street, signalling to each other	(music)
12	MLS sideview group of soldiers aiming rifles	(music)
13	MLS Two US soldiers lying down with guns aimed	Voice over: This force is comprised ...
14	MLS Two US soldiers moving forward	... of US Army Rangers and ...
15	LS US soldiers crossing road and moving towards building	... operators from the First Special Forces ...
16a	LS Humvee driving towards camera. Camera tilts up to	... operational Detachment Delta, an elite fighting unit also known as ...
16b	LS Black Hawk helicopter overhead	... Delta Force

And here is the mission briefing. It appears over an image of a Black Hawk helicopter with a soldier pointing his gun downwards.

Mission 1
Bandit's crossing
Date: 27 February 1993 – 1930 hours
Location: Jubba Valley

Situation:
UN forces are attempting to distribute food and provisions to local civilians. Intel reports that Habr Gadir militia may be planning to raid the distribution centres and take the supplies for their clan's use. You must prevent any militia unit from taking food shipments. Secure the village and ensure that enemy reinforcements cannot reach the UN convoy.

Figures 5.7 and 5.8 show the relevant 'scenarios':

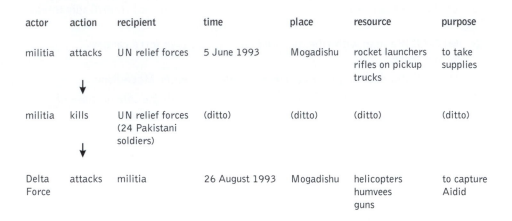

actor	action	recipient	time	place	resource	purpose
militia	attacks	UN relief forces	5 June 1993	Mogadishu	rocket launchers rifles on pickup trucks	to take supplies
militia	kills	UN relief forces (24 Pakistani soldiers)	(ditto)	(ditto)	(ditto)	(ditto)
Delta Force	attacks	militia	26 August 1993	Mogadishu	helicopters humvees guns	to capture Aidid

Figure 5.7   'Special operations' scenario (documentary introduction, *Black Hawk Down*)

The two segments are not identical, yet they draw on the same discourse. In both cases the UN provides relief supplies, is then attacked by the militia, after which Delta Force sets things right. But the discourse allows for some options. The goal of the mission may either be capturing the demonic anti-hero – the despotic warlord, the demonic terrorist leader, the ruthless tyrant – as in the documentary introduction, or providing protection for the food relief agency, as in the game. The operation itself, although provoked in both cases, may either be punitive, as in the documentary introduction, or preventative, as in the mission briefing from the game, where the militia only *plans* to attack. Such differences may relate to the fact that different media are used. To market a game in which the users are invited to kill a real person, rather than anonymous shadowy enemies, may be crossing a line that should not be crossed, even if that person is a demonic anti-hero. At other times, however, both options may be part of the same discourse, the punitive as well as the preventative option, for instance, and the motive of removing the threatening anti-hero, as well as the motive of protecting innocent and weak civilians, or defenceless relief agencies. All these options were much in evidence in the press and TV coverage of one and the same real war, the Iraq war which started more or less at the same time as the release of *Black Hawk Down*.

Actual instantiations of a discourse, such as those mapped in figures 5.7 and 5.8 draw only on part of the knowledge, the whole body of statements that has gradually accrued over the last 18 years to create the 'special operations' discourse of war. The full picture of the discourse would only emerge if we studied more texts and mapped the resulting scenarios on top of each other, using flowchart type bifurcations where two possibilities exist – for example, 'preventative' or 'punitive'. The examples I have given hopefully provide just enough detail to show that investigating a discourse is like

actor	action	recipient	time	place	resource	purpose
UN forces	provide relief supplies	local population	27 February 1993	Jubba valley		
↓						
militia	plan to attack	UN forces	(ditto)	(ditto)	w/ .50 calibre mounted weapons	to take supplies
↓						
Delta Force	attacks	militia	(ditto)	(ditto)	M16/203s M9 Berettas At4 Anti-Tank rockets	
↓						
Delta Force	prevents	militia's plans	(ditto)	(ditto)		
↓						
Delta Force	secures	village	(ditto)	(ditto)		

Figure 5.8   'Special operations' scenario (mission briefing, *Black Hawk Down*)

an archaeological dig which may seem to yield only fragments – statements and clusters of statements – but will, if you keep digging, eventually allow you to put the whole vase back together again.

Exercises

1   Think of a subject about which you know very little – in my case this would for instance be 'rhinoceroses' or 'Bogota'. Write down what you know about it in the form of a 'scenario'. Find someone else who also knows very little about this subject and ask him or her to tell you what s/he knows. How similar is his/her scenario to yours? Where does this scenario come from? Why does it contain the particular 'statements' it contains?

2   Take a short verbal text that represents a 'tourist discourse' about a village or town, for instance a description – and evaluation – of that village or town from a tourist guide. Now design two different kinds of illustrated 'texts' based on that discourse, for instance a board game and a web page for children.

3   Find some quotes from different contexts that ascribe different purposes to what is essentially the same activity – for example, advertising, waging a particular war? What is at stake for the writers or speakers in choosing the purposes they have chosen?

4   Collect a series of short texts – they do not have to be written texts – on a practice of your choice. This could be, for instance, a brief description of an arrest by the police in (a) a news report, (b) a crime novel and (c) a television series; or an account of a first sexual experience in (a) a magazine advice column, (b) a novel and (c) the lyrics of a song. Or anything else across a similar range of texts. Use the terminology introduced in this chapter to analyse what is included and excluded in each case and why.

5   Collect two series of about six photographs representing more or less the same subject matter – for instance, Africa; the countryside – one of them casting a negative and the other a positive light on the subject. What means are used to do so?

Note

Some of the material in this chapter appeared earlier in Swedish (Selander and Van Leeuwen, 1999). The material on discourses of war draws on research by D. Machin and T. van Leeuwen in the project Language and Global Communication, which is sponsored by a grant from the Leverhulme Trust to the Centre for Language and Communication Research, Cardiff University.

6 Genre

Speech acts

In the previous chapter I looked at discourse as a social semiotic approach to studying the 'what' of communication. In this chapter I will use the concepts of 'speech act' and 'genre' to outline a social semiotic approach to the 'how' of communication.

The term 'speech act' was coined by J.L. Austin (1962), a philosopher of language. Until the 1960s philosophers of language had seen language as predominantly a mode of representation, a resource for making statements about what is going on in the world. The task of language philosophy, as they saw it, was to formulate the precise conditions under which such statements would be true or false (see also chapter 8). Austin changed this. Some statements, he said, are neither true nor false. They *create* their own truth. They *become* true by the very act of uttering them. He called such statements 'performatives' and contrasted them to 'constatives', statements with a primarily representational function, which can therefore be true or false. He gave examples like 'I do take this woman to be my lawful wedded wife', as said in the course of a marriage ceremony, and 'I name this ship the *Queen Elizabeth*', as said while smashing a bottle against the hull of a ship (1962: 5), noting that these utterances can only perform their performative work under certain conditions, which he called 'felicity conditions': unless the sentence 'I take this woman to be my lawful wedded wife' is said in the setting of a recognized marriage ceremony, it will not perform the act of marriage. The same applies to less institutionalized performances. An apology, for instance, will only work as an apology if it follows an action which is recognized, in the given context, as requiring an apology.

Austin stressed that every speech act combines three simultaneous acts, a *locutionary act*, an act of representing something that is going on in the world – for example, referring to 'this woman' and predicating of her that she is the speaker's lawful, wedded wife – an *illocutionary act*, that is, the performance of a communicative act such as promising, warning, apologizing, commanding, etc., and a *perlocutionary act*, the causing of an effect on the hearer. Speech act theory has become widely applied in pragmatics, the study of language in use (see for example, Blum-Kolka, 1997), but unfortunately most pragmaticians neglect the perlocutionary act. This is a pity because there clearly may be a difference between the intended and the actual effect of a speech act. The Indian version of *Cosmopolitan* magazine contained the following piece of advice for managers: 'If you manage a lot of people, maintain their morale by showing you have a sense of humour'. For readers who are 'managees' rather than managers reading this piece of advice might diminish the effect of the manager's jokes, because they could now be seen as somewhat less than spontaneous.

Halliday (1985: 68) stresses that speech acts are dialogic:

> An 'act' of speaking ... might more appropriately be called an 'interact': it is an exchange in which giving implies receiving, and demanding implies giving in response.

He distinguishes four basic 'interacts' of this kind:

- *Offering information*
  The speech act of 'offering information' is expressed by statements, for example, 'The manager showed a sense of humour'. The preferred response, says Halliday, is agreement or acknowledgement, although it is of course also possible to disagree, or to remain noncommittal – for example, 'Mmmm ... ', 'Maybe ... '. Which response is preferred may depend on the context. In adversarial debates, for instance, disagreement is preferred.

- *Demanding information*
  The speech act of 'demanding information' is expressed by questions, for example, 'Did the manager show a sense of humour?' Note that the locutionary act stays the same: I am still referring to 'the manager' and still predicating of her that she has a sense of humour. The only thing that changes is the illocutionary act or, in Halliday's terms, the 'speech function'. The preferred response to the question is of course the answer, but there may also be a 'disclaimer' – for example, 'I don't know' – or a refusal to answer, although the latter will usually be seen as unfriendly, an admission of guilt, or an act of resistance.

- *Offering goods and services*
  This is the only one of Halliday's four speech functions which, in English at least, cannot be expressed by a specific grammatical category such as statement, question or command. It is usually expressed by a limited range of standard idioms such as 'Here you are'. When it comes to exchanging 'goods and services', Halliday says, the exchange is essentially non-verbal, and language is 'only brought in to help the process along' (1985: 68). The preferred response is acceptance, with or without some expression of thanks or appreciation, although, again, offers may also be rejected, or hedged – 'Not right now ... '.

- *Demanding goods and services*
  The speech act of 'demanding goods and services' is expressed by some kind of command, for example, 'Show that you have a sense of humour, managers'. The preferred response is an undertaking – for example, 'OK, I will' – although there may also be a refusal.

There are many different kinds of statements, questions and commands. Statements, for instance include 'promises', 'warnings', 'assertions', 'arguments', 'accusations', 'apologies' and many more. Jef Verschueren (1985) lists some 650 different speech acts, from 'abandon' to 'zip one's lip'. There are no separate linguistic categories for the expression of these. They are realized by *combinations* of linguistic, non-linguistic and contextual features (see Halliday, 1973: 75). A promise, for instance, is a statement which must minimally have the following three additional linguistic features: first person – 'I' or 'we'; future tense – because you can only promise something that has not yet been done; a verb of voluntary action – dying, for instance, is not a voluntary action, and hence you cannot promise to die. Whether an action is regarded as voluntary or not may depend on the context. In the Bible 'love' is a voluntary action – if it was not there could be no command to 'love thy neighbour'. But in certain romantic discourses it is not voluntary, you 'fall in love', whether you like it or not.

Changing any of the three minimum features necessary to realize a 'promise' will result in a different kind of statement:

I will help you tomorrow	1st person; future; volitional verb	promise
I will die tomorrow	1st person; future; non-volitional verb	forecast
I helped you yesterday	1st person; past; volitional verb	recount of event
You will help me tomorrow	2nd person; future; volitional verb	order

The same speech acts can, of course, also be realized by statements that contain an explicit speech act verb – for example, 'I promise to help you tomorrow', or 'I order you to help me tomorrow'.

Apart from the linguistic features of the speech act itself, other features might contribute, for instance features relating to the preceding text or the context – for example, to have a speech act of 'explaining' there has to be something that is to be explained – or features that are expressed non-verbally.

To summarize:

- Every linguistic utterance is at once a piece of representation – a 'locutionary act' – *and* a move in an interaction – an 'illocutionary act'.
- Speech acts come in pairs, and always involve an 'initial move' and a 'response'.
- There is a difference between the 'illocutionary act' – what the speech act is trying to do, for example, to *persuade* – and the 'perlocutionary act' – the effect of the speech act, for example, to *convince*. If the addressees know the language – say, English – and the conventions of the particular context in which it is used – say, advertising – they will understand that someone is trying to persuade them, but that does not necessarily mean they are going to be convinced.
- There are four basic types of speech act, each with a preferred response and possible alternative responses: the statement – offer of information; the question – demand for information; the command – demand for goods and services; and the offer – the offer of goods and services.

Multimodal communicative acts

Images have for the most part been studied as representations rather than as interactions. The key questions of image analysis have been: 'What people, places and things are represented in this image?' and 'What kind of connotative or symbolic meanings are associated with these representations?' (Van Leeuwen and Jewitt, 2001: 92). But clearly images are also used to *do* things to or for or with people: to persuade (advertisements), instruct (patterns for dress making), explain (diagrams in textbooks), warn (image of skull and crossbones on a door), and so on. Kress and Van Leeuwen (1996: 121) have extended Halliday's theory of 'speech functions' to images. Like linguistic representations, images can also either 'offer' or 'demand'. But where, in the English language, this is realized linguistically, in images it is realized by the system of the gaze. If a person (or animal) represented in an image looks at the viewer, the image realizes a 'demand': 'the gaze ... demands something from the viewer, demands that the viewer enter into some kind of imaginary relation with him or her' (ibid.: 122). If such a look is not present, the image is an 'offer'. It then '"offers" the represented participants to the viewer as items of information, objects of contemplation, impersonally, as though they were specimens in a display case' (ibid.: 124).

The precise nature of such offers and demands comes about through a combination of different visual and contextual features, just as in the case of the speech act. The picture in figure 6.1, for instance, combines a visual demand with a pointing finger, an imperious look, and a military moustache and uniform – both symbols of authority. Together these features modulate the demand into a very direct, maximally authoritative visual summons.

Figure 6.1   Kitchener recruitment poster (1914)

The linguistic speech act in figure 6.1 expresses another kind of demand. It is a statement with direct address, a verb which realizes a kind of request – 'need' – and an agent – 'your country' – who has, in the given context, the right to command the addressee – a moral right, based on patriotism. Taken together, these features create a hybrid speech act, a speech act which oscillates between bluntness and formality, directness (the direct address) and indirectness (the indirect demand). And then I have not even mentioned the typography, with its highly salient, large 'you'.

The question is, what do we have here? One or two speech acts? The same demand formulated twice, once in a rather direct way, and once verbally, in a more indirect, less personalized and more formal way? Or one single multimodal communicative act in which image and text blend like instruments in an orchestra?

If we take the first approach we will have to sequentialize what we in fact see in one glance and posit some kind of reading order that leads the eye from the picture to the text. The text then becomes a kind of caption for the picture. But is this the right approach? In the everyday face-to-face equivalent of the poster we would not dream of doing so. Imagine an actual uniformed man addressing us in this way. Clearly we would experience it as a single, multilayered, multimodal communicative act, whose illocutionary force comes about through the fusion of all the component semiotic modes: dress, grooming, facial expression, gaze, gesture – as show in figure 6.2. Perhaps the same approach should be used here. Perhaps speech acts should be renamed *communicative acts* and understood as multimodal micro events in which all the signs present combine to determine their communicative intent.

The example shows how many linguistic and visual features can combine into a single communicative act, and how many different kinds of communicative act can therefore be expressed. It also is an example which may at first sight seem monologic

image:
finger pointed at the viewer
unsmiling look at the viewer
military uniform
military moustache

language:
2nd and 3rd person combines
declarative
lexicalized request (need)
 authorized subject (country)

typography:
large and heavy you

stylistically cohere into ⟶ single communicative act

Figure 6.2   Multimodal communicative act

rather than dialogic. Yet it does of course have a preferred response – enlist in the Army – and hence also a dispreferred one.

So far I have mentioned speech acts, image acts and acts of non-verbal communication, such as facial expressions and gestures. But does the idea of the communicative act extend to all semiotic modes? Can we have 'music acts', for example? Or 'sound acts'? Or 'smell acts'? In Van Leeuwen (1999: 92) I began to look at the role of melody in realizing 'music acts'. Melodies often have an overall direction. They can tend upwards or downwards. In singing, going up in pitch requires an increase in vocal effort, and going down a decrease, a degree of relaxation. As a result rising melodies can be used to energize people, to rally people together for a common cause, for instance in national anthems and patriotic songs, or in upbeat advertising songs. Melodies with a descending pitch, on the other hand, can relax and soothe, and may therefore be used, for instance, in meditative, inward-looking hymns or in lullabies. The same applies to voices (see Van Leeuwen, 1992). The disc-jockeys of 'Beautiful Music' radio stations not only speak in low, relaxed voices but also allow their voice to go down a lot, so as to soothe and relax the listener, to 'sound like a warm, friendly adult' and to portray a 'relaxed manner' (ibid.: 237) while the disc-jockeys of Top-40 breakfast programmes speak at a pitch level well above their normal register and make much use of rising pitch, in order to energize the listener, to sound 'up' – 'Your sound has gotta be a "hey let's get it happening" sort of approach' (ibid.: 238). Such melodic features combine of course with features of tempo, rhythm, voice quality, etc. Like speech acts and image acts, 'sound acts' result from a *combination* of features.

Finally, as far as smell is concerned, we live in a world where supermarkets pump chocolate flavours and other enticing smells into their air-conditioning systems to encourage customers to buy more, where one debt collecting company was reported to have impregnated the paper of final notices with a synthetic version of human sweat to instil fear, and where perfumes help us express our identities and attract the other – or the same – sex. Smell does not just 'represent', or 'remind' us of other places and times, it is also and quite deliberately used to *do* things to, for or with people.

To summarize:

- The linguistic features of speech acts combine with other, non-linguistic and contextual features to create multimodal communicative acts.
- Many features can combine into a single communicative act, so it follows that many distinct types of communicative act, and many subtle modulations of these communicative acts, are possible.

Genre and discourse in storytelling

The term 'genre' is generally used to mean 'a type of text'. Texts become 'typical' when they have characteristics that can also be recognized in other, similar texts. The reason for this is that the people who produce the texts follow certain 'rules' –

prescriptions, traditions, ingrained habits, rôle models, etc. (see chapter 3). Three kinds of 'typical characteristics' characterize genres, characteristics of content, form and function. Genres such as the Western and the fairytale are usually characterized on the basis of their content. Westerns are typically set in a particular time and place and will use certain stock characters and typical plots. Fairytales, likewise, are set 'a long time ago, in a faraway country' and typically include at least some magical characters – sorcerers, witches, etc. – and events. As can be seen from the examples, the content-oriented approach to characterizing genres is common in literature and film studies. But it should not remain restricted to these text types. Content, the 'what' of the text, is clearly important in any kind of text. In social semiotics, however, content is studied under the heading of 'discourse', rather than under the heading of 'genre'.

Texts can also be characterized on the basis of the means of expression or media they use. The string quartet could be an example of this form-oriented approach to 'genre': a string quartet is a string quartet because it comprises four string instruments, regardless of what they play. This form-oriented approach is common in relation to forms of expression in which representation is not foregrounded or considered important – for example, music.

Finally, texts may be typical in terms of what they *do*. The genre of advertisement is defined by its function of selling products or services – and, today, increasingly, ideas. The genre of news is defined by its function of providing information about recent events of public interest. Combinations are possible too. The genre of magazine advertisement, for instance, is defined on the basis of its function – advertising – as well as its medium – the magazine. The social semiotic approach to genre has focused on the *function* of texts in social interactions, on what people *do* to or for or with each other by means of texts. As such doings unfold sequentially, this approach to genre has concentrated on the way in which different kinds of 'beginning–middle–end' structures help to enact communicative practices. But the social semiotic approach has also stressed that studying the text alone is not enough. The sequences of communicative actions that make up genres are embedded in social practices which contain other elements as well – actors, times, places, and so on (see chapter 5). Social semiotics should look, not just at the actions, at 'What is done here with words (or pictures, or music)?' but also at 'Who does it?', 'For whom?', 'Where?', 'When'?, etc. And if this aspect remains in the background in this particular chapter, it is only because I cannot speak of everything at once, not because it is less important.

Genre as defined in this way is, of course, only one of the three key textual resources I will discuss in this part of the book. Texts also represent. They are also *about* things, and they should therefore be studied not only from the point of view of genre but also from the point of view of discourse. Finally, as will be discussed in chapter 7, they also have stylistic characteristics, an aspect which, in the age of the 'lifestyle', is becoming increasingly important. The difference between discourse and genre can be illustrated with respect to stories. A well-known discourse-oriented approach to analysing the beginning–middle–end structure of stories was that of Vladimir Propp (1968), originally published in 1927. Propp noted that Russian folktales, despite their surface differences, contain typical events in typical sequences. Consider the following examples:

> *Folktale 1* A tsar gives an eagle to a hero. The eagle carries the hero away to another kingdom
> *Folktale 2* An old man gives Sucenko a horse. The horse carries the hero away another kingdom
> *Folktale 3* A sorcerer gives Ivan a boat. The boat takes Ivan to another kingdom
> *Folktale 4* A princess gives Ivan a ring. Young men appear from out of the ring and carry Ivan away to another kingdom

Clearly the characters differ in each story, but there is always a hero (Sucenko, Ivan, etc.), a helper (a tsar, an old man, a sorcerer, a princess) and a magical agent (an eagle, a horse, a boat, young men), and the hero is always given some means of transport and then transported to another kingdom. These are the recurring characteristics that allow us to recognize these stories as typical of their kind, and they are of course similar to the 'statements' (Foucault's term) and 'scenarios' I discussed in the previous chapter. Propp called these statements, these typical story events, 'functions' and gave them labels like 'Provision of a magical agent', 'Transference to another kingdom', and so on. He showed that there were, in all, 31 of these functions, and that although not every one of them occurs in every story they always have to occur in a fixed order.

Wright (1975: 143) applied this idea to the Western. 'Classical' Westerns, common from the 1930s to the 1950s, typically begin with a hero riding into a farming community – or some other community – which is threatened by unscrupulous villains – for example, ranchers. The hero initially keeps a low profile, but soon the community discovers that he has exceptional skills – that he is an ace gunfighter. They accept him, but also mistrust him a little, as he resembles the enemy in some ways – or even has links with the enemy. As the conflict between the community and the villains reaches a crisis, the hero intervenes and defeats the villains. Although the community now fully accepts him, he leaves and rides into the mountains.

Such typical plots may be fictional, but they nevertheless represent what goes on in the real world. Their 'mythical' nature, their remove from contemporary realism, allows them to represent key themes relevant to a wide range of contemporary social practices. In classical Westerns, for instance, the farmers represent progress and communal values in opposition to the ranchers' greed and selfishness, while the hero has characteristics of both: he is on the one hand an individualist, fiercely independent, and a gunfighter, but on the other hand he also respects and protects the community, rather than exploiting or destroying it. The story therefore 'argues' that (American) society does need communal values, but that communities are also weak and vulnerable. Society therefore needs men who possess individuality, independence and enterprise, but who also respect community values. This 'argument' clearly has affinities with that of the 'special operations' discourse discussed in the previous chapter. The fact that that discourse was brought into the domain of global politics by Ronald Reagan – who, as an actor, had starred in many Westerns – gives pause for thought.

There is another way of looking at stories, an approach which stresses the beginning–middle–end structure, not of the *represented* events, but of the events that constitute the telling of the story. Such an account of storytelling has been given by the sociolinguist William Labov (1972b). Note that each of the events is defined in terms of its communicative function, as something the storyteller *does* for the listener (or reader, or viewer). The story I use to illustrate Labov's analysis is from Julia Vosnesenskaja's *Women's Decameron* (1987):

1   *Abstract*
    The storyteller begins with a brief summary or indication of the topic of the story, to attract the listener's attention and interest:

    I fell in love for the first and last time when I was only five ... Don't laugh, first hear what sort of love it was. Perhaps you won't feel like laughing when you have heard the whole story ...

2   *Orientation*
    The storyteller introduces the setting – who is involved, when, where – and the event that kicks off the story, thus providing orientation for the listener. Elements of orientation may also occur later in the story, when new people, places and things are introduced.

    It was during the war. My father was in charge of a military aerodrome and my mother was a medical officer. They were both serving in the same unit and were so afraid of losing me in the general chaos of war that they dragged me around with them rather than entrust me to relatives or children's homes ... One day, a new pilot came to us straight from flying school, He was the youngest, only eighteen, but of course he seemed grown up to me, even quite old.

3   *Complication*
    The story moves into the events that make up the core of the story. In the case of my example, Volodka, the pilot, spends much time with Larissa, the storyteller, but then falls in love with a telegraphist, which makes Larissa jealous. Volodka does not return from a mission, then returns months later, badly burnt after a plane crash. When he leaves he promises Larissa he will marry her when she is grown up – she is the only one who does not mind his scars.

4   *Evaluation*
    Throughout the development of the story there may be moments of evaluation, moments when the storyteller answers the unspoken (or spoken) question 'So what?', 'Why should we find this interesting?' Here she anticipates and counters such a sceptical reaction: 'Don't laugh, It's true'.

They all had their eye on Volodka, and this Rayechka girl even had some success. But I got Volodka away from her. Don't laugh, it's true ...

5   *Resolution*
The final event, the outcome of the story, provides the listener with *meaning*. Stories are told to convey ideas about life, in this case the idea is that in real life there are no happy endings: Volodka, after having first been decorated as a Hero of the Soviet Union is revealed to be a traitor and a spy and perishes in the camps. The marriage with Larissa never happens.

6   *Coda*
This stage – which does not always occur – has the storyteller signing off and making a bridge from the resolution to the 'here and now' of the telling of the story – it is told in a maternity ward, to other new mothers – and to the relevance of the story for the storyteller and/or the listeners.

But I never did find a man like him. I received my doctorate and decided it was time to have a family by myself, without a husband. I've now borne my son, Volodka, and I'm going to bring him up by myself.

All stories can be described in terms of these two structures: the structure of the story told and the structure of the telling of the story. The same applies to non-narrative genres. They too, rely on three kinds of semiotic resources – 'discourse', a resource for structuring content, 'genre', a resource for structuring the interaction through which that content is communicated, and 'style', the resource I will deal with in the next chapter.

Labov's schema includes only the *actions* of the social practice of storytelling. It was based on boasting stories told by Harlem teenagers. These stories would typically be told to other teenagers in the school playground, but here they were told to researchers, and what these researchers recorded did therefore not include the 'original' who, when, where, etc. If the story had been recorded as it was told in the playground, there would, for instance, have been many interruptions. Listeners would have participated actively. Researchers recording authentic stories, on the other hand, are less likely to participate actively in the telling of the story. It is clearly important to study what kinds of stories are, in our society, told to whom, when, where, how, etc. Yet, abstract as it is – or maybe because it is relatively abstract – Labov's schema has been useful for studying many different types of story, as is demonstrated by the fact that I could easily apply it to a story which differs in many respects from those studied by Labov. Clearly, Labov was describing a semiotic resource, not a particular kind of text. Discourses and genres are best seen, not as types of text, but as semiotic resources that can be used in many different contexts – where their use may then be subject to context-specific rules (see chapter 3).

Genre as a staged and multimodal process

The text below is an example of the non-narrative genre of the magazine advice column. In magazine advice columns readers reveal their problems and experts provide solutions and advice. The example is 'typical of its kind', instantly recognized as exemplifying a standard format for going about the business of asking for, and receiving, help with problems of everyday life. In the right hand column I use functional labels to try and characterize the 'speech acts' that make up the text:

I lied on my CV   *Revealing a problem (confession)*
↓

Should I come clean with my boss?   *Appealing for help (question)*
↓

Yes   *Providing a solution (answer)*
↓

But be prepared for the possibility of losing   *Issuing a caveat (warning)*
your job if you have a scrupulous Boss
↓

The bright side: you will gain her respect if   *Predicting the result (prediction 1)*
you speak up and accept your mistake
↓

and having got this burden off your chest   *(prediction 2)*
will help you focus better on your work

The example demonstrates the key characteristics of the social semiotic genre theory (see for example, Eggins 1994: 25ff, Martin, 1992: 546ff):

- A genre consists of a series of 'stages' which are given functional labels, such as 'Revealing a problem', 'Appealing for help', 'Providing a solution', to indicate the communicative work done by each stage.
- Each stage consists of one or more of the *same* speech acts. For instance a 'Problem' stage may consist of one or more sentences realizing a confession (see below). In the above example the 'Problem' stage contains only one confession, but the 'Result' stage has two predictions.
- The sequence of stages as a whole realizes a particular strategy for achieving an overall communicative goal, in this case the solution of a problem.
- Because each stage is homogeneous in terms of the communicative acts it contains, it will also be relatively homogeneous in terms of the linguistic features that characterize it, for instance, the 'problem' stage of an advice column will have the linguistic characteristics typical of confessions – it will be a statement, in the first person, using past tense and a verb which expresses what is, in the

context, considered to be a deviant action or state – and the 'result' stage will have the linguistic characteristics typical of predictions – it will be a statement, in the second person, using future tense and a verb expressing what is, in the context, considered to be a non-volitional action, in this case an 'effect' of 'coming clean'.

But as I have already mentioned, speech acts can be modulated in different ways. Confessions may be blunt or veiled, predictions confident or tentative, and all this will modify the language used.

Genres, then, are semiotic resources, 'templates' for doing communicative things. As such, they are very versatile. The 'advice column' genre, for instance, can be applied to many contents, to beauty problems as well as gardening problems, health problems as well as relationship problems, and so on. But that does not mean that genres are neutral, value-free 'tools'. Genres are culturally and historically specific forms of communication and they realize culturally and historically specific power relations between the communicating parties. The 'advice column' genre, for instance, is one of the ways in which society enacts and perpetuates the relation between the 'helpless' and 'ignorant' lay person and the resourceful and knowledge-able professional 'expert'. The social critic Ivan Illich (1971: 19) has argued that the growth of professionalism in the nineteenth century gradually 'disabled' people, deprived them of their autonomy in fields of everyday life such as food, health, sexuality, and bringing up children:

> Professionals assert secret knowledge about human nature, knowledge which only they have the right to dispense. They claim a monopoly over the definition of deviance and the remedies needed. In any area where a human need can be imagined these professions, dominant, authoritative, monopolistic, legalised – and, at the same time, debilitating and effectively disabling the individual – have become exclusive expert of the public good.

In this way the advice column can be seen as one of the 'procedures of power' that constitute what Foucault (for example, 1978: 59ff) has called the 'microphysics of power', the way in which power is exercised through everyday routines and habits, including, importantly, everyday communicative practices.

Today the rule of experts is increasingly challenged by the rule of managers and bureaucrats. Doctors, teachers and other professionals complain that they can no longer determine autonomously, on the basis of their professional knowledge and ethos, what will count as illness and how it will be treated, what will count as educational knowledge and how it will be taught, and so on. As a result we may see advice columns gradually replaced by formats which offer people *menus* of options with which to help themselves, rather than one single authoritative solution. But as such menus are also put together by the agents of powerful social institutions this will not fundamentally change the situation. It will merely be a new strategy for enacting and perpetuating power.

So far I have used mainly linguistic examples. But the concept of genre is a *multimodal* concept. An influential early study of the genre of service encounters (Hasan, 1979) used the following key example – the right hand column again displays the functional labels:

Who's next?	*Sale initiation*
I think I am	
I'll have ten oranges and a kilo of bananas please	*Sale request*
Yes, anything else?	*Sale compliance*
Yes	
I wanted some strawberries but these don't look very ripe	*Sale inquiry*
They're ripe alright, they're just that colour, a greeny pink	
Mmm I see	
Will they be OK for this evening?	*Sale inquiry*
Yeah they'll be fine. I had some yesterday and they're good, very sweet and fresh	
Oh alright then. I'll take two	*Sale request*
You'll like them cos they're good	*Sale inquiry*
Will that be all?	*Sale compliance*
Yes	
That'll be two dollars sixty-nine please	*Sale*
I can give you nine cents	*Purchase*
Yeah OK thanks, eighty, a hundred, three dollars	*Purchase closure*
Come again	*Finish*
See ya	

The point is, the transaction is represented here as being realized by talk and by talk alone. To understand it, there is no need for any context, or any non-verbal communication. Shopping in a modern supermarket, on the other hand, does not happen in this way. Every single one of the component activities or 'stages' of Hasan's shopping genre must occur, but they are realized differently. Instead of asking about the quality of the products, they are visually inspected and handled silently. The checkout queue forms silently and the products are silently taken from the trolley and placed on the conveyor belt, although the checkout assistant will perhaps have been told to smile and say 'hello', inquire whether you have a loyalty card, and mumble a 'thank you'. In other words, shopping must still involve 'sale inquiries', 'sale compliances', etc., but their realization has become multimodal and does not necessarily involve talk. Some of the stages may be realized verbally, others through action, or through writing and visual communication – reading the price on the shelf, checking the sell-by date or the ingredients on the package. The same applies, for instance, to getting cash from an automatic teller machine. The directives issued by the machine may be visually or verbally realized and the responses will be mechanical actions. This again shows that genres are culturally and historically specific. Shopping happens differently in different cultures and periods. Even within our own culture we may still have, side by side, the old market where produce can be handled and where bargaining is still possible, the shop in which everything is done verbally, as in Hasan's example, and the modern supermarket.

Here is another example, taken from Paddy Chayevsky's 1953 television play *Printer's Measure* (1994) Note how some of the communicative acts, some of the micro events that constitute this 'apprenticeship episode', are realized by speech, others by actions such as looking up, scurrying down the shop, pulling out a letterhead, etc. Remember also that the individual stages, whether they are dominated by speech or action, are all in themselves also multimodal, as pointed out earlier in this chapter: Mr Healey's summons – 'Hey! Come here!' – once performed by an actor, is every bit as multimodal as Kitchener's call to arms in figure 6.1.

Mr Healey: Hey! Come here!	*Call to attention*

The boy looks up and comes scurrying down the shop, dodging the poking arm of the Kluege press, and comes to Mr Healey.

Mr Healey pulls out a letterhead, points to a line of print	*Demonstration*
Mr Healey: What kind of type is that?	*Quizzing*
Boy: Twelve point Clearface	
Mr Healey: How do you know?	*Probing*
Boy: It's lighter than Goudy, and the lower case 'e' goes up	
Mr Healey: Clearface is a delicate type. It's clean, it's clear. It's got line and grace. Remember that	*Instruction*
Beat it!	*Dismissal*

The boy hurries back to the front of the shop to finish his cleaning

All this applies not just to face-to-face interaction. The stages of print genres, too, may either be realized verbally or visually, or by means of other semiotic modes. In 'problem-solution' print advertisements, for instance, the 'problem' may be represented verbally, as in an advertisement for hearing aids which opens with the line 'Want to hear clearly?' or visually, as in an advertisement for headache tablets which shows a picture of a sufferer with a contorted face.

The boundaries between stages or groups of stages can also be indicated non-verbally. In face-to-face interaction this is often done by means of changes of posture or position (see Scheflen, 1963). The apprenticeship episode above, for instance, lasts as long as the two participants are facing each other, at the back of the shop. In printed or written text the different sections of the text may be given distinct graphic identities to clearly separate them from each other.

Of course, in some genres most of the work will still be done through language. But overall the relation between language and other semiotic modes is changing – in ways that are quite complex. In service encounters the increasing importance of *self service* creates a much greater role for visual communication and bodily action. At the same time, the increased use of *distance communication* has caused many 'manual' actions and transactions to become more verbal and 'dialogic', for instance instructions – for example, computer help screens and help lines – or medical checkups – telemedicine. And although visual structuring is replacing linguistic structuring in many types of print media, new types of screen genres – for example, websites – make much greater use of written language than older screen media such as film and television. To understand such changes and their products, the study of speech and writing and other semiotic modes needs to be much more fully integrated than has been the case in the past, when media studies paid scant attention to language, and linguistics scant attention to visual media.

Genre and globalization

The magazine *Cosmopolitan* was started in 1970 in the USA by Helen Gurley-Brown, the author of *Sex and the Single Girl* (1962). The key difference between *Cosmopolitan* and earlier women's magazines was that women were no longer shown in domestic settings, as (house)wives and mothers. They were either working or in pursuit of adventure and pleasure, more specifically sexual adventure. Like other new US magazines of the 1960s and early 1970s, *Cosmopolitan* highlighted sexuality in a new and 'liberated' way. Women were portrayed as expressing their freedom and independence essentially by being sexy – and this sexiness, in turn, was expressed essentially by their choice of consumer products.

Today the magazine, still under the editorship of Helen Gurley-Brown, has become truly global. The magazine appears in 48 different versions and the *Cosmopolitan* 'brand' has also diversified into television programmes, cosmetics and other products and services for women. Many of *Cosmopolitan*'s local versions are produced by local teams in local languages, and involve some locally produced material as well as rewritten imported materials. Yet the basic *Cosmo* 'philosophy' and 'brand identity', embodied by the slogan 'fun, fearless, female', has to be preserved in all local versions. This means in the first place preserving the essential aspects of the *look* of the magazine, especially its layout style. But it also involves genre. *Cosmopolitan* also helps create powerful global genres, which enact and perpetuate key power relationships, now on a global scale. These power relationships again centre around providing advice for life – in this case primarily in the areas of (women's) beauty, health, relationships, sexuality and work. Indeed, providing such advice is perhaps the single most important social function of the magazine as a whole, as becomes immediately obvious by looking at the readers' letters page(s) which open each version. Here are two examples from the British version (February 2002): 'Too often I have tried to be aggressive in order to get my own way in the workplace. However, I have found I'm more successful when I follow your suggestion of being assertive while remaining cool', and 'Thanks for your article *Banish PMS For Good*! .... having read this in *Cosmo*, I researched the topic more widely, and found a new way to tackle my anxiety and PMS'. Or, from the Indian version (October 2001), 'I don't often follow tips I read in articles, but your *24-Hour Sex Clock* in the September issue inspired me to go for it ... The results were wonderful and have helped me strengthen my bond with my husband', and 'We have made Xerox copies of your juicy therapy recipes and put them up in our kitchens'.

   Although all versions of *Cosmopolitan* contain traditional advice columns of the kind I have just discussed, many more articles use the 'hot tips' genre. The essential ingredients of this genre are (1) a general problem, or a desirable goal to be achieved, and (2) a number of tips. These tips do not form a step-by-step procedure but a loose set of suggestions, which do not have to be implemented in any particular order, and from which the readers can *choose*, although they can of course also decide to follow up all of the tips. The element of choice − choice is of course a key value of consumer society − is often highlighted in the titles of the articles. In the Indian version (October 2001) we have, for instance, *4 Falling in Love Styles*, *9 Ways to be a Bad Chick*, and more. The following example is from its 'Careers' page − all versions of *Cosmopolitan* have a 'Careers' page:

4 Ways to Win Them Over	*Goal*
Arindam Chaudhuri, author of *Count Your Chickens Before They Hatch* shares his mantras of **effective communication**	*(Restatement of) Goal*
Be audience-friendly. Follow the KISS (keep it short and simple) principle while addressing an audience. Get a wee bit of clarity in the way you speak and watch it make a difference in what people around you perceive	*Tip 1*
Be polite and polished. The fact is that what you say fades over time, but how you felt during that conversation remains with you for a long time	*Tip 2*
Bring on the humour. Managers who use wit in their presentations come across as more approachable. So if you manage a lot of people, maintain their morale by showing that you have a funny bone	*Tip 3*
Don't forget the LAW. Looks, action and words all matter. You don't have to be born with Aishwarya's looks to be a good communicator. What you need is a pleasing, smiling personality that endears you to everyone around you. So work at it.	*Tip 4*

And here is another 'hot tips' item, from the 'Careers' page of the Dutch version of *Cosmopolitan*:

Figure 6.3 'Cosmo Careers' (Indian) *Cosmopolitan*, October 2001: 58

Post-holiday stress?	*Problem*
In some jobs work keeps piling up while you are away on holiday. Stress makes you forget your beautiful holiday in less than a day	*(Elaboration of) problem*
With these tips that won't happen	*Link to tips*
If you need to keep something, put it in a folder	*Tip 1*
Before you go on holiday, book space in your diary for clearing the 'rubbish' after you return	*Tip 2*
Make sure you don't have any appointments on your first day back. That way you will have the time to look through the things that have piled up on your desk.	*Tip 3*

If you do have things to do, put them on a to-do-list	*Tip 4*
Throw out anything you don't need any longer	*Tip 5*
Want to read more? Why not look at *Time Management for Dummies* by Jeffrey J. Maier, ISBN 906789981 X	*Tip 6*

The two versions of *Cosmopolitan* make different assumptions about their readers. Like many other European versions, the Dutch version of *Cosmopolitan* assumes that the reader is an employee, an office worker. In the Indian version, on the other hand, the readers are addressed as either senior managers or self-employed – as fashion designers, actresses and models especially. Clearly Indian *Cosmopolitan* targets an elite, and whether the *Cosmo* lifestyle will eventually filter through to other layers of

Figure 6.4   'Carrière' (Dutch) *Cosmopolitan*, October 2001

the population is at the moment still an open question. Each version also has its own absences. In the Indian version there is an almost total absence of the less well-to-do sector of the Indian population. The magazine seems to inhabit an opulent middle-class enclave that is almost totally shielded off from the realities of other women's lives in India. In the Dutch magazine it is the employers who are absent. Stress at work seems to derive from the individual's inability to get herself organized, rather than from the way managers structure their employees' time. Both versions, each in its own way, thus support the way in which work is organized in contemporary global capitalism.

In terms of form there are striking similarities between the two versions. Both magazines have a careers page. Both careers pages contain a 'hot tips' feature. And the two 'hot tips' features have a similar layout, with a colour photograph on top, and colour correspondences between the photograph and the text – in the Dutch version the bullet points are in the same yellow as the top of the woman in the photograph, in the Indian version the top of the woman on the left and the lettering of the headlined 'tips' are in the same pale blue, while the background of the photo and the text block are in the same darker blue. Finally, the two articles also use the same genres. Both offer advice as a 'resource' for self help, a kind of discursive 'self service', rather than authoritatively solving the specific problems of individual readers – although in both articles the authoritative source of the advice is mentioned.

I now have to qualify something I said earlier. The 'stages' of a genre are not always homogeneous in terms of the speech acts or, more generally, communicative acts, they contain. 'Tip' stages in a 'hot tip' genre must at the very least contain one tip, one piece of advice, for example, 'Bring on the humour'. But they may also contain additional elements, for example: (1) *maxims*, pieces of general wisdom – for example, 'Politeness is a virtue because it creates lasting impressions' – which may or may not be attributed explicitly to an expert; (2) *case stories*, mini case studies in which women narrate their experiences, and which therefore also act as (somewhat oblique) tips, and (3), *predictions of results:*

Be polite and polished	*advice*
The fact is that what you say fades over time, but how you felt during that conversation remains with you for a long time	*maxim 1*
Politeness is a virtue because it creates lasting impressions	*maxim 2*

Or, from the Indian *Cosmopolitan*:

One way to optimise your orgasm odds is to have lengthy foreplay	*advice*
'In order to let go enough to climax, I have to be really worked up. So I ask him to get me there with oral sex first. When I'm about to go over that cliff, then I suggest we start intercourse,' says Kit, 27	*case story*

Or, from the Dutch *Cosmopolitan:*

Make sure you don't have any appointments on your first day back   *advice*
That way you will have the time to look through the things that   *prediction of*
have piled up on your desk   *result*

In other words, advice, in magazines like *Cosmopolitan,* draws on a range of semiotic resources, combining them according to the interests and purposes of the magazine. Advice is mixed with information to legitimate it by stressing its authoritative and/or rational basis, and it is mixed with narration to include women's own experiences and thereby create greater emotive resonance and identification. Case stories almost always act as oblique tips, although they could also embody negative experiences, warnings *not* to do (the wrong) things. But it seems that a positive approach is favoured in magazines like *Cosmopolitan* – one of Helen Gurley-Brown's publications is titled *The Power of Positive Writing.*

The 'hot tips' genre is by no means the only global genre employed in *Cosmopolitan.* Another one is the 'Q&A', in which a standard set of questions is posed to different interviewees, either within the same article, or as a recurring column in each issue. The Indian version has a regular 'Cosmo Cover Info' feature in which the cover girl of the month is asked questions like the following – needless to say this genre also offers covert (style) advice:

   Name any can't-do-without item in your wardrobe
      A pair of blue jeans from Express

   What's your casual day look and evening glam garb?
      I'm most comfortable in a T-shirt and jeans. For an evening out, I usually opt
   for skirts and outfits with spaghetti straps

All these genres have one thing in common. They have a *visual* identity. They are recognizable at a glance, not on the basis of their linguistic features, but on the basis of their layout. They form *visual* 'templates' for writing not unlike those offered by computer software programs such as Powerpoint.

So what is global here is the visual rather than the verbal – the photographic illustrations, too, are increasingly similar, not least because they are increasingly obtained from global image banks – and form rather than content – although I have of course tried to show that forms create their own social meanings. *What* we say about sexuality and work is not the most important, what is important is *that* we talk about work and sexuality, and that we do so by means of specific genres and combinations of genres that can help create and maintain specific forms of global symbolic power. Let me try an analogy. Universities provide students with lectures and seminars that are based on very different beliefs. In one room there may be a lecture on total quality

Figure 6.5   'Cosmo Cover Info' (Indian) *Cosmopolitan*, October 2001

management, in the next a lecture on Marxist economics, in one room a lecture on sociobiology, in the next a lecture on the feminist critique of popular culture, and so on. However, the *format* of these lectures is the same. They take place in the same kind of room, last for the same amount of time, are examined according to the same examination rules and so on. It is this set of practices, not the beliefs that are propagated in lecture theatres, that (1) enacts and maintains the power relations that characterize universities, and (2) creates and perpetuates a form of unity between all these divergent activities, a set of common meanings, despite the very different ideologies espoused in the lecture rooms. Such a model also underlies the practices of global media like *Cosmopolitan*. What exactly is communicated in the different versions of *Cosmopolitan* is very different, but it is communicated through the same layouts and genres, and it links women's work, sexuality and consumer products together in the same way.

Exercises

1   Analyse the speech acts in a piece of television or movie dialogue between lovers, or in the lyrics of a love song of your choice.
2   Think of at least four 'dress acts', 'things we can do with dress' and find examples, for example magazine pictures or movie stills – or make your own original photographs.
3   Find an example of a predominantly verbal recipe. Describe the genre and its use of multimodality.
4   Make a new version of the recipe, using visuals – with or without accompanying text – for all the stages, making your own photographs and/or drawings.
5   Discuss the power relations enacted by questionnaires.

Note

The material on *Cosmopolitan* in this chapter relies on research by David Machin, conducted as part of the 'Language and Global Communication' research programme of the Centre for Language and Communication Research, Cardiff University, and sponsored by the Leverhulme Trust. This work is discussed more fully in Machin and Van Leeuwen (2004).

7 Style

The *Concise Oxford Dictionary* defines 'style' as 'a manner of writing, speaking or doing, especially as contrasted with the matter to be expressed or thing done'. This is a good definition. It includes discourse ('the matter expressed'), genre ('the thing done') and style, and it is multimodal, involving not just 'speaking and writing', but also 'doing'. Until now, social semiotics has in the main concentrated more on discourse and genre than on style. Yet, as 'lifestyle' begins to replace social class as the main type of social grouping and source of social identity, the idea of style is clearly becoming increasingly important in contemporary society:

> Lifestyle experimentation has taken place among people for whom occupational and economic roles no longer provided a coherent set of values and for whom identity has come to be generated in the consumption rather than in the production realm.
>
> (Zablocki and Kanter, 1976: 270)

In this chapter I will try to update the social semiotic approach to style, following the lead of Fairclough, who applied all three concepts – genre, discourse and style – to an analysis of the language of New Labour:

> Styles (for example, Tony Blair's style) are to do with political identities and values; discourses (for example, the discourse of the 'Third Way') are to do with political representations; and genres are to do with how language figures as a means of Government (so the Green Paper constitutes a particular genre, a particular way of using language in governing) ... These are only analytically separable – in actual cases they are always simultaneously in operation. So any speech by Tony Blair for instance can be looked at in terms of how it contributes to the governing process (how it achieves consent, for instance), how it represents the social world and the political and governmental process itself, and how it projects a particular identity, tied to particular values – that is, in terms of genre, discourse and style.
>
> (2000: 14)

Fairclough here applies these definitions specifically to the field of politics, but they can be extended beyond politics and applied to other spheres as well. They are of immediate relevance to the theme of this chapter, as they link style to 'identities and values' in much the same way as the sociological literature on lifestyles (see, for example, Chaney, 1996).

Three kinds of style

In this section I will describe three approaches to the idea of 'style'. I present them, again, as an inventory, a menu, a repertoire, and not as mutually exclusive. Even if there is now a shift in dominance from 'social style' to 'lifestyle', all three continue to exist side by side, in practice as well as in theory, and can be combined in different ways. Their common point is that they are all concerned with articulating and enacting the relation between individual freedom and social determination, even if they do so in different ways.

Individual style

The idea of 'individual style' foregrounds individual difference. Although the ways in which we speak and write and act are always to some extent socially regulated, there usually is room for individual difference, for 'doing things our way'. This kind of style is perhaps the oldest. The Romans already had a saying *stilus virum arguit* – 'the style announces the man' – and the word 'style' comes from 'stilus', the Latin word for 'pen'. Handwriting is a good example of individual style. As histories of handwriting (for example, Sassoon, 1999) show, it has always been socially regulated, most recently through the ways it has been taught in the school system, yet everybody has their own recognizable handwriting, their own individual style. Individual style has also come to play a strong role in literature, music and the arts, where 'achieving your own style' was, and to some extent still is, the ultimate mark of distinction, while 'genre pieces' were less highly valued. But, as the example of handwriting already shows, everybody has their own style in many of the things they do, including the an-on-ymous producers of 'genre pieces'.

What kinds of meaning does individual style express? Some say, none. To them, individual style is a mark of identity, a kind of fingerprint. The individual style of a voice allows you to recognize who the speaker is, the individual style of handwriting who the writer is, and so on. In some cases the ability to recognize individual style becomes a field of special expertise, for instance the expertise of the art historian, who can ascertain whether or not a painting is a genuine Rembrandt or Vermeer on the basis of style, or the expertise of the forensic linguist who can prove, on the basis of stylistic characteristics, that two documents were – or could *not* have been – written by the same person.

For others, style does have meaning – expressive meaning. Style expresses feelings, attitudes to what is said – or written or painted or acted – and it expresses the personality of the speaker – or writer, or painter or actor. This can either result from deliberate decisions, as in the case of literature, the arts, the theatre, etc., where styles may be deliberately cultivated (or imitated), or not, as in the case of ordinary people's voices, handwriting styles, styles of walking, and so on. The French stylistician Guiraud called the latter 'expressive' and the former 'im-pressive':

> The stylistics of expression is a study of the stylistic value of means of expression. There are expressive values which give away the feelings, desires, characteristics and social origin of the speaking subject, and there are im-pressive values which are deliberately produced and get across the impression the speaking subject seeks to create.
>
> (Guiraud, 1972: 57)

This view of style was common in French structuralist semiotics (for example, Rifaterre, 1971), and also underlies psychological approaches to individual style, for instance in the study of colour preferences (see chapter 3), in certain approaches to 'body language', or in graphology. Here 'expressive' colours, gestures, aspects of handwriting and so on are seen as expressive of 'moods' and symptomatic of personality traits, rather than as deliberate uses of semiotic resources 'to get across the impression the speaking subject seeks to create', as Guiraud put it. In relation to literature, Barthes criticized 'expressive values' (1967a: 17). Expressive style, he said, has only a 'biographical and biological frame of reference', not a historical one, and is the author's 'prison', from which he can only be set free by 'a colourless writing, freed from all bondage'.

'Expressive' as well as 'im-pressive' individual styles are acts of individual creation, in the one case guided by the unconscious, in the other deliberate. It follows that they cannot be socially regulated. They live in the interstices of social regulation, like grass growing between neatly laid, rectangular flagstones. They exist because, and to the degree that, social regulations cannot cover every detail of our behaviour, and thereby leave room for the expression of individuality. They also exist where people break the rules, go beyond conventions, as in the case of unconventional and innovative artists. Interpreting 'individual style' can therefore only be based on the principle of experiential metaphor. There are no written rules or traditions to cover what escapes or transcends the social. If, for instance, someone's handwriting is irregular, it can be interpreted as also *meaning* 'irregularity', on the basis of our experience of making marks on paper (see chapter 2) – as betraying momentary agitation and mental turmoil, for instance, or as the handwriting of a person who does not easily submit to rules and regularities and chafes against restraints.

Hodge and Kress (1988: 118) interpreted the handwriting of a poem by Sylvia Plath in this way, as betraying despair – Sylvia Plath was to commit suicide fourteen days after she wrote the poem:

> In the title and first three lines, the writing is relatively clear ... It is 'correct', incorporating the standards of writing which win approval in classrooms. As the text continues, however, these standards of clarity begin to be challenged by many deletions, with words and letters closer together, written at different angles, with no gaps between stanzas ... The despair this writing expresses was very real, as Sylvia Plath's actions were to show.

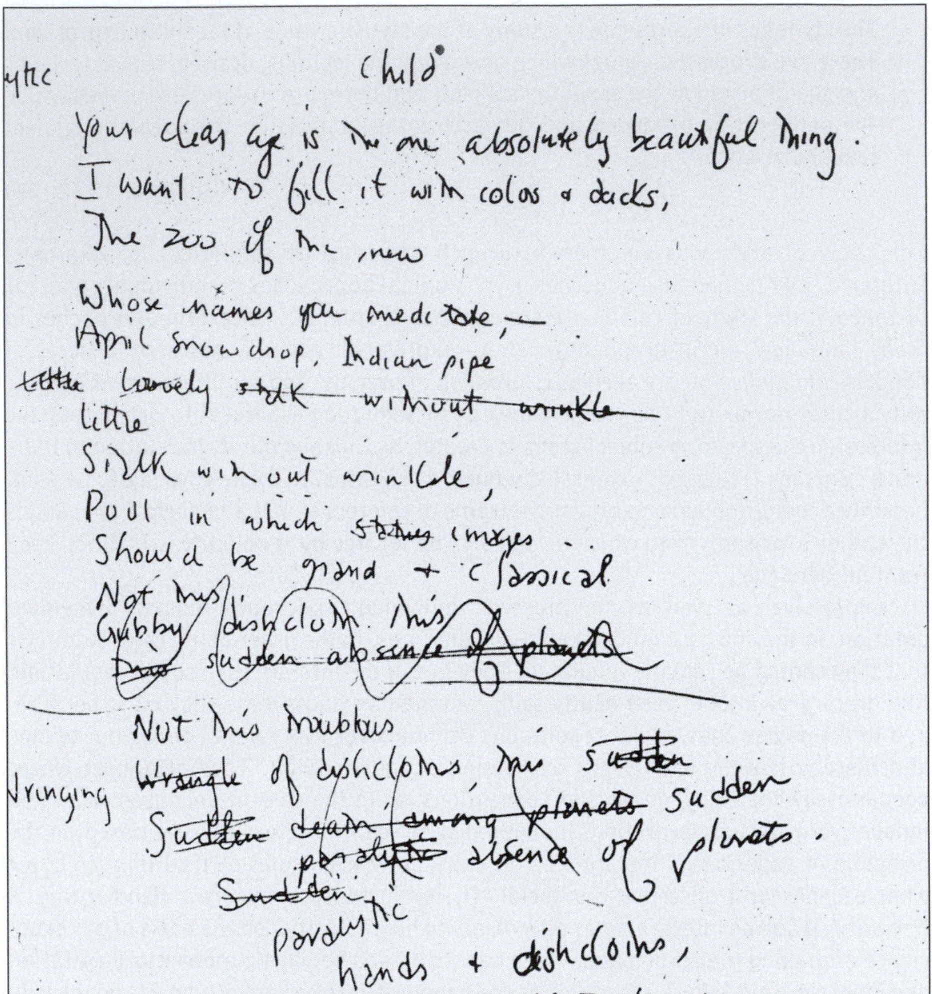

lytic

Child

Your clear eye is the one absolutely beautiful thing.
I want to fill it with colors & ducks,
The zoo of the new

Whose names you mediate ~
April snowdrop, Indian pipe
little lovely stalk   without   wrinkle
little
Silk without wrinkle,
Pool in which status images
Should be grand + classical
Not this/dishcloth. This
Grubby /dishcloth. This
Drag sudden absence of planets

Not this troublous
Wringing wrangle of dishcloths, this sudden
Sudden death among planets sudden
paralytic absence of planets.
Sudden
paralytic
hands + dishclothes,
This windows gaze without planets.
black paper
this black paper, without moon or planets.
Not this troublous   black da
Wringing of hands dishcloths, this ceiling
Ceiling, without moon or planets.
Ceiling, without planets. with no constellations, a
Without stars or planets.

Figure 7.1   Manuscript of Sylvia Plath's *Child,* 28 January 1963

Printing the poem in a volume of poetry then removes the expression of chaos, and restores order (ibid.: 119):

> The signifiers have stabilized the semiotic act by assigning it to a recognized genre, poetry. They also, at the same time, decisively remove it from the individual who produced it. The handwriting declared an individuality and lack of control which would be embarrassing to reveal. The poem, in print form, sanitizes it, by removing material traces left by the material social being, Sylvia Plath.

Social style

The idea of 'social style' foregrounds the *social* determination of style, the idea that style expresses, not our individual personality and attitudes, but our social position, 'who we are' in terms of stable categories such as class, gender and age, social relations, and 'what we do' in terms of the socially regulated activities we engage in and the roles we play within them. Social style is not internally, psychologically motivated, and it does not follow from our moods or from our stable and consistent 'character'. It is externally motivated, determined by social factors outside our control. In all this the idea of the individual does not disappear, yet its value and importance diminish.

Social style came to play an increasingly important role in the sociolinguistics and stylistics of the 1960s and 1970s. Alongside the traditional interest in regional varieties of language, there was now a growing interest in other varieties of language, for instance varieties related to social class (Bernstein, 1972; Labov, 1972a), or to power and status difference (Brown and Gilman, 1960), or to the styles of occupational fields such as the media and the law (Crystal and Davy, 1969; Leech, 1969). The idea of style, which had been so strongly associated with individual style, now transformed into the idea of 'language variety' – 'sociolect' and 'register' are two other terms. 'Stylistic features' became 'variety markers' (Crystal and Davy, 1969: 83) and 'sense of style' became an 'instinctive knowledge of linguistic appropriateness' (ibid.: 7), an awareness of social rules and the 'competence' to follow them. This view influenced social semiotics, of course, as it focused on the *use* of semiotic resources in social contexts. Thus Kress (1988: 126) defined 'style' as comprising both 'the organisation of linguistic features in text' and 'the effects produced in the complex interrelation of producer of the text, text, and consumer of the text, in their specific social positionings', and Hodge and Kress (1988: 82) saw style as a 'metasign', that is 'a marker of social allegiance (solidarity, group identity and ideology)', and made 'accent' their main example, for example, the Australian accent, which they related not only to Australian speech, but also to Australian (male) hair styles.

The idea of 'social style' regards stylistic features as 'markers'. Stylistic features tell you where someone comes from, what their gender, age and class is, what kind of activities they are engaged in, what role they play vis-à-vis other participants of these activities, and what form or medium of communication they are using – monologue and dialogue are also said to be styles, for instance, as are speech and writing. This applies not just to language but also, for instance, to the language of dress, as we have already seen in the case of traditional Moravian Slovakian dress, which can 'mark' gender, age, marital status, class, occupation and day of the week ('Sunday best'). Social semioticians can, of course, go beyond these meanings and interpret social styles not just as markers but also as expressing feelings and attitudes, this time *social* feelings and attitudes, or ideologies. Because they are innovative, and cannot rely on prescription or tradition or established cultural connotations, such interpretations will necessarily have to be based on the principle of the experiential metaphor.

Hodge and Kress (1988: 92–3) have interpreted the Australian accent in this way. To give just two examples, 'strine', as Australian speech is also known, has a preference for open vowels. Hodge and Kress interpret this as expressing 'energy' and 'lack of constraint' – closed vowels would have expressed 'constraint, control, culture'. Again, Australians pronounce the word 'beauty' as *bewdy* and use it to indicate 'general approval' – it can describe 'a fast horse, a good deal, a fine shot in cricket' and much more. So, Hodge and Kress argue, the 'lax' pronunciation – calculated to contrast with 'correct' English pronunciation – together with the way the word is used, 'conflates the categories of gender (male/female) and the aesthetic (art/non-art) and thereby constitutes a refusal to create a separate category of elite "high" culture'. But in making such interpretations, social semioticians subvert the rule of social style, which is that of tradition or the written word, with its appearance of arbitrariness. Under the rule of 'social style', style is only a 'marker', and not expressive, and other interpretations would not be accepted or understood. Under this rule, the social and the individual both exist, but strictly segregated. The social belongs to the public world, and is a matter of strictly regulated, formal obligations. The individual belongs to the private world and it alone provides room for individuality and self-expression. The world in which these two styles exist side by side, you could say, is a world of men in very similar grey suits and white shirts, whose individuality can at best be expressed through subtle variations in the kinds of ties they are wearing or the ways in which they button up their jackets – and who yet all have unique individual characters, even if they do not express them by means of their appearance.

Lifestyles

'Lifestyle' combines individual and social style. On the one hand it is social, a group style, even if the groups it sustains are geographically dispersed, scattered across the cities of the world, and characterized, not by stable social positionings such as class, gender and age, or comparatively stable activities such as occupations, but by shared consumer behaviours (shared taste) shared patterns of leisure time activities (for example, an interest in similar sports, or tourist destinations) and shared attitudes to key social issues, for example, similar attitudes to environmental problems, gender issues, etc.: 'People use lifestyles in everyday life to identify and explain wider complexes of identity and affiliation' (Chaney, 1996: 12). Lifestyles are also social because they are signified by *appearances,* so much so that just about any set of attitudes can be, and is, conveyed by styles of dress and adornment, interior decoration, and so on. As Chaney puts it:

> Strongly held beliefs and commitment to family values are likely to be symbolised by particular types of aesthetic choice, just as militant feminism is likely to be associated with particular ways of dressing, talking and leisure.
>
> (Chaney, 1996: 96)

For this reason the groups created by lifestyle can be called 'interpretive communities' (Fish, 1980). Through their appearance, people can announce their 'interpretations' of the world, their affiliation with certain values and attitudes. On the same basis they can also recognize others, across the globe, as members of the same 'interpretive community', as announcing the same taste, the same values and the same ideas.

The consumer goods they use to do so, meanwhile, are increasingly homogeneous for reasons of economies of scale. Therefore their producers have begun to elaborate symbolic systems to transform them into lifestyle signifiers, to differentiate them in terms of the kinds of expressive meanings that were traditionally associated with individual styles: feelings, attitudes, personality traits. But these expressive meanings, these 'new rhetorics of desire and personal involvement' (Chaney, 1996: 152) are now deliberately produced by designers and advertisers, and globally disseminated through the experts and role models featured in the global media, which, in the short space of 20 years, have become the key mediators of lifestyle (Hanke, 1989). Finally, 'lifestyle' is social because of the role it plays in marketing, where traditional social indicators such as class, gender, age, etc., have been replaced by 'lifestyle market segmentation' techniques (Michman, 1991) which classify consumers through a mixture of consumption patterns and attitudes. This classification of Florida newspaper readers is typical of the kind of labels used in market research of this kind. The figures indicate the market share of each group:

> Young, bored and blue (12)
> Tomorrow's leaders (3)
> Achievers (5)
> Mr Middle (18)
> Senior solid conservatives (7)
> Winter affluence (2)
> Ms Restless (3)
> Expanded outlook (2)
> Midlife optimists (21)
> Domestic inactives (10)
> Nostalgics (5)
> Mrs Senior traditionalist (12)
>
> (Michman, 1991: 1–3)

Yet, lifestyles are also individual. Unlike traditional 'social style', lifestyle is diverse. It diminishes homogeneity, increases choice and does away with the requirement to dress according to your age, gender, class, occupation and even nationality – distinct styles for men and women, the young and the old, and for different social classes and occupations may not have disappeared, but they are gradually becoming less important. Although individuals can be made aware of the fact that their choices are also the choices of millions of 'people like them', across the globe, they nevertheless *feel* that their style is primarily individual and personal, and that they are making creative use of the wide range of semiotic resources made available to them by the culture industries. This is further enhanced by the fact that 'lifestyle' identities are unstable and can be discarded and re-made any time. As a result there is a need to constantly monitor the lifestyle media and the environment: 'Modern consumers are physically passive, but mentally very busy. Consumption is more than ever before an experience which is to be located in the head' (Bocock, 1993: 51).

The meanings expressed by lifestyle no longer derive from the unconscious. Like writers, artists and actors in the past, people now create their identities quite deliberately, or 'reflexively' – perhaps this explains the exalted status of writers, artists, actors, etc. in contemporary consumer society. In the words of 'style icon' David Beckham:

> I don't think we should be sheep and follow anyone else. We're individuals and should be prepared to show that in our behaviour. Clothes are just one way of expressing your individuality, but it's an important one for me. I also think of dressing as a way of being artistic and art is something I'm quite into. I probably would have gone to art school if I hadn't been a footballer.
>
> (2000: 94)

As lifestyle identities can be disposed of at will, they are often said to be acted out 'with a degree of self-irony and self-satire' (Chaney, 1996: 12). This can be a good thing, a sign that people are aware of what they are doing. At the same time, it would seem that people distance themselves from their identities in this way, as if to say, this is not really me, it is only a game. I cannot help wondering whether people, in the long run, will be able to manage without a sense of continuity and consistency. Perhaps the popularity of expressing one's identity by changing one's body, or by marking it with permanent markings such as tattoos, shows that there is still a need for permanence.

Unlike the signifiers of 'individual style', the signifiers of lifestyle rest primarily on connotation, on signs that are already loaded with cultural meaning, yet not subject to prescription or tradition. More specifically, they rest on *composites of connotation*. Perhaps this is best explained with a few examples. If handwriting is an 'individual style' of writing, revealing the writer's unique and consistent personality, whatever the context, and if 'social styles' are homogeneous but vary according to context – for example, free handwriting for a personal letter, 'printed' handwriting for forms, typewriting for business letters – then lifestyle writing is characterized by the computer, which, like the typewriter, provides socially standardized, mass-produced letterforms, but, unlike the typewriter, gives users a wide choice of letterforms to allow them to personalize their written communications, regardless of whether these are private or public. An article in Dutch *Cosmopolitan* (October 2001: 75) shows that font choice has already become a new territory for the popular graphologist's expertise in interpreting writing as betraying individual characteristics:

> According to psychologist Aric Sigman the font you choose on your computer for writing letters reveals a great deal about your personality
> Courier New = a little old-fashioned
> **GEORGIA** = you have flair
> **Helvetica** = modern
> Times New Roman = creates confidence
> Universal = anonymous
> Comic Sans = attracting attention
> **Verdana** = professional

To take a second example, sports dress, as worn on the field during a training session, is a social style, a style that 'marks' a type of activity and, despite its relative uniformity, leaves some room for individuality – for instance in the colour of the trousers, the type of top worn, or the optional extra of the black or white woollen hat – as worn by David Beckham in a photo which we were not allowed to reproduce here.

Lifestyle dress works differently. It is a composite of connotations. A well-cut, expensive white shirt – connotations: elegance, a touch of formality, etc. – may be combined with drill trousers with a camouflage motif – connotations: jungle adventures, toughness, the resourcefulness of the commando, etc. – and sports shoes – connotations: affinity with healthy living, exercise and sport, etc. Another example is provided by a photograph of David Beckham in Beckham (2000) which we were not allowed to reproduce. The drawing in figure 7.2 gives an impression. David Beckham is not only a style icon but also a role model. His identity, as portrayed in the media, combines aspects of the rebel and the model citizen. Although often portrayed as a troublemaker, he nevertheless also speaks up for disadvantaged children, campaigns against racism, and stands for clean living, family values and the new masculinity – he is happy to change nappies and 'not scared of his feminine side' (Beckham, 2000: 95). The pictures of him and his family that circulate in the public domain may emphasize different aspects of this complex identity at different times. But they always portray his identity through his appearance, through the way he is dressed, wears his hair, poses, and also through the setting in which he is photographed. In the photograph on which figure 7.2 is based, he wears a bandana (bandanas are often associated with rebels) black clothes of a fashionable loose cut (characterizing him as fashionable and a bit of an 'artist'), but also sports shoes (and a kick) – and he is photographed against a background of well-to-do respectability. Such contradictions are typical of the way lifestyle role models are portrayed. They allow us to think and talk of ourselves as individuals, or even rebels, and yet fit in with the social scheme of things.

Figure 7.2   Beckham (after a photograph in Beckham, 2000)

The three styles I have described in this section continue to exist side by side. Hand-writing, although more marginal now, is still as individual as it always was. 'Social styles' are still required in many domains – for example, university essays. Yet, the 'lifestyle' approach is gradually making inroads everywhere. In the rest of this chapter I will return to the example of *Cosmopolitan* magazine, and try to describe its linguistic style as 'lifestyle', so as to investigate the 'possible parallels between the use of language and the use of symbolic markers in lifestyle practices' (Chaney, 1996: 46).

Language style as lifestyle

Linguistic style can also be based on the principle of lifestyle. In this section I will attempt to analyse the style of *Cosmopolitan* magazine in this way. This means asking two questions:

1   How can the writing style of *Cosmopolitan* be described as a 'composite of conno-
    tations', and what identities and values does it express?

We have seen that lifestyles are put together from existing styles which have lost their
specific functions as regional dress, period dress, uniform, etc., and which combine to
form hybrid styles that express a particular combination of meanings deriving from
connotations – from the associations we have, in the shared, global popular culture,
with the places, times and other contexts from which the original styles originated.
    The principal styles on which *Cosmopolitan* draws are (1) the style of advertising,
(2) the style of the fashion caption, (3) the style of expert discourse, (4) street style –
the slang of the trendy, and the young, and (5) conversational style. These mix to
different degrees with traditional magazine feature writing style – the traditional,
socially 'appropriate' style for magazines – in the same way that lifestyle dress may be
combined with, or tempered by, for instance, traditional 'white collar' work dress.

2   How diverse is this style? How does it negotiate between the individual and the
    social, or, in this case, the local and the global?

Lifestyle entails, on the one hand, a loss of uniformity and a gain of space for individual style, but, on the other hand, individual lifestyles draw on deliberately designed
and globally distributed semiotic resources that are definitely *not* individual. *Cosmopolitan* magazine clearly contributes to increased global cultural homogeneity –
comparing the magazine's Dutch, Spanish, Indian and Chinese versions to earlier
women's magazines from these same countries leaves no doubt about this. On the
other hand, the magazine is localized into 48 different versions, many of them in
languages other than English. It has also created room for difference. Although the
editors of the local versions all have to undergo compulsory training by the Hearst
corporation, and although the languages into which the magazine is localized must all
develop the *Cosmopolitan* style, by imitating the kinds of neologisms English copywriters have developed and by using focus groups to learn about the language of local
young and trendy people, there *is* room for local accents. Here I will draw on five
versions of the magazine – the US, Dutch, Spanish, Indian and Chinese versions – in
an attempt to explore this aspect of *Cosmo* style.

Advertising style

Advertising style developed not just to sell products and services but also to model the
identities and values of consumer society. It was the first 'corporate' language
variety, and it played a key role in what Fairclough (1993) has called the
'marketisation' of discourse. Now that consumer society is coming into its own, so is
advertising style. It is rapidly spreading beyond the confines of actual advertisements
and infiltrating other genres, for instance the 'advertorials' of magazines and the
burgeoning lifestyle sections of the print media. Displaced from its original function,

advertising style connotes a preoccupation with consumer goods and their meanings and attractions, and with the identities and values advertising has traditionally celebrated – glamour, success, hedonism, sensuality, sexuality. I will discuss three aspects of this style in a little more detail: direct address, evaluative adjectives and poetic devices.

Direct address

Advertising style makes a great deal of use of direct address for both ideological and practical reasons. Ideologically, it has always sought to address *you*, personally, and so to transcend its nature as a mass medium. Practically, advertisements need to persuade readers and viewers to do or think certain things and hence they are replete with imperatives – which also address readers and viewers directly. This excerpt from Indian *Cosmopolitan* (October 2001) is not an advertisement but it is full of imperatives and instances of 'second person' address – for the sake of ease I have italicized them – even though there are also remnants of 'proper' magazine reporting style – for example, attributed statements such as '"Too many accessories can kill your style … "', says hairstylist Jojo'.

> SUPERSLEEK STRANDS
> 'Too many accessories can kill *your* style. Sleek hair that is off *your* face looks really glamorous,' says hairstylist Jojo. *Fake* a poker straight mane with this simple tip from him. 'Before styling, *use* a good conditioner on *your* hair. *Blow-dry* your mane using a round brush. Then *spray* an anti-frizz product on *your* dry hair. *Divide your* tresses into sections and *run* a straightening iron through the whole length. *Finish* with a spritz of a shine enhancing product,' he suggests. Jojo likes L'Oreal Professionel's Tec-ni-Art Liss Control+, RS 339, Tec-ni-Art Spray Fixant Anti-Frizz, RS 399, and Tec-ni-Art Gloss Shine & Hold Spray, ES 399.

Indian *Cosmopolitan* is published in English, but the same advertising-like features occur in non-English versions, for instance in the Dutch version (October 2001):[1]

> *Gebruik in plaats van een vloeibare eyeliner een potlood of oogschaduw die je mooi uitwerkt*
> Literal translation: '*Use* instead of mascara an eye pencil or eye shadow which *you* apply beautifully'

Or in the Spanish version (October 2001):

> *Aprovecha para exfoliar tu piel y recuperar su luz*
> Literal translation: '*Take* advantage to exfoliate *your* skin and recuperate its glow'

Or in the Chinese version (October 2001):

> *Fu yu pi fu tan xing, gai shan song chi qu xian*
> Literal translation: '*Give your* skin elasticity, *tighten* those loose curves'

Adjectives

Adjectives play a key role in advertising style because many adjectives can apply both to the advertised product – the signifier – and to the values it signifies. For instance, in the US version (October 2001):

> Dramatic, passion-inspiring purple is the season's hottest hue. To instantly make any outfit feel more ' fall 2002', just add a taste of plum

Here 'dramatic' and 'passionate' can both be seen as a description of the colour – the signifier – and as a 'mood' or 'personality trait' the reader can express by means of the colour. Similarly in the Dutch version of the magazine (October 2001):

> *Heerlijk warme, zachte stoffen, lieve bloemen en zoete pastels in combinatie met wit. Zo wordt je huis een op-en-top winterpaleis, voor het ultieme prinsessengevoel*
> (Deliciously warm, soft fabrics, dear flowers and sweet pastels in combination with white. That's how your house becomes a winter palace, for the ultimate princess-feeling)

Clearly adjectives like 'warm', 'dear' and 'sweet' can apply to the fabrics as well as to the reader who chooses them to decorate her home, i.e. the 'princess' in her 'winter palace'. This ambiguity gives the adjective a key role in advertising. It welds together the signifier – the colour – and the signified – the personality traits of the user – making them seem like two sides of the same coin. Cook (1992: 162) has commented in some detail on the referential ambiguity of adjectives in advertising.

Poetic devices

Advertising style also makes abundant use of poetic devices. Here is another example from the Indian *Cosmopolitan* (November 2001):

> Flaunt that gorgeous body
> A sure shot way of upping your sinister sister image is showing off that bold bod – the right way. Give up the tedious treadmill at the gym for a sexy stretchy session of yoga to attract attention to all the right places.

Note the alliterations and half-rhymes: 'sinister sister image', 'bold bod', 'tedious treadmill', 'sexy, stretchy session'.

This use of poetic devices has again both a practical and an ideological function. The problem of 'recall' is a major practical problem in advertising and a major theme in its trade and research journals. How can we make sure that people will remember the brand, the product, the message? Poetic devices – and music – can help. In societies without alphabetic writing, knowledge had to be stored in memory and therefore often took the form of epic poems, with standard metres and an abundance of poetic devices (Ong, 1982). We can see this mnemonic function of poetic devices in the few traditional proverbs and sayings we still remember, for example, in the parallelisms and repetitions in 'Red in the morning, shepherd's warning, red in the night, shepherd's delight'. Advertising has revitalized this tradition with its ear-catching language and musical jingles.

But poetic devices also make advertising style more entertaining and pleasurable than, for instance, technical descriptions of products or instruction manuals. Advertising style pioneered 'edutainment', the combination of instruction – for instance, on how to make yourself beautiful or how to keep your teeth white – and pleasure, thereby undermining the traditional split between the serious and the popular, between high art and low art – and between the higher and lower classes and their different tastes (think also of the way advertising has incorporated high art, classical music, etc.). Advertising's emphasis on pleasure is therefore not just expressed through the pleasurable activities it portrays or alludes to but also through its linguistic style.

This theme is closely related to another aspect of advertising, its *transgressive* nature. Advertising is deliberately unconventional, deliberately bent on breaking rules and defying taboos, as in the above quote where women are encouraged to flaunt their femininity unashamedly. Again this is not just a matter of content but also of style. Advertising style also breaks rules of spelling – 'Mudd. Pure Inddulgence' – grammar – 'B&Q it' – and vocabulary – by concocting often punning neologisms: examples from the October 2001 US *Cosmopolitan* include 'bootylicious' and 'denim-ite'. The Chinese version of the magazine delights in creating such neologisms, for example:

> *yan yi zhen wo mei li*
> (Show me real charm)

> *mi mei du zhu*
> (Gamble on glam)

> *yi tou hu mei de jon se juan fa ji yi shuang lan bao shi ban de yan tong*
> (Foxy-charming curly hair and diamond-blue pupils)

And so does the Dutch version. I remember how neologistic compounds such as *winterbleek* ('winter-pale'), *natuurzacht* ('nature-soft'), and superlatives such as *krachtproteïne* ('power-protein') and *superlicht* ('super-light') were first introduced when commercials began to appear on Dutch television in the 1960s. I was not the only one who felt it forced the Dutch language and sounded alien – but in time that perception has paled.

This breaking of rules is always tongue-in-cheek, so that we can at once enjoy the transgression and dismiss it as 'not serious', 'only a joke', 'ironical'. The message is at once received and denied. I have already mentioned that lifestyle sociologists see irony and self-parody as a key feature of modern lifestyle identities. In advertising they have played an important role for a long time, traditionally to allow advertisers to appeal quite openly to the consumer's greed, envy and lust – and get away with it, because, after all, it is only tongue-in-cheek.

However, in this respect there are differences between the localized versions of the magazine. The Indian version takes the tongue-in-cheek approach to extremes, as if to make it absolutely clear that it's only a game, accompanied by much nervous laughter and giggling. Compared to the USA and Western Europe, India is still very much a man's world, where the gospel of *Cosmopolitan* has by no means been fully accepted. The Spanish version on the other hand is more subdued and serious. The use of rhyme and alliteration is for the most part restricted to the headlines and the body of the texts uses a more formal style. The subtitle of the magazine, for instance, is not 'Fun, Fearless, Female' as in the USA and the UK, but 'The Woman who is Changing the World'. In Spain there is still a certain reluctance to mix information and entertainment. There are, for instance, no tabloid newspapers and attempts to introduce them failed within a few weeks (Papatheodorou and Machin, 2003). There are also well-patrolled boundaries between high culture and popular culture. Members of the editorial staff[2] of the magazine stress that they seek to take the business of women's status in society seriously as Spain is still quite sexist, and the magazine often carries items on further education for women and women's rights which would never appear in the US or the UK version.

This seriousness is not only a matter of content but also of style. In Spain it is very important to show your level of culture and education through the way you speak and write. Introducing elements of 'street language' in your speech is just not done in Spain. The Chinese version, on the other hand, has adopted the *Cosmo* style with enthusiasm: 'Let's compete to see who is more joyfully casual'. There are economic reasons for this, because they see it as a style that will attract advertisers. At the same time, in creating a Chinese version of *Cosmo* 'poetics' they draw on classical Chinese styles, such as the symmetrical arrangements of words in the 'antithetical couplet', rather than on Western poetic devices. Apparently market reform has been accompanied by a revitalization of traditional forms in China, for instance a return of traditional characters (Scollon and Scollon, 1998) even in popular culture texts imported from the USA, Hong Kong and Japan (Nakano, 2002).

Yue guang zhi wen, mi zi zhi lian
(Moonlight's kiss, mi zi's love)

Zai sheng huo zhong, mei li de xiao, you ya de chou
(In life, beautifully smile, gracefully worry)

The style of the fashion caption

I have already touched on the style of the fashion caption in chapter 3. It has much in common with advertising style, including the use of direct address, adjectives and poetic devices, yet it is instantly recognizable as a style of its own – the examples are from the October 2002 US version of *Cosmopolitan*:

> Dramatic passion-inspiring purple is the season's hottest hue. To instantly make any outfit feel more 'fall 2002', just add a taste of plum

> Check out these stellar deals on faux fur – the season must-have that'll keep you feeling cosy and looking foxy as hell

> A sweet peasant skirt and sexy tank look lovely on a low-key date at the movies or a dive bar

As Barthes (1983) has shown, the fashion caption is a 'metalinguistic' statement, an entry from an ongoing, constantly changing and playfully written dictionary of fashion. It links a signifier – an outfit, or an item of clothing, or some aspect of it, for example, a colour – to a signified, in this case, to either or both of two kinds of signi-fied: (1) the simple assertion 'this is in fashion', which can be phrased in myriad ways – for example, 'the season's hottest', 'feel "fall 2002"', 'the season must-have' – and/or (2) a meaning which either indicates, for instance, the type of activities or the time of day for which the outfit is suitable – 'a low-key date at the movies or a dive bar' – and/or a 'mood' or 'personality trait' – 'dramatic', 'passionate', feeling cosy', 'foxy', 'sweet', 'sexy', lovely'. And it does so in a way which is 'imperative' – 'must have' – and inescapable, an edict that must be followed, yet at the same time playful and plea-surable – 'hottest hue', 'feel fall', 'look lovely on a low-key … ' – so that the fashion caption, like advertising style, is a proto-form of 'edutainment', of learning what to do in a playful, pleasurable and entertaining way. Originally confined to actual fashion spreads, the style of the fashion caption, with its function of introducing people to the latest symbolic meanings of consumption goods, has now infiltrated many other domains so as to connote, wherever it goes, the overriding importance of being in fashion and up to date with the latest.

The style of the expert

'Social style' rests on the rule of tradition, or on formal written rules. Lifestyles, on the other hand, rest on the rule of the role model and the expert – including, perhaps, the fashion expert who defines this season's meanings and values. To connote this, *Cosmopolitan* style is shot through with the style of the expert, whether it is that of the psychologist, the beautician, the dietician, or the *trend deskundige* ('trend expert'), for example, Hilde Roothart ('from the *Trendslator* company'), who is quoted in the

Dutch version of *Cosmopolitan* (October 2001: 74) as distinguishing between people who 'make their own style' and people who 'slavishly follow styles' and who concludes:

> Really cool people are not followers. They are the vanguard. They think of new things and make new combinations. I expect we are at the start of a period which stresses originality, being creative instead of following others.

Some of the key characteristics of expert style include a more formal vocabulary with technical terms – for example, 'anger management' and 'inferiority complex' – a preference for abstract and general nouns – for example, 'the phenomenon of gossip' instead of just 'gossip' –, a limited vocabulary of verbs – mostly 'be', 'have' and 'mean' and their synonyms – and an objective, third person form of address which, in magazines like *Cosmopolitan*, often contrasts with the second person address that derives from advertising and conversational style. Here is an example of a journalist using elements of expert style (Dutch *Cosmopolitan*, October 2001). Note the shift from the 'subjective' second person in the first sentence to the 'objective' third person in the second sentence:

> *We kennen allemaal … de buikpijn, het schaamtegevoel en de boosheid als je hoort dat jij degene bent over wie de verhalen gaan. Het fenomeen roddelen heeft een slechte reputatie, het woord an sich heeft dan ook een negative betekenis.*
> (We all know … the pain, the shame and the anger when finding out that *you* are the butt of the stories. As a result the phenomenon of gossip has a bad reputation, and the term on its own a negative meaning)

Apart from the style of the psychologist, as in the example above, *Cosmopolitan* also draws on the style of the doctor, the beautician, the dietician, and so on. Here a journalist uses the style of the expert dietician, in the Dutch version (October 2001):

> *Soms sla je in alle haast een maatijd over. En soms is het verlangen naar een vette snack sterker dan het gezonde verstand. Het gevolg: veel Nederlanders krijgen te weinig mineralen en vitaminen binnen. Bijna iedereen mist wel iets, blijkt uit onderzoek van TNO*
> (Sometimes you skip a meal. And sometimes your desire for a greasy snack is stronger than your common sense. The result: many Dutch do not consume sufficient minerals and vitamins. Almost everybody lacks something, according to research by TNO)

And here is the style of the beautician, in the Spanish version (October 2001):

> *La piel de los labios es muy finita, no tiene glándulas sebáceas, de manera que no produce lípidos o grasa como el resto de la piel y por esa razón se encuentra más desprotegida*

(The skin of the lips is very fine and does not have sebaceous glands and so does not produce its own oils like the rest of the skin. Therefore it finds itself unprotected)

In its use of expert style, the Spanish version is again more conservative. It does not like mixing expert style with other styles. This makes the expert information in the magazine more authoritative and 'top down' and again expresses the importance the Spanish attach to formal knowledge and the use of 'proper' style in information oriented writing.

The style of the street

Being up to date is an important aspect of lifestyle. Both the consumer goods and the identities and values they express are often short-lived and in need of constant updating. This can be connoted by 'street' vocabulary, by using a sprinkling of the latest slang expressions of the young and the trendy.

The US version is full of slang of this kind: 'for a smokin-hot style', 'showing off your gams' (legs), 'if you have a good butt', 'mattress-mambo sex', and so on. And, as has already been seen, the Indian version takes it to extremes, with 'vamp varnish' for nail polish, 'mane' for hair, 'smoochers' or 'pouters' for lips, 'chicas', 'sirens', 'vixens', 'babes' and 'chicks' for girls, and so on. In many non-English versions, trendiness is almost synomous with the English language. The Dutch version, for instance, is full of English words – in the translations below I have italicized the words that were in English in the original:

> *Saaie novembermaanden vragen om een lekker opvallende make-up, die niet ophoudt bij een beetje mascara en gekleurde lippen. Smoky eyes, roze wangen en lippen, en vooral: glamorous glans!*
> (Dull November months call for a nice eye-catching *make-up* which doesn't stop at a little mascara and coloured lips. *Smoky eyes*, pink cheeks and lips and above all: *glamorous* gloss!)

> *Een roze blush op je wangen geeft je winterbleke gezicht een warme gloed. Plaats de blush hoog op de wangen voor het gewenste effect.*
> (A pink *blush* on your cheeks gives your winter-pale face a warm glow. Place the *blush* high on the cheeks for the desired effect)

The Chinese version also makes a lot of use of English – and employs market research to make sure the readers know the English words:

> *nu ren yu shou dair de guan xi ke yi shi hen ou miao de, si best friend you si fan*
> (The relation between women and their handbags can be very subtle, like a *best friend* and also like a *fan*)

ni de mei li Must-Have shi shen me?
(What is your beauty *Must-Have*?)

fei yang shen cai shi party qian shi party hou?
(Glowing with health and radiating vigour, before and after the *party*)

The Spanish version, on the other hand, avoids slang. Although it occasionally modifies words – for example, *protagonista* to *prota* – to give a youthful feel, this remains the exception rather than the rule. In the main the Spanish version prefers a formal, traditional and homogeneous style.

Conversational style

Cosmopolitan style also draws on conversational style, to bring a sense of informality to the stylistic mix. Conversation is essentially private speech, dialogue between equals. But, ever since the 1920s, elements of conversational style have systematically and deliberately been introduced in public communication, where they can give a flavour of equality to forms of communication which are in fact deeply unequal, for instance media communication – where viewers and listeners cannot talk back – and political communication.

David Cardiff (1989) has documented how, during the late 1920s, the BBC quite deliberately developed a conversational style for radio speakers, complete with fully scripted hesitations and errors, so as to sound more 'natural' and to soften the new intrusion of public speech into private living rooms. He also showed how, in the early days of BBC radio, 'vox pops' were fully scripted – and then read in the studio by taxi drivers with Cockney accents – in time 'people-in-the-street' would learn to produce exactly the same kinds of vox pop 'spontaneously', without any need for a script. In the USA the 'spontaneous' reactions in entertainment radio programmes and advertisements were also pre-designed, as in this excerpt from a 1920s script (Barnouw, 1966: 168):

> 'I am so happy to be here. I do these exercises every morning and I am sure I keep my figure just through these exercises. Thank you (GASP OF RELIEF). My gawd, I'm glad that's over.'

A decade later, in Nazi Germany, Goebbels would exhort radio speakers to use conversational speech and local dialects so as to 'sound like the listener's best friend' (Leitner, 1980: 26). As noted by Bell and Van Leeuwen (1994: 36):

> A new form of public speech developed, a genre which retained the logical structure and advance planning of the formal public monologue speech, but mixed it with elements of informal, private conversation – in a planned and deliberate way, and in order to develop a new mode of social control.

Politicians also started to use the conversational style as part of an attempt to present themselves to voters as ordinary people, 'just like you and me' – for instance Roosevelt's famous 'fireside chats' of the 1930s. Everywhere the traditional boundary between the public and the private – a boundary intimately connected to style – was erased. In *Cosmopolitan* this is also the case, not just because the magazine uses the same discourses to represent the public life of work and the private life of love (see Machin and Van Leeuwen, in press), but also by using elements of conversational style. Local versions of the magazine have followed suit. The Chinese version, for instance, makes much use of conversational idioms which formerly would not have been used in writing:

du yi wu er
(the only one in the world)

zong qing xiang shou
(enjoy to one's most)

nong jia cheng zhen
(let false become true)

The following excerpt from a Dutch *Cosmopolitan* editorial (October 2001) uses a wide range of conversational devices: incomplete sentences, contractions like '*m'n*', typical conversational fillers like '*je weet wel*' ('you know'), slang words like '*tutten*', informal spellings like '*friet*' (instead of 'frites', the official, French, spelling), trendy evaluatives like '*onwaarschijnlijk fantastisch*' ('implausibly fantastic'), indications of intonation and timing ('*heeeel*') and so on. In many ways it sounds just like a trendy contemporary Dutch conversation, but it is not. It is an editorial in which the writer has cleverly worked in the highlights of the month's issue:

> *Ben ik raar?*
> *Vorig weekend was ik bij m'n Antwerpse vriendin Linde. Letter tutten samen. Je weet wel, eerst winkelen, dan mossels met friet lunchen en het hele leven doornemen. Beetje over de liefde, beetje over de lijn, en heeeel veel over de nieuwe kleren die we nog willen. En over Cosmo natuurlijk. Ik raakte helemaal op dreef toen ik haar vertelde dat we zo'n onwaarschijnlijk fantastische Bel&Win-actie hadden gemaakt.*
> (Am I weird?
> Last weekend I was in Antwerp with my friend Linde. Having a nice girly time. You know, bit of shopping first, then lunch with mussels and chips and discussing the whole of life. Bit about love, bit about the [waist]line, and looooots about the new clothes we still want. And about *Cosmo* of course. I really got going when I told her about this absolutely brilliant Phone&Win action for our lingerie special ... ')

In conclusion, I have tried to show that *Cosmopolitan* style is a hybrid of different styles, chosen for the connotations they bring, for the way they help express the magazine's identity and values. Like the media styles of the 1920s and 1930s, this style has been quite deliberately designed. And although local versions adopt it in their own specific ways, overall it is a *global* style. The local languages may differ, but the message of the style does not.

Exercises

1   Take photographs of people wearing the same uniform in different ways – for example, school children, football players. Ask people from the same group – for example, children from the same school, players from the same club – what they think of the differences.
2   Collect pictures of a star or celebrity posing in a range of different styles as well as articles about him or her from popular newspapers and/or magazines. Describe how his or her appearance expresses the identities and values for which he or she stands according to the media.
3   Collect or make pictures of people with dreadlocks. What did dreadlocks originally mean? How did they acquire fashion and lifestyle value?
4   Select a picture of a living room – or other room – from a 'Beautiful Home' type magazine, and analyse it as a 'composite of connotations'.
5   Design a poster for a singer or band that expresses the singer's or band's musical style through colour and typography, using the principle of the 'composite of connotations'. Explain your choices.

Notes

1   Translations are by Theo van Leeuwen (Dutch), David Machin (Spanish), and Sally Zhao (Chinese)
2   Interviews were carried out by David Machin as part of the research project Language and Global Communication, conducted at the Centre for Language and Communication Research at Cardiff University, and funded by the Leverhulme Trust.

8 Modality

The concept of modality

'Modality' is the social semiotic approach to the question of truth. It relates both to issues of representation – fact versus fiction, reality versus fantasy, real versus artificial, authentic versus fake – and to questions of social interaction, because the question of truth is also a social question – what is regarded as true in one social context is not necessarily regarded as true in others, with all the consequences that brings. Linguists and semioticians therefore do not ask 'How true is this?' but '*As how true* is it represented?' They are concerned not with the absolute truth but with the truth as speakers and writers and other sign producers *see* it, and with the semiotic resources they use to express it. The two do not necessarily coincide. It is perfectly possible to represent something that does not exist as though it does. Realist fiction thrives on this. And it is equally possible to represent something that actually exists or has existed, as though its existence is in doubt – think for instance of Holocaust-denying 'historians'.

The text below comes from the ENCARTA interactive multimedia encyclopaedia (Microsoft, 1995). It deals with the religious beliefs of Native Americans, hence with what, according to Native Americans, the world is really like. It contains three different voices: the voice of the Native Americans, that of 'the Europeans' and that of the writer of the article. The question I am asking here is: As how true are the truths of these different voices represented? I have italicized the words and phrases that seem relevant to answering this question.

> *Most* Native Americans *believe* that in the universe there exists a spiritual force that is the source of all life. The Almighty of Native American *belief* is not *pictured as* a man in the sky; rather it is *believed* to be formless and to exist throughout the universe. The sun is *viewed as* a manifestation of the power of the Almighty, and the Europeans *often thought* Native Americans were worshipping the sun, when*, in fact,* they *were* addressing prayers to the Almighty, of which the sun *was* a *sign and symbol*.

As how true is the voice of the Native Americans represented here? First of all, their version of reality – 'there exists a spiritual force that is the source of all life', 'the sun manifests the power of the Almighty' – is called a *belief* and a *view.* Ever since science has taken over from theology and philosophy as the main arbiter of truth, 'belief' has been opposed to proven fact and the dominant truths of Western societies have had to be grounded in science. The cultures of native peoples do not have such a division between science and theology, and this, in our eyes, makes their truths less true than ours, however attractive and ecologically sound they may now seem to many of us. Second, the sun is called a *sign and symbol* of the Almighty. This also lowers truth value, because the 'sign' of a thing is not the thing itself. Finally, the Native American beliefs are represented as not shared by all – '*most* Native Americans believe...' – and as beliefs that were held in the past – 'they *were* addressing prayers' – and are therefore not necessarily valid in the here and now.

The voice of the 'Europeans' is also given low modality. Their version of Native American beliefs is represented as false – '*they often thought...*' – because 'thinking' has a lower truth value than 'knowing' – it is more 'subjective' – and the past tense suggests that their view is no longer tenable today. It is not clear to whom the view that 'God is a man in the sky' is ascribed, but it is obviously represented as less than true. To say that God '*is pictured as* a man in the sky' clearly has lower modality than to say that God '*is* a man in the sky'.

The truth of the writer of the encyclopaedia article, finally, has high modality: '*In fact*, they were addressing prayers'. Note that he or she uses a Christian vocabulary to interpret the beliefs of Native Americans – '*the Almighty*', '*addressing prayers*' – while '*worship*', the word used in connection with the mistaken earlier version of the 'Europeans' can have negative associations – after all, you can worship the wrong things (for example, money), but it is hard to think of a context in which 'addressing prayers' is negative. Clearly the writer assigns different modalities, different degrees of truth, to these different versions of reality, using the modality resources of English to do so: frequency terms like *often, many*; cognition verbs such as *believe, picture as, view as*; modality adjuncts such as *in fact*; tense, and so on. And what is more, s/he does so with great confidence in his or her judgement, as though s/he knows exactly what Native Americans believe. Even if some readers were to disagree, even if they were to think, for instance, that the sun really *is* the Almighty, they would still also realize that the writer does not see it that way, and that the truth of the encyclopaedia, that accepted compendium of society's knowledge, is a powerful one and difficult to challenge by someone who is not a recognized expert.

Authoritative texts, then, can use the modality resources of language to impose a view of the truth that is hard to counter. If you read back over what I have just written you will see I do it myself all the time. It is a pretty unavoidable part of writing an academic text. But the same modality resources can also be used in dialogue, to *negotiate* a truth to which the participants of the dialogue will then agree to bind themselves for all practical purposes, whether they say so in so many words or not. This example is from the John Grisham thriller *The Runaway Jury*. Jack Swanson, working for a tobacco company facing a major litigation trial, interviews a friend of one of the activists who infiltrate themselves into juries to try and get verdicts against the tobacco companies:

> '*Are you sure* her real name was Claire Clement?'
> Beverly withdrew and frowned. 'You *think maybe* it wasn't?'
> 'We *have reason to believe* she was someone else before she arrived in Lawrence, Kansas. Do you remember anything about another name?'

'Wow. I just *assumed* she was Claire. Why *would* she change her name?'
'We'd love to know.'

At first Beverly is sure that Claire Clement is the real name of her friend. She has never had any reason to doubt it. So her first reaction is to attach low modality to Swanson's implied doubt, both verbally ('You *think maybe...*'), and non-verbally ('she withdrew and frowned'). Then Swanson bids for a somewhat higher modality value. He still calls it a 'belief', but a *reasoned* belief. This persuades Beverly to move a step towards Swanson's position. Her earlier certainty begins to crumble. She now recognizes that it is possible that her assumptions about Claire may have been unfounded. Yet she still has her doubts, otherwise she would have asked 'Why *did* she change her name?' instead of 'Why *would* she change her name?' She is not yet completely convinced.

Whether based on imposition by an authority or authoritative text or on a consensus reached in dialogue, modality always requires two parties, the speaker or writer and the hearer or reader who, willingly or grudgingly, falls in line with the accepted or agreed version. As Hodge and Kress have put it:

> Social control rests on control over the representation of reality which is accepted as the basis for judgement and action ... Whoever controls modality can control which version of reality will be selected out as the valid version in that semiotic process. All other versions can exist briefly, but are deprived of force in the longer term unless a group refuses to let that force be negated. The sanction of modality ultimately has its source in the agreement of a group of people.
>
> (1988: 147)

The linguistic resources of modality clearly have a very important role to play in society. They allow people to create the shared truths they need in order to be able to form groups which believe the same things and can therefore act cohesively and effectively in and on the world – and they also allow people to downgrade the truths of others, with all the potential consequences that may have, from freezing people out of a group of friends to religious and ideological wars.

Linguistic modality

Linguists' interest in modality has traditionally centred on a specific grammatical system, that of the modal auxiliaries – *may, will,* and *must.* These neatly express three *degrees* of modality: low, median, and high. It follows that, for linguists, truth is not an 'either–or' matter (true or false), but a matter of degree:

She *may* use another name (low modality)
She *will* use another name (median modality)
She *must* use another name (high modality)

These three degrees of modality can of course also be expressed by related nouns – for example, *certainty, probability, possibility* – adjectives – for example, *certain, likely, possible* – and adverbs – for example, *certainly, probably, maybe*.

Halliday (1985) added an important dimension. He realized that modality not only allows us to choose degrees of truth, but also *kinds* of truth. The examples cited above are all based on the idea of probability. They represent values on a scale that runs from 'Yes, true' to 'No, false'. The yardstick for this kind of truth goes something like this: the higher the probability that what-is-asserted really exists, or has really occurred, or will really occur, the higher the modality of the assertion. Another kind of truth is *frequency modality*. This is based on a scale that runs from 'Yes, always' and 'No, never' – or 'Yes, everybody' to 'No, nobody'. Here the truth criterion goes something like this: the more often what-is-asserted happens, or the more people think or say or do it, the higher the modality of that assertion. The linguistic resources used to realize this therefore again express *degrees* of frequency, for example, *always–often–sometimes, most–many–some*, etc.

> She *sometimes* uses another name (low frequency modality)
> She *often* uses another name (median frequency modality)
> She *always* uses another name (high frequency modality)

Halliday also distinguished between *subjective modality* and *objective modality*. In the case of subjective modality, the truth criterion goes something like this: the stronger my inner conviction about the truth of an assertion, the higher the modality of that assertion. In the case of objective modality the idea of objective truth is *explicitly* expressed. Again, this does not mean that the assertion actually *is* objectively true, merely that it is represented as such. In both cases the assertion is preceded by a frame ending in 'that', for example, '*It is a fact that* (she uses another name)' or '*I have the impression that* (she uses another name)'. In the case of subjective modality this frame has a person as the subject and uses a 'verb of cognition'. It is these verbs which then express the degrees of modality, for example, *know–believe–guess*.

> *I have a feeling that* she uses another name (low subjective modality)
> *I am fairly confident that* she uses another name (median subjective modality)
> *I am convinced that* she uses another name (high subjective modality)

In the case of objective modality, the frame begins with '*it is*' or '*there is*', and it is this which explicitly expresses impersonal objectivity. The frame then uses nouns or adjectives to indicate the degree of modality, for example:

> *It is possible that* she uses another name (low objective modality)
> *There is a good likelihood that* she uses another name (median objective modality)
> *It is a fact that* she uses another name (high objective modality)

Different social groups and institutions prefer different kinds of truth. Frequency modality is preferred, for instance, in the quantitative social sciences and in administrative practices which use social science discourses – for example, opinion polls – and it is also highly regarded in journalism. Subjective modality is used in fields that are considered personal, such as romantic love, psychotherapy, art, certain kinds of religion. As objectivity is the most highly valued kind of truth in the dominant institutions of Western societies, subjective modality is often used in connection with people who have comparatively little social power, for example, women, children, consumers, patients, or, as we have seen, native peoples. In media interviews the expert is usually asked questions which seek to elicit objective modality – 'What IS the case?' – and the ordinary person-in-the-street is usually asked questions which seek to elicit subjective modality – 'What do you FEEL about it?' Clearly social groups and institutions differ not only in the truth values they assign to different versions of reality, but also in the *kinds* of truth they use to do this. As most of us belong to more than one social group and operate within several social institutions, we must, for all practical purposes – and whatever we really believe – be seen to adhere to different truths in different contexts, at least if we want to be seen to belong.

I can now summarize my analysis of the 'Native American beliefs' text more fully, in the table below. This shows up the writer's ambivalent attitude towards Native American beliefs even more clearly – s/he makes them seem at once untrue (on a scientific level, perhaps) and true (on a more abstract, symbolic and subjective level). Clearly modality is not an either/or business. It can express complex and ambiguous attitudes that are not easy to tabulate. It also shows that modality analysis is ultimately an interpretation, albeit one that lays its cards on the table. In many cases the choices are not clear-cut. Should 'sign and symbol' be seen as 'median' or 'low' for instance? Are there really only three degrees or many more? It is also clear that there are still gaps in the theory. What kind of modality is expressed by tense, for instance? But all this does not make the idea of modality invalid. It merely shows that there is plenty of scope for further thought and further development.

What is modalized	Linguistic realizations	Degree of modality	Kind of modality
God is the source of	most	high	frequency
life and manifested	believe (3 times)	median	subjective
in the sun	view as	median	subjective
	present tense (3 times)	high	?
	past tense (2 times)	low	?
	sign and symbol	median	subjective
God is a man in the sky	picture as	low	subjective
Native Americans	often	median	frequency
worship the sun	think	low	subjective
	past tense	low	?
Native Americans see	in fact	high	objective
the sun as a sign and			
symbol			

The study of modality began in the philosophy of language, as a concern with the absolute, context-independent truth of assertions. Then it moved to linguistics, which, as we have seen, started to emphasize the *expression* of truth values, but still remained mainly concerned with the modality of representations. Halliday moved this a step further when he observed that the same modal auxiliaries can express 'what exists' and 'what is allowed'. For instance, '*may*' can express not only *possibility* – 'She may be using another name' – but also *permission*, or its opposite – 'You may not use another name' – and '*must*' can express not only the certainty of logical truth but also the absoluteness of a social obligation. Thus there is a close connection between degrees of representational truth and degrees of social obligation. Philosophers have recognized this as well, through their concept of 'deontic' logic, the logic of obligation and permission (Von Wright, 1956). All this laid the foundations for the social semiotic view that modality should be thought of as central to social life. Social semiotics stresses the fact that modality 'ultimately has its source in the agreement of a group of people', to quote Hodge and Kress again, and that social groups and institutions define their own truths, and relate them in their own ways to the truths of others.

The linguistic resources for expressing modality clearly go well beyond the grammatical system of modal auxiliaries. We have seen how the past tense can express that an assertion is no longer valid, whereas the present tense can give it a sense of universal and timeless truth – compare 'nineteenth century scientists *said* that ...' to 'Scientists *say* that ...'. A further way of expressing modality, very important in journalism and academic writing, is through the 'saying verbs' that frame quoted and reported speech: 'Scientists have *claimed* that ...' clearly has lower modality value than 'Scientists have *shown* that ...'. As Kress and Hodge have said:

> There are a large number of ways of realising modality: non-verbal and verbal, through non-deliberate features (hesitations, *ums*, *ers*, etc.) and deliberate systematic features which include fillers (sort of), adverbs (probably, quite better), modal auxiliaries (can, must), and mental process verbs (think, understand, feel) and intonation
>
> (1979: 127)

This has been taken up more fully as social semiotics developed (for example, Hodge and Kress, 1988). According to social semioticians modality is not restricted to language but is a multimodal concept. All means of expression have modality resources. The question of truth emerges in all of them, even if the kinds of truth they allow and the ways in which they express degrees of truth will be different.

Visual modality

The advertisement in figure 8.1 is fairly typical of its kind. The top part of the page shows the 'promise' of the product – how beautiful or glamorous or successful you will become if you buy the product, or how cool or soft or luxurious it will feel or taste or smell. The bottom part provides factual detail and/or a picture of the product itself. In other words, the modality value of the two parts of the advertisement differ. The top shows what you *might* be or *could* be (low modality), the bottom what *is* and what you can actually buy right now in the shop if you want to (high modality). This is expressed through subtle differences in the way certain means of visual expression are used. In figure 8.1, for instance, the photograph of the woman is in a slightly sepia-tinted black and white, whereas the glasses and the case are in full colour. Again, the photo of the woman is in soft focus, whereas glasses and case are depicted in sharp detail. This illustrates the way visual modality works. Increases or decreases in the degree to which certain means of visual expression are used – colour, sharpness, etc. – express increases or decreases in 'as how real' the image should be taken.

Figure 8.1   Web Eyewear advertisement (*Marie Claire*, April 1996)

According to Kress and Van Leeuwen (1996), the following means of visual expression are involved in judgements of visual modality:

- Degrees of the *articulation of detail* form a scale which runs from the simplest line drawing to the sharpest and most finely grained photograph.
- Degrees of the *articulation of the background* range from zero articulation, as when something is shown against a white or black background, via lightly sketched in or out-of-focus backgrounds, to maximally sharp and detailed backgrounds.
- Degrees of *colour saturation* range from the absence of saturation – black and white – to the use of maximally saturated colours, with, in between, colours that are mixed with grey to various degrees.
- Degrees of *colour modulation* range from the use of flat, unmodulated colour to the representation of all the fine nuances and colour modulations of a given colour – for example, skin colour or the colour of grass.
- Degrees of *colour differentiation* range from monochrome to the use of a full palette of diverse colours.
- Degree of *depth articulation* range from the absence of any representation of depth to maximally deep perspective, with various other possibilities in between – for example, simple overlapping without perspectival foreshortening.
- Degrees of the *articulation of light and shadow* range from zero to the articulation of the maximum number of degrees of 'depth' of shade, with options such as simple hatching in between.
- Degrees of the *articulation of tone* range from just two shades of tonal gradation, black and white – or a light and dark version of another colour – to maximal tonal gradation.

All these means of visual expression are gradable. They allow the relevant dimension of articulation to be increased or reduced. What is more, the different parameters may be amplified or reduced to different degrees, resulting in many possible modality configurations. These configurations cue viewers' judgements of modality, of 'as how real' images (or parts of images) are to be taken. Newspaper cartoons, for instance, tend to have reduced articulation of detail, background, depth, and light and shade, and no articulation of colour and tonal gradation. By comparison, the articulation of these same parameters in news photographs is much amplified. This corresponds to their modality value: cartoons are taken as visual 'opinions' and hence as less factual than news photographs, which are held to provide reliable, documentary information.

It is not the case, however, that modality always decreases as articulation is reduced. If this were so, simple line diagrams would always have low modality and be judged as 'not real'. But despite the fact that their articulation is usually greatly reduced, scientific line diagrams are clearly to be read as images with high truth value, and not as fictions or fantasies. After all, they are science. This means that there is no fixed correspondence between modality judgements and points on the scales of articulation described above. Instead the modality value of a given configuration depends on the kind of visual truth which is preferred in the given context.

In many contexts *naturalistic modality* remains dominant. Its view of visual truth is more or less as follows: the more an image of something resembles the way we would see that something if we saw it in reality, from a specific viewpoint and under specific conditions of illumination, the higher its modality. This, at least, is the theory, because in reality naturalistic modality judgements depend very much on the way in which the currently dominant naturalistic imaging technology represents the visual world. When black and white was the norm, colour was regarded as 'more than real'. In film, for instance, it tended to be used for relatively unrealistic genres such as musicals and Westerns. Serious contemporary realist drama tended to be in black and white. Today colour is the norm and black and white tends to be lower in modality, used for representing the past, dreams, fantasies, etc., as in figure 8.1.

In *abstract modality*, common in scientific visuals and modern art, visual truth is abstract truth. The more an image represents the deeper 'essence' of what it depicts, or the more it represents the general pattern underlying superficially different specific instances, the higher its modality from the point of view of the abstract truth. This is expressed by reduced articulation. Specifics of illumination, nuances of colour, the details that create individual differences are all irrelevant from the point of view of the essential or general truth. This is seen, for instance, when naturalistic and abstract visuals are combined. Children's books about dinosaurs have detailed naturalistic pictures of dinosaurs in primeval landscapes to excite the imagination, and simple line drawings to help them recognise the essential attributes of different kinds of dinosaur or to explain the process of fossilization (figure 8.2).

The distinction between naturalistic and abstract modality resembles that between 'naturalism' and 'realism' in debates about art and literature. Here 'naturalism' often has a pejorative meaning. It is seen as representing the world only superficially, 'in terms of its outwards appearance rather than its inner reality' (Williams, 1976: 260). 'Realism', on the other hand, especially in specific forms such as 'psychological realism' or 'socialist realism', can 'include or emphasise hidden or underlying forces or movements, which simple "naturalistic" observation could not pick up and which it is the purpose of realism to discover and express' (ibid.: 261). This sense of 'naturalism' as 'accurate external representation', which is also the one used in this chapter, should not be confused with the more specialized use of the term in nineteenth century literature and drama, where it related to the very faithful description of the social environments which were held to determine or influence characters, actions and events.

In *technological modality*, visual truth is based on the practical usefulness of the image. The more an image can be used as a blueprint or aid for action, the higher its modality. Many maps are of this kind, and so are patterns for dress making, architectural drawings and the assembly instructions of 'do it yourself' kits. The corresponding modality configurations will tend towards strongly decreased articulation. Perspective, for instance, will be reduced to zero, as foreshortening would make it difficult to take measurements from the image.

Learning from fossils

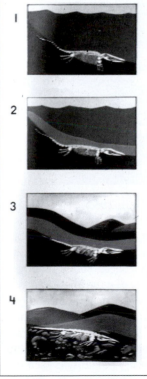

We can learn a lot about reptiles from their **fossils.** Our pictures show how a fossil is made.

1. Millions of years ago the **skeleton** of a dead animal sank to the bottom of a lake.

2. Layers of mud covered the bones.

3. The layers of mud turned into rock and the lake dried up.

4. Wind and rain wore away the rock over millions of years so we can find the fossil bones on the ground.

Figure 8.2   Dinosaurs (from Bailey, 1988: 10, 17)

Figure 8.3   St John of the Cross (Salvador Dali, 1951)

Finally, in *sensory modality*, visual truth is based on the effect of pleasure or displeasure created by visuals, and realized by a degree of articulation which is amplified beyond the point of naturalism, so that sharpness, colour, depth, the play of light and shade, etc., become – from the point of view of naturalistic modality – 'more than real'. Colour, for instance, is now used not to denote general meanings such as 'desert' or 'water' on maps or to express the essence of something in an artistic image (abstract modality), nor for its resemblance to reality (as in naturalistic modality), but for its soothing, or stirring, or unsettling effect – a whole psychology of colour has evolved to elaborate this. Needless to say, sensory modality is used in contexts where pleasure matters: in food photography and perfume ads, for instance, and also in contexts which try to create an intensity of experience akin to that of the dream or the hallucination, for example, in certain kinds of surrealist art, or in horror films. Salvador Dali's *St John of the Cross* (figure 8.3), with its 'more than real' articulation of perspective and light and shadow, is a famous example.

I can now summarize my analysis of Figure 8.1 more fully:

What is modalized	Visual realization	Degree of modality	Kind of modality
A woman with sunglasses behind a car window	Reduced detail Minimal background Black and white Normal depth Normal representation of light and shade Reduced tonal range	Lowered	Naturalistic (Could also be seen as median abstract ('the essence of fame'))
Sunglasses on a case	Sharp detail No background High colour saturation High colour modulation High colour differentiation Normal depth High representation of light and shade High tonal variation	High	Naturalistic (tends towards the 'sensory')

Visual truth in the age of the digital image

Photography is often thought of as *reproducing* rather than representing reality. It is seen as inherently truthful and reliable because of its technological nature, because its images are formed not by the hand of the photographer but by nature, by the light which reflects from the subject and then affects the photographic emulsion. In Peirce's terminology (see chapter 3), the photographic sign is 'indexical', a sign *caused* by its referent. Digital images, on the other hand, can *look* like photographs, yet the people, places and things they show may never have existed before the lens of a camera. The computer is essentially a synthesizing, rather a recording technology. It forms images on the basis of stored information about the geometrical forms and surface textures of the people, places and things that are to be represented.

Photojournalists have much invested in the reliability and trustworthiness of photography. Hence they are concerned about the digital image and its immense potential for manipulation. In the age of the digital image, how can photojournalism continue to fulfil its role of reporting reality? How can the public continue to trust journalistic images to show what really exists and really has happened? In a widely cited article Ritchin (1990) proposes a form of certification in which photographs will be labelled as not having been manipulated or as having been 'ethically manipulated'. He also suggests relying on the reputation of the photographer as another guarantee for the truth of the photograph. But both criteria are external. The photograph itself will no longer carry the visible signs of its truthfulness. From the point of the semiotic theory of modality, it never did, of course. It could always only carry the signifiers of its *claim* to truthfulness. It could always only show *as how true* it sought to be taken, not how true it really was. And it has always been possible for 'untrue' things to be photographically represented as though they were true, and the reverse. Price recounts a famous case:

> In 1936 the American photographer Arthur Rothstein photographed a steer's skull that had been bleached by the sun and left lying on the earth. A simple still life, then, but one that was clearly intended to exemplify the contemporary crisis in agriculture. He took two photographs of this object, the most famous of which shows it resting on cracked, baked, waterless earth. The second, however, revealed it as resting on the less symbolically charged ground of a stretch of grass. The photographer acknowledged that he had moved the skull a few metres to obtain a more dramatic pictorial effect. When this was discovered there was an outcry from Republican politicians, who claimed that the public had a right to see photographs that were objectively true rather than those that had been manipulated for purposes of rhetoric or propaganda.
>
> (2000: 76–7)

In other words, there was a conflict between two kinds of truth criteria. On the one hand there was the naturalistic truth criterion according to which Rothstein should have recorded reality just as he found it. On the other hand there was the abstract truth criterion according to which a photograph should not just record its subject but also say something about it. Both kinds of truth have always existed in photography. There have always been genres in which photographers arranged the reality before the camera, and genres which did not allow this. The latter, of course, also carried the outward signifiers of their adherence to the naturalistic truth: a lack of artificial lighting, a lack of overly stylized composition, a lack of darkroom manipulation of the image. Conflicts only arise when a discrepancy is revealed between the 'how true' and the 'as how true' of what is taken to be a naturalistic image, when, for instance, a journalistic picture looks as if it has been recorded with a traditional camera but has in fact been computer-generated. Where a deeper, abstract truth is preferred, the problem does not arise. This is so in the case of socialist realism, for instance, as illustrated by this quote from Bertolt Brecht:

> Less than at any time does a simple reproduction of reality tell us anything about reality. A photograph of the Krupp works or GEC yields almost nothing about these institutions. Therefore something has actually to be constructed, something artificial, something set up.
>
> (quoted in Benjamin, 1972: 24)

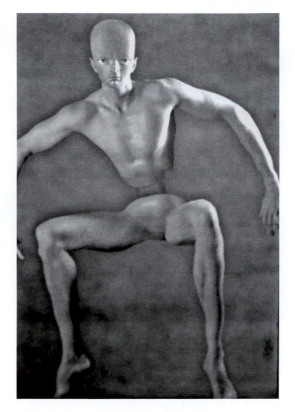

Figure 8.4   Six Stills (Corinna Holthusen, 1998)

This is so also in the case of art photography. Figure 8.4 is constructed from 6 slides, with the aid of computer manipulation and its modality is clearly meant to be abstract. Although the articulation of detail is photographic, the picture has strongly reduced colour – a greenish monochrome – and background. It does ask us to believe that this creature really exists, or at least to suspend our disbelief for a time. It asks to see this creature as a telling representation of contemporary hybrid identity – and so affirms the reality of an abstract idea, that of hybrid identity.

It is so even in the case of science, which increasingly works with computer simula-tions and visual modelling rather than with photographic records, because it too is ultimately more interested in the deeper, more general truth than in the specificities of external reality.

But, again, visual modality is not an either/or business. It allows complex and subtle modality configurations that can mix the naturalistic and the abstract, or the sensory and the abstract, or the naturalistic and the sensory. Figure 8.5 is a photo-graph by Joseph Kudelka, a highly regarded documentary photographer. It was taken in Spain, in 1976, hence still during the Franco era. It clearly depicts some kind of

Figure 8.5   Spain, 1976 (Joseph Koudelka)

parade or procession, and it clearly signifies itself as a documentary photograph: black and white, taken with natural light, and not likely to have been specially arranged for the camera. Yet, from a naturalistic point of view, the people and the flags have low modality, because their silhouetting causes a complete elimination of the articulation of detail and of tonal gradation. The street on the other hand has high modality. Through this contrast in modality the photographer expresses a more abstract truth. Something like this, perhaps. This street has been here for a long time. It has seen the sun rise and set countless times. It has seen processions come and go countless times, as fleeting and unreal as shadows. All this political and military and religious fervour, what does it all amount to in the end?

   This shows two things. First of all, there are always several visual modality cues at once, and they can contradict each other. Some can signify naturalism and some abstraction for instance, as in this case. And as a result at least two interpretations are possible, a naturalistic and an abstract one. As in the case of Rothstein's photograph of the sun-bleached steer's skull, some will prefer one kind of interpretation, some another – and who prefers what will have to do with their interests and values. Second, from the point of view of the abstract truth, would the message have been any different if the image had not been a photograph, but, for instance, a 'photo-realist' painting? Or even a computer-generated image? I think not. And that is important. It means that the decline of traditional photography does not necessarily spell the end of observational truth. What matters in the end is not that this image has been produced by means of a photo-chemical process. What matters is the quality of observation to which it testifies, together with the quality of the photographer's visual thinking, of his or her practical understanding of the visual resources produced by centuries of visual art.

Modality in other semiotic modes

There is no room for discussing the modality of other semiotic modes in the same amount of detail. Instead I will give one further example and then return to the relation between truth and norms, between the way we picture reality and the way we conduct social life.

As is discussed in detail in Van Leeuwen (1999), the modality of sound can be approached along the same lines as the modality of visual communication. This is perhaps best illustrated with an example. Imagine three different locomotive sounds. The first is purely musical. Perhaps it is the locomotive from Honegger's symphonic poem *Pacific 231*. In this piece, the whistle is played by strings abruptly sliding up, while brass, strings and timpani play the chugging of the engine, first low and slow, then gradually faster as the machine gathers speed. Only conventional musical instruments and conventionally stylized patterns of sound are used. The sound is both recognizably a locomotive (but represented abstractly, reduced to its essential features) and recognizably music, hence emotively appealing. In other words, the modality is *abstract-sensory*.

The second would be an average quality audio recording of an actual locomotive. Here too, we will recognize the whistle and the chugging, but there will be other noises as well, clicks, squeaks, hisses, the grinding of wheels, and so on, and the 'melody' and 'rhythm' will not be as regularized and stylized. This is *naturalistic sound modality*. You hear more or less what you would have heard if you could transport yourself back to the era of the great steam engines.

The third might be a scene from a film in which the sound of the locomotive is meant to frighten the viewer. Perhaps a character is lying flat between the rails, unable to move as the train approaches. Now the sound will be 'sensurround', exaggerated, overwhelming, a deafening roar, heightened reverb, ear-piercing grinding of wheels on rails, a shrill and screaming steam whistle. What matters here is not in the first place that we get a naturalistic sense of 'being there' but that the sound *terrifies* us. The recording aims at *sensory modality*, at emotive impact without the abstraction that characterizes representational music.

In other words, as in visual modality, there are both degrees and kinds of sound modality. The truth of a given recording will be cued in by the degree to which that recording uses certain means of aural expression: pitch range – narrow vs wide – loudness range, amount of variety in the duration of sounds, amount of variety in the steadiness of sound – for example, degrees of 'vibrato' in music – sound texture – smooth–rough; tense–lax etc. – and so on. There is no space here to explore this in detail, but one point needs to be made. The same means of aural expression can be used representationally and interactionally, to represent the world and to *present* oneself, to use a distinction from the work of Martinec (2001: 117). Take pitch range. It can clearly be used for representation. Representing a howling wind, for instance, will require a wider pitch range than representing a drizzly rain. But we also use it in our everyday speech. And here the yardstick of modality will be not closeness to reality but closeness to *normality*, to the pitch range that is regarded as 'normal' in the given context. If our pitch range is narrower than normal, we might be regarded as too restrained, too dull, lacking in energy and self-projection. If we exceed the norm, we might be seen as too excessive, too emotional. Moreover, such norms may vary for different kinds of people and different kinds of situation. According to McConnell-Ginet, women use a broader pitch range and more rapid and frequent changes of pitch than men: 'Part of women's being emotional in our culture derives from our sounding emotional' (McConnell-Ginet, 1977: 77). A very narrow pitch range is normal in certain kinds of liturgical chanting, which may even use a complete monotone, with only one lower note to signal the end of a line. In this context it is not appropriate for people to assert themselves.

Finally, norms of this kind vary historically, as illustrated by this quote:

> Medieval and early Renaissance music tended to move in stepwise progression at a normal to medium pitch, befitting man's humble subjection to the deity; but with the growth of human self-realisation, music drama, in the hands of Monteverdi and others, began to introduce more and more liberty of pitch movement to express the rhetoric of human passion; until, by the end of the nineteenth century, violent emotional unrest beat against the natural limits of audible pitch.
>
> (Cooke, 1959: 109)

The same is true for other semiotic modes we use to present ourselves rather than (only) for representation, dress, for instance. In the theatre and film we use dress to represent, but, as discussed in chapter 7, in everyday life we use it to present ourselves, to say something about who we are and how we want to be seen. This, too, will invoke norms by reference to which we may either be judged too restrained or too excessive, and which will vary both contextually and historically. There clearly is a close connection between the way we represent the world and the rules and norms of everyday social behaviour, and this duality is the essence of modality, the key to its social importance.

Exercises

1   Compare the modality of two different kinds of newspaper article dealing with the same issue – for instance a report and an editorial from the same newspaper, or articles from two newspapers which differ in readership or outlook – and try to explain the differences. It is best to take an issue about which there is difference of opinion in the given context.

2   Collect five images of a particular kind of object – for example, a car – from each of at least three different sources – for example, advertisements, technical manuals, news articles, art works. Compare the three categories in terms of visual modality and attempt to explain the differences.

3   Describe the modality of a dream scene from a dramatic production – film, TV or stage. What aspects of image and sound and perhaps also of dress, acting, speech, and so on make the scene dreamlike?

4   Does it make sense to speak about the modality of food? What kind of truth criteria do people have in mind when they say things like 'This is not true bread' or 'This is real fruit juice', and how would degrees of these kinds of truth be expressed through the food itself, through its packaging and through its advertising?

5   Take a simple line diagram or chart and change it to make it more 'sensory'. What needs to be changed? Is it a good idea to do this, and, if so, why – or, if not, why not?

PART III

Multimodal cohesion

In this part of the book I introduce four ways in which different kinds of semiotic resources are integrated to form *multimodal* texts and communicative events:

- *Rhythm*
  Rhythm provides coherence and meaningful structure to events unfolding over time. It plays a crucial role in everyday interaction as well as in time-based media such as film and music.
- *Composition*
  Composition provides coherence and meaningful structure to spatial arrange-ments. It plays a crucial role not only in images and layout but also in three-dimensional spatial arrangements such as exhibition displays and architecture.
- *Information linking*
  Under this heading I discuss the cognitive links between the items of information in time – as well as space-based media, for instance the temporal or causal links between words and images in multimodal texts.
- *Dialogue*
  Under this heading I explore how the structures of dialogic exchanges and forms of musical interaction can be used to understand the relationships between the semiotic modes used in multimodal texts and communicative events.

Again, although I discuss these dimensions one by one, they never occur in isola-tion. Although rhythm will play the lead role in time-based media and composition in space-based media, in other cases – for example, film – the two combine.

9 Rhythm

In this chapter and the next I discuss two major sources of cohesion in multimodal texts and communicative events – composition in time, or *rhythm*, and composition in space, or *layout*. Rhythm provides cohesion in texts and communicative events that unfold over time – conversations, oral storytelling, music, acting, dance, film and television, etc. Layout provides cohesion in texts that are spatially organized – pages, screens, paintings, museum exhibits, buildings, cities, and so on. Some kinds of text combine the two types of organization. In films the composition of the shots and the arrangements of the sets and locations are spatially organized, while the action, the dialogue, the music and the other sounds are organized according to the rhythmic principles discussed in this chapter.

Apart from being the two single most important sources of cohesion in multimodal texts and communicative events, rhythm and layout have something else in common. They form the key link between semiotic articulation and the body. They are the 'life-blood' of semiotics. Rhythm is a basic biological given. Human action is by nature rhythmically co-ordinated, and, as micro-analytical studies have shown (see Hall, 1983), so are human interactions. As we act together and talk together we synchronize. The rhythms of our actions become as finely attuned to each other as the parts of different instruments in a musical performance. They have to be. If they were not, things would go drastically wrong. We would fall over ourselves and trip others up. Successful social action and interaction would become impossible. The same applies to layout. Our sense of layout derives from our sense of balance (see Arnheim, 1982). Layout is a matter of positioning things in or on a space – ... a bit this way ... a bit that way ... just a little bit up here ... just a little bit down there ... etc. – until a sense of balance has been achieved so that the arrangement feels 'just right'. And balance is as fundamental as rhythm. Without it we fall down. Everything stops and action becomes impossible.

Perhaps terms like 'organizing', 'structuring' and 'providing cohesion' are not really appropriate here. Rhythm does not just provide some kind of formal structure, some kind of scaffolding to keep the text from collapsing, or some kind of cement to hold it together. It also plays an indispensable part in getting the message across. The old Ella Fitzgerald song has it right: 'It don't mean a thing if it ain't got that swing.' As well as that, rhythm is indispensable in fusing together the meanings expressed in and through the different semiotic modes that enter into the multimodal composition, for instance the meanings expressed by the action, the dialogue, the music and the other sounds in films. As I will show in the next chapter, all this is equally true of layout. But I will start with rhythm, trying to show just how it does its work of organizing (and '*vitalizing*', blowing life into) texts and communicative events.

Rhythm and meaning

The essence of rhythm is alternation – alternation between two states: an up and a down, a tense and a lax, a loud and a soft, a night and a day, an ebb and a flood, and so on. Such alternation between two 'opposite poles' is so essential to human perception that we perceive it even when, 'objectively', it is not there. Psychological experimentation has discovered that, when listening to a series of absolutely identical, evenly spaced click noises, people will, at regular intervals, hear one of the clicks as stronger than the others (Allen, 1975). They will hear a regular alternation between two different 'states', even when there is no physical basis for it. But 'state' is of course the wrong word here, because time never stops. In rhythmic organization structure and process become one.

Measures and pulses

Rhythm divides the flow of time into measures – also known as 'rhythmic feet' in connection with speech rhythm and poetic metre – which, to our senses at least, are equally long and marked by an explicit pulse – called 'stress' in the case of speech and 'beat' in the case of music – which falls on the first sound (syllable, note, or other sound) or movement (gesture, dance step, etc.) of the measure, and which is made more prominent, more 'attention-catching' by means of increased loudness, pitch or duration, or, in the case of movement, some other form of increased force.

Tempo results from the duration of the measures and this, again, is closely linked to the body. Musical tempo, judging by the metronome, ranges from 40 pulses to 208 pulses per minute – the human heartbeat ranges from about 50 to about 200 pulses per minute. Again, 90 pulses per minute is not only a medium tempo for music, but also the average rate of easily paced walking in adults. In the following example, from the dialogue of the *The Firm* (Sydney Pollack, 1993), the measures are indicated by forward slashes and the pulses by bold italic. The measures with three syllables – for example, /*why* do you/ – were spoken faster to give them the same length as the measures with two syllables – for example, /*think* I'm/. A second representation of the dialogue (figure 9.1) is added to show that rhythm is not an alternation between 'steady states', but a wave-like motion – where the dividing line between the measures goes is in the end an arbitrary decision:

Why do you/*think* I'm/ *work*ing like/*this*//

Why do you *think* I am *wor*king like *this*

Figure 9.1   The rhythmic structure of dialogue

This 'pulsing' plays a key role in articulating meaning because it foregrounds the sounds or movements that carry the key information of each measure, for example, '*why*', '*think*', '*work*' and '*this*' in the example above. If you heard only these syllables you might still get the meaning. If you heard 'do you I'm like' you would not. These non-pulsed syllables flesh out the information in more or less predictable ways and help construct the melody line that conveys the emotional key of the utterance. To put it another way, the 'opposite poles' created by rhythm are never equal. One of them always carries most of the information that is important for the participants in the given context, and it is usually – although not always – the one which is articulated most energetically or in some other way has 'most' of something – for example, the day has the most light and is therefore the most important to people needing to carry out activities in the daylight. This inequality between two 'opposite poles' is another basic given of human perception.

The form of rhythmic structuring I am describing here is common to all time-based texts and communicative events. Figure 9.2 shows the opening line of Tchaikovsky's Fifth Symphony. The pulses – indicated by arrows – fall on the notes that are most important for getting the musical message across. The first pulse falls on a 'minor third', the note that causes the music to be in a minor key, and hence 'sad'. The second pulse moves up from this, trying to 'rise above the gloom', as it were, but only a little. It seems to be held back by some kind of musical gravity. The third pulse then falls back into the same old 'gloom'. Thus the message becomes something like a 'failed attempt to lift the spirits'.

Figure 9.2   First two bars of Tchaikovsky's Fifth Symphony

In the following example, which represents somebody repeatedly and insistently knocking on a door, there are two silent measures: the timing of the wait between the door knocks continues the regular beat (ONE/two three/ONE two three) which is set up by the pattern of the knocking, and the pulses in these measures are felt rather than heard:

/***knock*** knock knock/ (*silent pulse*) – – / (*silent pulse*) – – / *knock* knock knock/

Rhythmic phrases as frames for communicative acts

I now move to another important aspect of rhythmic organization: rhythm organizes measures – up to seven or eight at a time – into *phrases*. In the case of speech rhythm, these are also called breath groups, as their duration is similar to that of the cycle of breathing, on average nine to 25 syllables, or three to five seconds – it is longer during sleep. Between these phrases there is some kind of break – a short pause, a drawing out of the final sound or movement, or perhaps a change of tempo or some other discontinuity. A phrase may begin with a short, incomplete measure, also known as 'anacrusis'. One of the pulses, usually the last one, will be more salient, more attention-catching than the others.

Phrasing is of key importance in semiotic articulation as phrases form a kind of 'frame' for – and are therefore co-extensive with – the communicative acts I discussed in chapter 6. The extra-salient pulse then carries the highlight, the crucial moment of that communicative act, for instance, in figure 9.2, the note that finally reveals the failure to 'rise above the gloom'.

There is a difference here between the rhythms of semiotic articulations and other kinds of rhythms. Semiotic articulations, whether in the form of speech, music, dancing or other types of communicative action, are segmented in phrases, but other rhythms, for instance the rhythms of nature and the rhythms of repetitive human work, are not 'chunked' in this way and carry on as a continuous wave form, without having breaks after up to seven or eight measures. This contrast is often used in texts and communicative events. A continuous rhythm provides an ongoing background or setting, and a 'chunked' rhythm provides the message that is set in that 'setting', for example, a drum machine may play continuous repetitive rhythmic patterns, without a break, while a voice and/or other instrument(s) articulates phrases on top of this.

Rhythmic moves as frames for generic stages

Here, finally, is the third key aspect of rhythmic organization: rhythm also organizes phrases – again, up to seven or eight at a time – into *moves*. Between these moves there is a more distinct boundary, for instance a significantly longer pause, and perhaps also overall changes in tempo, pitch level, loudness or, in the case of movement, posture and position. Just as phrases form a kind of time frame for communicative acts, so moves form a kind of time frame for the stages of the generic structure of time-based texts and communicative events and the most salient phrase in a move will be the one that clinches the communicative work done in and through the stage demarcated by that move. In dialogue stages can consist of several moves or 'turns', as will be discussed in chapter 12.

The examples below show how rhythmic structuring contributes to 'getting the message across' and also bring out how the different 'tracks' of films – the action, the dialogue, the music and the other sounds – are rhythmically co-ordinated with each other and with the camera movements and the editing points of the film. Often one of these tracks provides the *guide rhythm,* the basic rhythm to which the other rhythms are synchronized during the editing process. In some scenes *action* will provide the guide rhythm (figure 9.3), in others it will be the *dialogue* which provides the basic rhythmic drive of a scene (figure 9.4) or the *music* (figure 9.5). The example in figure 9.5 is an example in which images have been cut to music – but note that music is often written after picture editing has been completed, in which case it is timed to the already edited film.

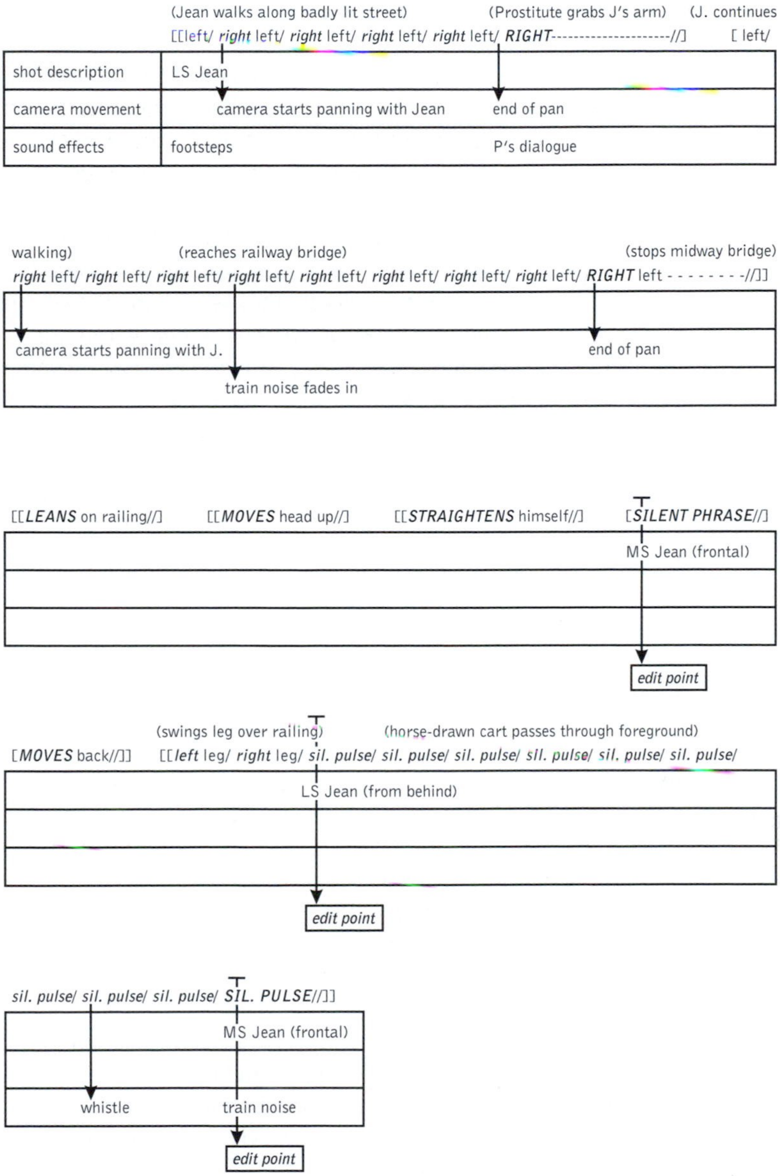

(Jean walks along badly lit street)   (Prostitute grabs J's arm)   (J. continues

[[left/ *right* left/ *right* left/ *right* left/ *right* left/ ***RIGHT***--------------------//]   [left/

shot description	LS Jean	
camera movement	camera starts panning with Jean	end of pan
sound effects	footsteps	P's dialogue

walking)   (reaches railway bridge)   (stops midway bridge)

right left/ *right* left/ *right* left/ *right* left/ *right* left/ *right* left/ *right* left/ *right* left/ ***RIGHT*** left - - - - - - - -//]]

camera starts panning with J.		end of pan
	train noise fades in	

[[***LEANS*** on railing//]   [[***MOVES*** head up//]   [[***STRAIGHTENS*** himself//]   [***SILENT PHRASE*//]

	MS Jean (frontal)

edit point

(swings leg over railing)   (horse-drawn cart passes through foreground)

[***MOVES*** back//]   [[*left* leg/ *right* leg/ *sil. pulse*/ *sil. pulse*/ *sil. pulse*/ *sil. pulse*/ *sil. pulse*/ *sil. pulse*/

LS Jean (from behind)

edit point

sil. pulse/ *sil. pulse*/ *sil. pulse*/ ***SIL. PULSE***//]]

	MS Jean (frontal)
whistle	train noise

edit point

Figure 9.3   Rhythmic analysis of a scene from *Hôtel du Nord* (Marcel Carné, 1938)

The scene from *Hôtel du Nord* (Marcel Carné, 1938) analysed in figure 9.3 follows a highly dramatic incident. Jean (Jean-Pierre Aumont) and his girlfriend Renée (Annabella) have made a suicide pact and locked themselves into a hotel room. Jean has shot Renée but has been prevented from shooting himself by a knock on the door. He has escaped the hotel room via the balcony and now walks along badly lit, gloomy streets, in deep despair. He stops on a railway bridge, obviously intending to commit suicide by throwing himself in front of a train. Just as he has climbed over the railing, and as the train has nearly reached the bridge, a cart drawn by a white horse passes through frame, close to the camera, obscuring Jean from view. When the steam from the locomotive has cleared, we discover that Jean has not jumped. He climbs over the railing and walks back in the direction he came from to give himself up.

The scene unfolds in three moves. The first move *signposts* what is about to happen. It tells the audience that Jean *may* commit suicide, thus setting up anticipation. The move is driven by the rhythm of Jean's footsteps and ends when a prostitute tries to attract his attention, thus slowing him down. Note that the camera movement also ends here. At this point the audience will wonder what Jean is going to do. Is the prostitute going to play some role in the story, and if so how? But no, he walks on. The second move is again driven by the rhythm of Jean's footsteps and ends as he stops walking, midway across the bridge. Now the audience can envisage the possibility of suicide. Note that the train noise is brought in at the exact moment when the railway bridge becomes visible, and that the camera movement also ends at this point.

So the second move *delays* the inevitable climax of the scene, and in that way creates further suspense. As Jean gets ready to jump the tempo slows down. Then there is a silent pulse, a moment of hesitation, of doing nothing, and at that very moment the film cuts to a frontal shot, to reveal Jean's anguish.

The third move provides the *resolution*, but again holds back the moment of revelation as long as possible. The guide rhythm is that of Jean's movements and we continue to 'feel' this rhythm as the horse and cart obscure him from view. At the tenth measure, well after we would have expected the move to end, we hear the whistle of the train, but still Jean is obscured from view. Exactly at the moment of the twelfth pulse there finally is a cut to a frontal view revealing that Jean has not jumped.

Clearly rhythm plays a crucial role here in the *way* the story is told, in the game of revealing and withholding story information from the viewers to maximize both their active involvement in anticipating the events and their passive abandon to the story's suspense.

The scene from *The Firm* (Sydney Pollack, 1993) analysed in figure 9.4 occurs when young lawyer Mitch (Tom Cruise) arrives home in the early hours of the morning, after having stayed back at work to try and find information about a suspicious accident that has befallen two of his colleagues. His girlfriend Abigail (Jeanne Tripplehorne) has waited up for him and is upset.

Here rhythm structures the interaction between Mitch and Abigail. There are five moves. The first, consisting of several communicative acts – direct appeals, a rhetorical question, and then, finally, an attempt to justify himself – is Mitch's *plea* for

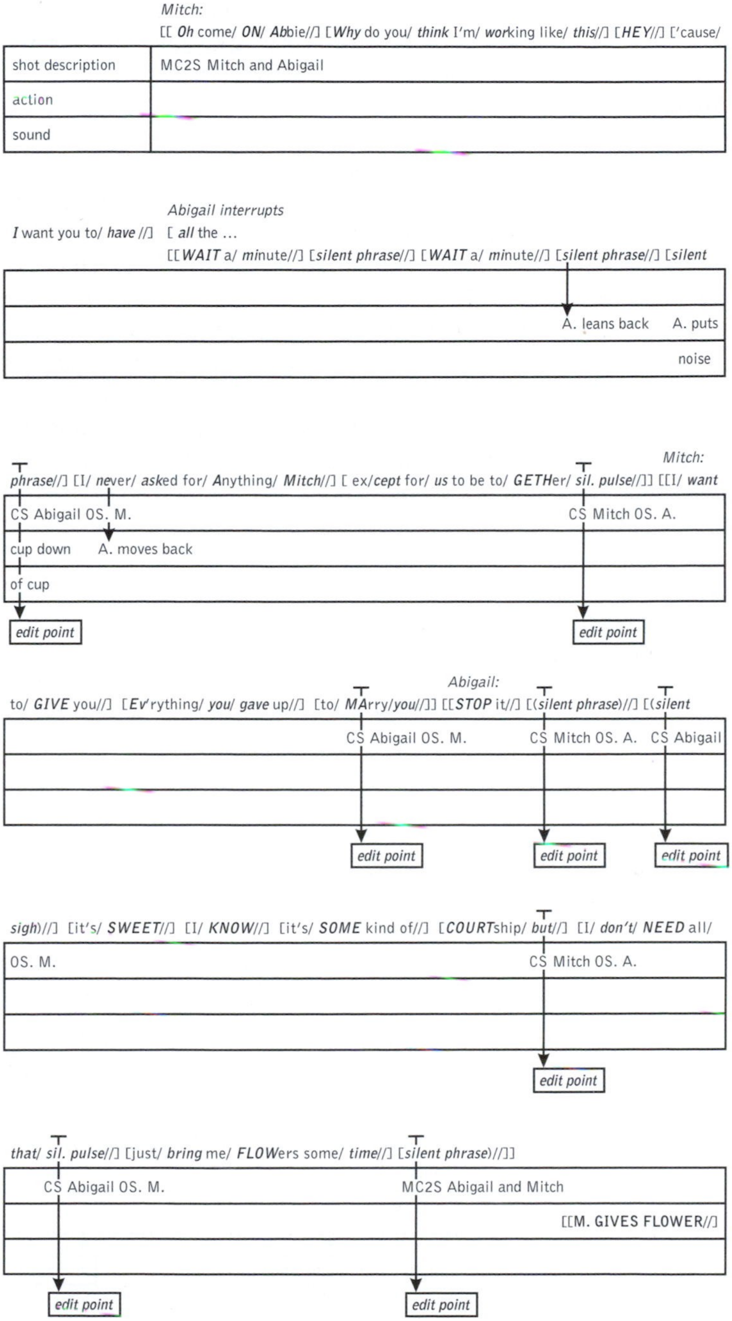

Mitch:
[[*Oh* come/ *ON*/ *Ab*bie//] [*Why* do you/ *think* I'm/ *work*ing like/ *this*//] [*HEY*//] ['cause/

shot description	MC2S Mitch and Abigail
action	
sound	

Abigail interrupts
I want you to/ *have* //] [*all* the ...
[[*WAIT* a/ minute//] [*silent phrase*//] [*WAIT* a/ minute//] [*silent phrase*//] [*silent*

	A. leans back	A. puts
		noise

Mitch:
phrase//] [I/ *never*/ *ask*ed for/ Anything/ *Mitch*//] [*ex*/*cept* for/ *us* to be to/ *GETH*er/ *sil. pulse*//]] [[I/ *want*

CS Abigail OS. M.	CS Mitch OS. A.
cup down A. moves back	
of cup	
edit point	*edit point*

Abigail:
to/ *GIVE* you//] [*Ev'*rything/ *you*/ *gave* up//] [to/ *MA*rry/*you*//]] [[*STOP* it//] [*(silent phrase)*//] [(*silent*

	CS Abigail OS. M.	CS Mitch OS. A.	CS Abigail
	edit point	*edit point*	*edit point*

sigh)//] [it's/ *SWEET*//] [I/ *KNOW*//] [it's/ *SOME* kind of//] [*COURT*ship/ *but*//] [I/ *don't*/ *NEED* all/

OS. M.	CS Mitch OS. A.
	edit point

that/ *sil. pulse*//] [just/ *bring* me/ *FLOW*ers some/ *time*//] [*silent phrase*//]]]

CS Abigail OS. M.	MC2S Abigail and Mitch
	[[M. GIVES FLOWER//]
edit point	*edit point*

Figure 9.4   Rhythmic analysis of a scene from *The Firm* (Sydney Pollack, 1993)

forgiveness and understanding. He is cut short by Abigail's *refusal* to see his devotion to work as a gift to her. First she stops him in his tracks, to gain the floor, then follows the refusal itself. In the third move Mitch insistently *repeats his plea*. The fourth move, by Abigail, is again a *refusal*, but one in which she makes a small step in his direction. Again she begins by stopping him in his tracks, but the tempo slows down and she speaks more softly and haltingly, and more understandingly, ending by saying 'just give me flowers'. The final, non-verbal move of the excerpt, is a *peace offering*. Mitch suddenly produces a red rose, after which they make up.

   Clearly here the moves are stages in a stylized version of a lover's quarrel. I should add that the transcript covers only the second part of the quarrel – in the first, Mitch tries to avoid the whole issue by inventing a road accident in which he had to help a pregnant woman, a story which he tells in a humorous way. But Abigail is not in the mood for jokes, so Mitch changes tactics.

   The scene analysed in figure 9.5 is from an anonymous travel film called *Latin American Rhapsody*. The excerpt shown is part of a sequence which opens with the clichéd phrase 'South America, land of a thousand faces …' The film then moves to a series of short scenes, first of different kinds of human and animal faces, then of different kinds of landscapes and cityscapes. Figure 9.5 analyses one of these, a scene showing faces of mothers with young children. It is marked off from the preceding and the following moves by a break in the music, a drum roll, and it contains three rhythmic phrases, three melody lines played on a flute. There are four shots, each beginning on the first pulse of a melodic phrase, except for the last one, which begins on the silent pulse that comes at the moment where a fourth phrase might be expected to begin, but where in fact the last note of the

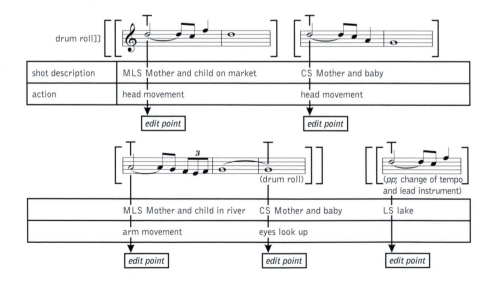

Figure 9.5 Rhythmic analysis of a scene cut to music

third phrase is lengthened to signal the end of the move. Note that in each shot the onset of the movements made by the people in the shot is synchronized to the music by means of the editing process. The transition to the next move is also signalled by a change in loudness and a change of tempo and instrumentation, as indicated in the transcript.

Here the rhythmic organization demarcates stages that form mini 'catalogues' – in the case of our excerpt a 'catalogue' of different mothers and children – within a larger 'catalogue' – a 'catalogue' of different 'faces' of the land and its inhabitants – in other words, the structure is thematic rather than narrative, a structure governed by creating contrasts and similarities between shots rather than chronological ordering.

To summarize:

- Rhythm divides the flow of time into *measures* of equal duration. Tempo results from the duration of these measures.
- Each measure begins with a *pulse*, a sound or movement which is 'stressed', made more prominent by means of loudness, pitch, relative duration, tension, etc., or by means of some form of increased vigour in movement. The pulses mark the sounds and movements which carry the greatest information value in the given context.
- Measures are grouped together in *phrases* of up to seven or eight measures. The phrases are marked off from each other by boundaries, breaks or changes in the regular rhythm of the pulses. These boundaries may be unobtrusive or strongly marked. The phrases demarcate communicative acts.
- Each phrase has a key pulse, the *main pulse*. The main pulse marks the key moment of the communicative act.
- Phrases are grouped together in *moves* of up to seven or eight phrases. These phrases are marked off from each other by boundaries that are perceptually more salient than phrase boundaries, for instance by longer pauses. The moves demarcate stages in the generic structure of the text or communicative event.
- Each move has a key phrase, the *main phrase*, which marks the crucial communicative act of the stage.

Rhythmic regularization

In everyday speech and movement the number of syllables and movements contained in each measure varies. If there are many syllables or movements in a measure they will be executed rapidly, if there are less they will be drawn out. This ensures that all measures are equally long, despite the different numbers of sounds or movements they contain. As far as tempo is concerned, while in music and dance the tempo remains constant for longer stretches of time, in everyday speech and movement it changes quite often. The example below is an excerpt from an informal interview with a newsreader (Van Leeuwen, 1984: 88). The number of syllables varies from one – for example, in 'em' – to five – for example, in 'not just because I'm'; the number of measures per phrase varies from one – again, 'em'– to three; and after the fourth phrase – 'far easier to read' – the tempo suddenly speeds up, to slow down again in the sixth phrase.

[*I*'ve read/ *news* at all/ *SORTS* of/ *pla*ces and the the//] [*blokes* that/ *write* the news/ *HERE*//] [*EM*//] [*CER*tainly//] [*far*/ *EA*sier to/ *read*//] [and that's/ *not* just because I'm/ *wor*king here/ *NOW*//] [than/ *A*ny news I've/ *read* anywhere/ *else*//]

When the same speaker changes to news reading, his speech becomes more regular. Now almost all the measures have three syllables, except for final measures, measures that conclude phrases. The number of measures per phrase also becomes more regular (four), and the tempo not only becomes faster, but also more constant:

[the con/ *tai*nership/ *A*sian Re/ *NOWN*//] [is/ *due* to leave/ *BRIS*bane to/ *day*//] [with a con/*sign*ment of u/ *ra*nium/ *YEL*lowcake//

In a textbook of broadcasting technique, a former head of training at the BBC condemned this kind of rhythmic regularization (Evans, 1972: 50): 'Newscasters sound monotonous simply because their speech rhythms are too regular'. But as all newsreaders do it, it cannot be because of a lack of skill. Perhaps newsreading, like other formal, official types of speech, *has to* sound impersonal and official. One way of achieving this is then to 'regulate' what should or should not be stressed, not on the basis of the amount of information in the to-be-stressed syllables, but on the basis of an impartial, mechanical 'rule', which will guarantee an impression of regularity.

In metric poetry, music and dance, rhythmic regularization goes even further. Metric poetry will have exactly the same number of syllables in every measure but the last, for instance two, as in this Gershwin song:

It's/ *ve*ry/ *clear*, our/ *love* is/ *here* to/ *stay*//

Or three, as in the Rogers and Hart song 'My Funny Valentine':

/*My* funny/ *Va*lentine,/ *sweet* comic/ *Va*lentine/
/*you* make me/ *smile* with my/ *heart*//

Or four, as in these lines from 'These Foolish Things':

A/ *ci*garette that/ *bears* a lip stick's/ *tra*ces//
An/ *air*line ticket/ *to* romantic/ *pla*ces//

The number of measures per phrase (line) may also be regularized, for example, four (tetrameter), as in 'My Favourite Things', or five (pentameter), or six (hexameter), or more.

/*Rain*drops on/ *ro*ses and/ *whis*kers on/ *kit*tens//
/*Bright* copper/ *ket*tles and/ *warm* woollen/ *mit*tens//

And finally there can be regularization of the number of phrases (lines) in a move (stanza).

The social semiotics of metre goes back to Aristotle's *Poetics*. For Aristotle metre had meaning. Some metres were 'high' and 'noble', others 'common' and 'ignoble', for example, the dactylic hexameter was 'heroic', while the 'iambic' and 'trochaic' were 'metres of movement':

> The heroic has dignity, but lacks the tones of the spoken language. The iambic is the very language of ordinary people, so that in common talk iambic lines occur oftener than any others: but in a speech we need dignity and the power of taking the hearer out of his ordinary self. The trochae is too much akin to wild dancing: we can see this in tetrameter verse, which is one of the trochaic rhythms.
>
> (Aristotle, 1954 [4th century BC]: 180–1)

Now as then, the significance of metrical patterns derives from the kind of sources I discussed in chapter 2, that is, either from provenance, from 'what the pattern reminds of', 'where it comes from' – for example, from 'the language of ordinary people' – or from experiential meaning potential, from the meaning latent in the pattern itself and in the actions needed to articulate it. In the case of monosyllabic stress, for instance, every syllable is stressed, and every syllable is therefore made equally important. This meaning potential is then narrowed down differently in different contexts. In one context everything may be stressed to convey excitement, in another for didactic reasons, to make sure that not a word will be missed. Grandmaster Flash in 'The Message' uses the pattern to convey exasperation, in a line whose long drawn-out monosyllabic rhythm clashes with the rhythm of the bass and the drums and contrasts with much of the rest of the song in which most measures have four syllables and a pulse coinciding with the main pulse of the drums – some/*times* it makes me/ *won*der how I/ *keep* from going/ *un*der//:

> *Don't*/ *push*/ *me*/ *I* / *am* / *close*/ *to* / *the* / *EDGE*//

The semiotic potential of tempo also derives from the meaning latent in the signifier, on the slow, medium or fast tempo itself. This then becomes more specific in context. The relatively high tempo of newsreading which I mentioned before helps convey the *recency* and *immediacy* of the news. As Raymond Williams (1974: 116) put it, in news, 'the sense of hurried transmission from all points establishes a sense of ... surprising and miscellaneous events coming in, tumbling over each other, from all sides.' But in other cases high rates of speech may illustrate the subject matter spoken about, for instance in horse racing and other types of sports commentary.

Musical tempo is usually held more or less constant for the whole of a piece. The amount of measures per phrase and the amount of phrases per move also tend to be regular – usually a multiple of four. The amount of notes per measure usually varies but there is nevertheless a regularity in that each measure is either counted in duple time – *one* two/ *one* two/ etc. – or in triple time – *one* two three/ *one* two three. In

Western music duple time has historically been associated with collective dances, especially procession dances such as the *allemande* and the *polonaise*. In the Baroque era collective dancing went into decline and the 'variety of the concrete types of movement (dance) narrowed down to a walk or promenade where only the mechanical continuity of the steps existed as the organising force of the community' (Marothy, 1974: 239). 'Collectivity' became a matter of public parades and military marches, rather than dances, and of the expression of national ideals rather than community values, as is the case, for instance, when people dance in a circle. Triple time is the more artificial metre. As most of the things we do – walking, running, etc. – have a binary rhythm, triple time is different from the everyday. This can then be 'coloured in' by the context. It can for instance become 'noble' or 'dignified' – high status is often signalled by artificiality. In dance, triple time became associated with the 'closed couple dance'. In older forms, such as the *volte* or the *minuet*, 'couple dancing' still involved some engagement with the whole group. Dancers would 'open out' towards the other people in the ballroom, bowing and gesturing towards them in stylized ways, but in the waltz the couple became a world on its own, physically together in the ballroom with others, yet not communicating with them, and behaving as if they did not exist, thus symbolizing the relative isolation of the 'nuclear family unit' from the community. In addition the waltz was seen as replacing the 'stiffness' and 'artificiality' of court dances, and creating space for self-expression and individuality. Thus rhythmic patterns helped symbolize what was then a new division in social life, or at least a much stronger division than before, the division between the public and the private, the regimented and the individually self-expressive, the communal and the romantic, which I also touched on in chapter 7 in relation to individual and social styles.

To summarize:

- Rhythmic structure can be regularized in four ways: (1) by regularizing the tempo, and/or (2) by regularizing the amount of sounds or movements per measure, and/or (3) by regularizing the amount of measures per phrase, and/or (4) by regularizing the amount of phrases per move. This allows many degrees and kinds of rhythmic regularization.
- The meaning of patterns of rhythmic regularization may be based on provenance, as for example, in the case of duple and triple time in music, or on experiential meaning potential, as for example, in case of the meanings of monosyllabic rhythm and tempo.

Semiotic time and social time

I will end this chapter by discussing three broader types of rhythmic patterning: (1) measured and unmeasured time, (2) metronomic and non-metronomic time, and (3) monorhythm and polyrhythm.

Measured and unmeasured time

The mode of rhythmic organization I have discussed so far is that of *measured time*, time you can tap your feet to, at least where it concerns the timing of human activities, because some of nature's rhythms are a bit too slow for feet tapping. But measured time has an 'other', *unmeasured time*, time which does not have a clear beat and appears to flow on continuously. Our vocal apparatus is in principle unable to produce such continuous noises because we must breathe from time to time, although we can produce an ongoing movement with our body, by swaying to and fro, or round and round. Unmeasured sound often has sacred significance, based, ultimately, on the fact that it is 'not human', which in a religious context is then narrowed down to 'more than human', 'divine'. Special instruments and techniques may be devised to produce such sacred sounds, for example, the pipe organ or the circular breathing technique of Aboriginal didgeridoo playing. Swaying the body also has sacred significance and often plays a central role in meditative practices.

Unmeasured time can have other meanings as well, and these will also derive from the given that unmeasured time is 'not human'. In music it may, for instance, be used to denote the grandeur of nature, or the vastness and loneliness of outer space – electronic drones. Measured and unmeasured time may also be combined. This happens for instance in classical Indian music. The *raga* begins with a continuous sound, a drone, on which, after a while, the measured timing of melodic phrases is superimposed. The drone is played on the tambura, a string instrument, and:

> ... is not supposed to be 'interesting', like the piano accompaniment to a modern song, but is the medium in which the melody lives, moves and has its being ... It is heard before, during and after the melody: it is ageless and complete which was in the beginning, is now and shall ever be.
>
> (Coomaraswamy, quoted in Tagg, 1984: 25)

Metronomic and non-metronomic time

In my discussion of the rhythmic coordination of image and sound in film, I might have given the impression that rhythmic coordination is *metronomic*, a matter of precise synchronization of the rhythms of image, music and sound being completely 'in step' with each other. But this is not necessarily always the case.

It is true that, in Western societies, there has been, over the past few centuries, an increasing stress on synchronization in social life. All kinds of activities began to be scheduled in minute detail to start and end at exact times to which all participants had to adhere if they were not to miss the beginning of the news, or the train, or worse if they were not to be frowned upon or penalized. Inevitably this increased stress on high synchronization and the 'metronomic' timing of social activities developed its 'other'. In private life, the demands of synchronization could be relaxed a little: to arrive all-too punctually at a party is misunderstanding the subtle and often unwritten rules of social time. In other words, two kinds of time developed, the metronomic time of work and public institutions – schools, hospitals, the media, etc. – and the less metronomic, freer time of private life. As a result people developed an acute sensitivity to the difference between 'objective' clock time that always progresses at the same speed, and subjective 'psychological' time, which feels as though it sometimes slows down and at other times speeds up. The difference between the two kinds of time became an important cultural theme exploited, for instance, in philosophy (for example, Bergson, 1965), in film, which is uniquely able to stretch or compress time for dramatic reasons, and also in music. One of the key 'sentimental' devices of nineteenth century 'salon music' – and many other kinds of music – is suspension, delaying pulsed notes that are significant in the melody. In the twentieth century leisure time music was deeply influenced by Afro-American music in which the accompaniment – the musical 'environment', one might say – does usually have a regular beat, but the soloists who express themselves *in* that environment will anticipate or delay the beat. As I have discussed in more detail elsewhere (Van Leeuwen, 1999: 58ff) classic jazz singers like Billie Holiday hardly ever time their words to coincide neatly with the beat. Tagg has described this as a 're-humanisation of time' and saw an element of subversion in it:

> Pulse beats can be missed out and strong beats in the metre anticipated by either half a beat, one beat or even two beats, this causing agogic effects which subvert the implacable exactitude of natural science, computers and clock time. Over this already partially rehumanised version of humanly produced regularity, other instruments (for example, cymbals, hi-hats, rhythm guitars, keyboards) perform riffs including accentuations at microcosmic loggerheads (out of phase by a quaver usually) with the implicit or explicit beat (pulse) ... The rhythms and sounds of our times are in this way brought to a higher degree of stylisation through this musical resocialisation.
>
> (Tagg, 1990: 112)

In other kinds of contemporary music, however, for instance in disco, there is, says Tagg, 'not the same extent of subversion of clock time, not the same human appropriation of the mechanical pulse' (1984: 31–2).

Monorhythms and polyrhythms

The example in this chapter might also have given the impression that rhythmic co-ordination always requires a single 'guide rhythm', a single 'clock' – baton of the conductor, rhythm of the drum machine, guide rhythm in a film sequence – to which all have to synchronize their watches, so to speak. It is true that this monorhythmic approach is still dominant in Western semiotic and social time. But it, too, does have an 'other', *polyrhythm*. In polyrhythm each person – each instrument, each of the tracks of the movie, etc. – follows his or her or its own internal clock. Imagine a large open square with people crossing in all directions, at their own pace, yet perfectly co-ordinated with each other as they weave in and out without ever colliding. Everyone follows their own rhythm yet the whole is co-ordinated, because everyone takes everyone else into account. Imagine what the trajectory of a person crossing that square would be like if all the other people were left out. He or she would seem to zigzag for no good reason – because we would no longer be able to see the rhythms of the other people in the square 'weaving in and out' which caused the zigzagging. The same is true for polyrhythmic music: the parts would make no sense on their own and 'give the impression of a rhythm tripping along clumsily or meaninglessly accented' (Chernoff, 1979: 52). Not surprisingly societies where polyrhythmic forms are domi-nant are what Hall (1983) has called 'polychronic' societies, societies where the regime of the clock has never become as dominant as it has, for instance, in North America and (especially Northern) Europe, and where people are better able to attend to several things at the same time, prioritize people and networks over procedures and schedules, and find many things more important than 'getting there on time'.

Two further aspects of polyrhythmic music must be discussed:

1   It is difficult for all participants to start at the same time. As Chernoff describes it (1979: 45, 47):

Instruments must find their entrance, not by counting from the main beat, but in relation to other instruments. The use of 'staggered' independent entrances in the cross-rhythmic relationships of the music indicates an important characteristic of African music.

2   There is no need for synchronization. Polyrhythm is semiotic pluralism. Different rhythms co-exist without having to conform to each other, and the 'beat' emerges from the way these rhythms engage and communicate with each other (Chernoff, 1979: 157). It is never stated and must be found by the listener, whose listening thereby becomes much more active than would be the case in monorhythmic music (ibid.: 50):

In African music, it is the listener or dancer who has to supply the beat: the listener must be actively engaged in making sense of the music. The music itself does not become the concentrated focus of an event, as at a concert.

Polyrhythmic music and dance forms such as salsa and other genres of Latin and African music are becoming increasing popular. If it is true that forms of musical timing are in an active relationship with forms of social timing, that musical timing reflects, enacts, celebrates, critiques, subverts or proposes forms of social timing, this interest in polyrhythmicality may signal that metronomic time and synchrony are losing their grip on social life. Although the remaining state institutions – schools, for instance – continue to enforce punctuality and fixed hours of attendance, in other spheres of life, including the workplace, time is becoming 'increasingly fragmented, heterogeneous and multiple' (Paolucci, 1996).

To summarize:

- Measured time is time with a regular pulse, time you can tap your feet to. It is also the time of human activities, including semiotic activities. Unmeasured time is a form of time in which no regular pulse can be discerned. Its meaning potential is 'out of time', and it is therefore often used to signify the 'eternal', the 'sacred', the 'supernatural', etc.
- Metronomic time is a form of measured time with very precise and unvarying timing, often aided or produced by mechanical or electronic technology. In non-metronomic time, metronomic timing is subverted by anticipating or delaying the beat or by other means, for instance local increases and decreases in tempo.
- Monorhythmic time is a form of measured time in which all the sounds and movements participating in a text or communicative event synchronize their timing to the same pulse. In polyrhythmic timing this does not happen. The participating sounds and movements use different, overlapping rhythms, without the whole becoming unstructured.
- Social time and semiotic time are closely related, with semiotic time symbolizing, enacting and celebrating (or critiquing and subverting) social time.

Exercises

1   Transcribe a short dialogue scene from a mainstream feature film – two minutes or so, with at least four or five cuts – following the method described in this chapter. What appears to have determined the choice of the edit points in this scene?
2   Record examples of rhythmically regularized speech – children's ditties, market vendors' chants, religious chants, etc. What kinds of rhythmic regularization are used and why?
3   Record some television commercials and try to ascertain what guides their rhythm – the guide rhythm may change in the course of a commercial.
4   Listen to the sounds of the city and of nature, and record your observations in a diary. Do you hear phrases or ongoing rhythms? Are the rhythms regular or irregular? Measured or unmeasured? (And so on.)
5   Record and mix two versions of a short sound piece, using sound effects and ambient sounds and only very minimal dialogue.
    The first version has three components. Track one has six or seven phrases articulating an event – for instance: (1) Actor opens and closes front door and walks outside. (2) Actor pauses. (3) Actor shouts 'Hey!' (4) Actor shouts 'NO!!!!' (5) Sound of brakes and impact of crash. (6) Pause. (7) Siren. Track two has the setting – for example, street atmosphere with traffic – and Track three contains a

few additional sounds, not directly related to the action and acting as percussive accents – for example, distant dog barks, or car horns, or gulls shrieking. Use the action of track one as the guide rhythm for positioning these accents.

For version two add a fourth track: music. Remix, using the music as the guide rhythm.

Evaluate the differences between the two tracks.

Note

Some of the material in this chapter was discussed in more detail in two earlier publications: 'Rhythmic Structure of the Film Text', in T.A. van Dijk, ed. (1985) *Discourse and Communication – New Approaches to the Analysis of Mass Media Discourse and Communication*, Berlin, Walter de Gruyter; and *Speech, Music, Sound*, London, Macmillan, 1999, chapter 3.

10 Composition

Although the term 'composition' is also used in relation to language and music, I use it here only in relation to semiotic modes that are articulated in space. Composition is about arranging elements – people, things, abstract shapes, etc. – in or on a semiotic space – for example, a page, a screen, a canvas, a shelf, a square, a city. As Arnheim (1974, 1982) has shown, it is based on our sense of balance, hence on a very physical and intuitive process, for instance the process of placing something exactly in the centre, or of getting something that is on the right and something that is on the left in perfect balance. But this process is at the same time a semiotic process: 'the function of balance can be shown only by pointing out the meaning it helps to make visible' (Arnheim, 1974: 27).

The elements of a picture or page layout are balanced on the basis of their *visual weight*. This 'weight' derives from their perceptual *salience*, which, in turn, results from a complex interaction, a complex trading-off relationship between a number of factors: relative size; sharpness of focus – or, more generally, amount of detail and texture shown; tonal contrast – areas of high tonal contrast, for instance borders between black and white, have high salience; colour contrasts – for instance the contrast between highly saturated and 'soft' colours, or the contrast between red and blue; placement in the visual field – elements not only become 'heavier' as they are moved up, but also appear to be 'heavier' the further they are moved towards the left, due to an asymmetry in the visual field; perspective – foreground objects are more salient than background objects and elements that overlap other elements are more salient than the elements they overlap; and also quite specific cultural factors, such as the appearance of a human figure or a potent cultural symbol, which may override pure perceptual salience.

In symmetrical compositions left and right are evenly balanced, but balance becomes more eventful when one side is visually heavier than the other so that the balancing centre has to be shifted away from the geometrical centre of the space. Achieving and maintaining balance in unbalanced situations is a fundamental human experience, a basic given of our existence as biped creatures, and as a result our sense of balance informs all our activities including our semiotic activities. It forms an indispensable matrix for the production and reception of spatially articulated messages. It is also the source of our aesthetic pleasure in composition. The pleasure we derive from moving elements about until the result feels 'just right', or in arranging things to perfection in front of a camera lens, is directly related to the pleasure of almost losing and then regaining balance which we experience as children when we are lifted up and swung through the air, or when we swing on a swing until it moves so high that by right we should fall off, yet still hold on, a pleasure which Freud has famously related to sexuality (1977 [1905]: 121). It is even more directly related

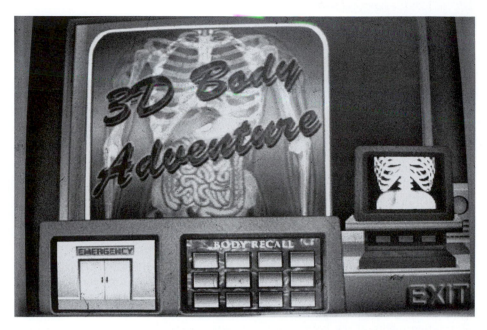

Figure 10.1   Page from 3D Body Adventure (Knowledge Adventures, 1993)

to the pleasure which, as children, and not only as children, we experience when we build with blocks and explore how far we can go in unbalancing things before a structure topples over. In actual buildings elements which seem to hover on the edge of losing balance, and yet maintain it, are often sites of power – the balcony, jutting out from the wall, on which the monarch will appear, or the pulpit, jutting out from the pillar of the cathedral, from the which the priest will hold his sermon: challenging gravity is itself a source of salience.

Figure 10.1 shows the first screen of a CD-ROM titled '3D Body Adventure'. It is a very multimodal composition, combining verbal/typographical, pictorial, musical – there is a softly tinkling melody in the background – and kinetic elements – the picture of the skeleton is slowly rotating. The top of the screen shows a range of media on a desktop. A slide is projected on a screen. A video monitor shows an animated sequence. Half-hidden behind the monitor, a loudspeaker plays soft music. In other words, the top part of the semiotic space represents what we might call 'information media', media to read, look at and listen to. The bottom part of the screen, on the other hand, represents things the user can *do*. It offers games to play, media to interactively engage with. 'Emergency', for instance, is a game which mixes laser surgery and the shooting gallery – the player zaps brain cells in a race against time – 'Hurry doctor, save the patient'. And in 'Body Recall' body parts must be matched with their names. Thus the composition of the screen uses the vertical dimension to separate information-as-knowledge from information-as-action, or information-as-education from information-as-entertainment. Exactly the same use of space can be observed in many other contexts. In school textbooks the exercises, test questions and assignments – the things students must *do* – tend to be found on the bottom of the page. In advertisements the coupons which readers can cut out, fill in and send off, or the telephone numbers they can ring and the addresses where they can buy the product, are all on the bottom of the page.

But the composition does not only separate out these two elements, it also gives them a specific value in relation to each other. It makes 'knowledge' and 'education' something that is '*up*' and '*high*', and entertainment something that is '*down*' and '*low*'. 'Up' and 'down' are basic dimensions of our spatial experience. But they have also acquired a wide range of metaphorical extensions, in our everyday language as well as in other semiotic forms. Lakoff and Johnson (1980) devote a whole chapter to 'up' and 'down' metaphors. 'Up' can stand for positive affects, and power, but also for an excess of abstraction and unworldly idealism – 'head in the clouds'. 'Down' can stand for negative affects and a lack of power, but also for a realistic, 'down-to-earth', 'feet on the ground' attitude. As a first approximation to the meaning of 'up' and 'down' in figure 10.1, we might say that 'entertaining activities' are here represented as 'consolidating' – giving a firm '*footing*' or' *grounding*' to – authoritatively presented ('*high*') knowledge. Reversing the two, putting the games on top and the information media at the bottom, would create a very different meaning, perhaps something like 'knowledge provides a foundation ("*grounding*") for ("*highly*" regarded) active experiences'.

The screen also uses the horizontal dimension to separate the domain of the still image, on the left, from the domain of the animated '3D' image on the right. In addition the left is the domain of what has already been formulated *for* the users, while the right is the domain of what users can do *themselves*, because they can rotate the skeleton with their mouse so as to view the image from any angle and exit the screen at will. Note that the monitor straddles the boundary between 'up' and 'down': like interactive games, user-activated 3D viewing still has some entertainment value because of its novelty, but, like information media, it also has instruction value – the animated skeleton can serve as a stand-in for an actual skeleton and make a good learning aid for students. In other words, as we move from right to left, we move from the traditional 2D diagram or drawing to the new, animated 3D diagram or drawing and from the traditional passive learner to the new, active learner.

Finally there is foreground and background: the loudspeaker is placed *behind* the monitor in keeping with the role that sound and image play here. All of the information is provided visually and the soundtrack only offers soft background music. But foreground and background do not only exist in naturalistically represented spaces such as the desktop depicted here. They exist whenever one element overlaps another. They also exist, for instance, when words are superimposed on a picture: the picture then becomes a background, a context for the words. And they exist in the case of frames-within-the-frame, such as the frame that contains the 'Emergency' and 'Body Recall' games: interactive games are literally and figuratively *foregrounded* over traditional information media, represented as positioned 'in the environment of' more traditional media and modes of presentation.

In the next few sections I will discuss these dimensions of semiotic space one by one: horizontality, verticality, centrality, and 'the third dimension'.

Given and new

Throughout history and across different cultures, the distinction between left and right has been an important source of meaning and often also of morality. In his article 'Left and Right in Icon Painting', Uspensky (1975: 37) quotes many examples in which the left is associated with negative and the right with positive moral values: 'On the right the righteous proceed in joyfulness into Paradise, on the left the sinners go into torment'; 'On the right or good side is Mount Sinai, on the left or bad side Mount Lebanon'. But 'good' and 'bad' are not the only meanings we give to left and right. Left is also associated with the past, and right with the present – time moves from left to right. When there is both 'general' and 'specific' information, the 'general' is usually placed on the left, and the 'specific' on the right. Apparently left and right can take on many different meanings, even within the same cultural tradition.

Perhaps this is because the difference between left and right is not as obvious as that between up and down. As children we have to learn to tell our right from our left. Like most natural objects, our bodies are balanced, horizontally symmetrical. The actual slight asymmetry of human faces usually surprises people. It has to be pointed out before it is noticed, except in the case of extreme asymmetry which is usually considered ugly. Human action, on the other hand, *does* bring left and right into play. Many activities are executed with one hand only and not only is there no equality between left and right in this matter, the 'proper' division of labour between the two hands is important enough to warrant detailed description in the sacred books of the culture: 'Then the priest shall take some of the log of oil, and pour it into the palm of his own left hand, and dip his right finger into the oil that is in his left hand' (Leviticus 14: 15–16).

Another key source of meaning is the direction in which we write. In spoken language, sentences – and larger chunks of speech – begin with the 'Given', with something that has already been mentioned or is assumed to be known by the listener, and then move to the 'New', to the information the speaker wants to impart (Halliday, 1985: 277). When we move from speech to writing, 'before' and 'after' are 'transcoded' as 'left' and 'right', at least in Western writing. The examples below link two ideas together: 'the idea of eternal return' and the 'mysterious nature' of that idea. The first sentence is most likely to be used in a context where 'the idea of eternal return' has already been introduced and explained. The 'mysteriousness' of that idea would be the *new* information here. The second sentence is most likely to be used in the context of a discussion of 'mysterious ideas'. We would already know that we are getting information about mysterious ideas, but we would not yet have heard about this particular mysterious idea. Thus putting things on the left or the right is a way of conveying information value, of indicating the relevance of information for particular listeners or readers or viewers in particular contexts.

    The idea of eternal return is a mysterious one
    GIVEN →   NEW

    The most mysterious idea of all is the idea of eternal return
    GIVEN →   NEW

    The given and new principle is not restricted to language. In music, the first few notes of a series of musical phrases often repeat themselves, perhaps with minor variations. What determines 'where the music goes' – up or down in pitch, into which harmonic territory, etc. – is the notes with which each phrase culminates, as shown in figure 10.2, where the 'new' moments are moving up by half a step each time.

Figure 10.2 Given and new in musical phrases

    Or imagine a typical piece of screen acting. An actor enters a room, walks across to a table, then picks up a note someone has left there for him, reads it and frowns. The first part of the 'action phrase' is predictable and contains little information. It is what one would expect anyone to do when coming home. The new on the other hand provides the action which will move the plot forward and make a difference to what follows.

    Actor walks to table in middle of room, then picks up a note and frowns
    GIVEN →   NEW

In the same way, 'before' and 'after' become 'left' and right' not only in writing but in all (Western) space-based semiotic modes. Slimming advertisements using a 'before'–'after' approach show the 'not-yet-slim' model on the left and the successfully slimmed-down model on the right. The left is not only before, it is also given, and as such relates the information to the viewer: 'this is you as you are now' – or maybe 'if this is you as you are now, read on'. The right is not only after but also new: 'this is what you can become if you use our product'. However, similar advertisements in Chinese language magazines reverse the order, and have the before on the right and the after on the left.

Figure 10.3   Front page of *Täglich Alles*

Laying the table is another spatially based semiotic mode. The sociologist Norbert Elias has described its history. In 1530 Erasmus wrote about table manners in a treatise called *On Civility for Boys*: 'Your goblet and knife, duly cleansed, should be on the right, your bread on the left,' (quoted in Elias, 1978: 89). Two centuries later, LaSalle wrote a similar treatise, *The Rules of Decency and Christian Civilisation*. Spoon and fork had now been added: 'The spoon, fork and knife should always be placed on the right' (ibid.: 97). One thing remained constant. The utensils that constituted something new had to be on the right, whereas the traditional bread, still broken by hand, remained on the left.

Figure 10.3 shows a typical front page from the Austrian newspaper *Täglich Alles*. The top section of the page has a clear given–new structure. The left contains mainly words: the masthead, in blue, and the editorial, printed on a cream ground. The right contains a large, salient photo of a celebrity, usually from the world of show business or sport. In other words, the dynamics is from the traditional 'fourth estate' role of the newspaper and the verbal nature of its discourse, to the new role of the press as a much more visually oriented local adjunct to the global worlds of show business, consumption, tourism, sport, and so on. It is the latter which is both most salient and new.

To summarize, if two elements are polarized – one representing one kind of thing, the other another – then the element placed on the left will be presented as though it is given, that is, although it is something already known to the receiver of the message and hence not in question. The element on the right will be presented as new, that is, as something not yet known to the receiver and hence the important part of the message, and the part that might potentially be acted on, that might for instance be denied or confirmed, or followed up by some other action. Note that the given is never *objectively* given, nor the new *objectively* new. Things are *treated as* given or new in the context of a specific communication situation.

Ideal and real

In contrast to left and right, 'up' and 'down' are fundamentally different in our everyday experience. Like most things in nature, the human body is vertically asymmetrical. In our environment there is always the chasm between the heavens above, eternal and unchanging – from our human perspective at least – and the earth below, constantly changing, constantly giving and taking life. It is no wonder that metaphors of verticality play such a role in construing and maintaining social difference. People with power become the 'high and mighty', the 'upper' classes, people without power the 'lower' classes, and at the 'bottom' of the social hierarchy we find people who are 'down and out'. The thrones, pulpits and benches of kings, priests and judges are elevated above the seats of others and, in many cultures, the low have to lower themselves even further by bowing or prostrating themselves before their rulers. Towers and tall buildings are symbols of power everywhere – the Tower of Babel made even the Almighty worry that His power would be challenged. To complicate matters further, verticality is tinged with moral values, so that 'high' becomes good and 'low' bad – and also with pleasure, so that 'high' and 'up' come to stand for positive, pleasurable affects, and 'down' and 'low' for negative feelings. But there is another side to this. 'High' may become too high – too abstract or too idealistic, too 'ethereal', no longer touching base. And 'low' can be positive, for instance when it is associated with 'keeping your feet on the ground' and a realistic 'down-to-earth' attitude.

Left and right are dynamic and action-oriented. On the horizontal plane we can move in every direction with equal facility. The action painter Jackson Pollock apparently worked on the floor. 'I feel nearer, more a part of the painting, since this way I can walk around it, work from the four sides, and literally be in the painting' (quoted in Arnheim, 1974: 32). Aboriginal sand painters also worked this way. The horizontal plane is the plane of activity, or of the floorplan, the map, on which the trajectories of activities can be marked. The vertical plane, on the other hand is the plane of the spectacle, or of the façade of the building, the plane on which static categories are fixed and spatial order and structure created. Gravity comes into play here. Movement requires effort and cannot flow as freely.

It is from this complex of actual bodily experiences of high and low that the semiotic use of 'high' and 'low' in composition derives. In Kress and Van Leeuwen (1996) we adopted the term 'ideal' for 'high', for the upper section of the semiotic space and the term 'real' for the lower section. It is difficult to formulate the principle that unites the many different – although always related and motivated – values which 'ideal' and 'real' can assume in actual communicative practices. This is the formulation we came up with (ibid.: 193): When a composition polarizes top and bottom, placing different, perhaps contrasting, elements in the upper and lower sections of the semiotic space, the elements placed on top are presented as the ideal and those placed at the bottom as the real. For something to be ideal means that it is presented as the idealized or generalized essence of the information – and that means that it is usually also its ideologically most salient part. The real is then opposed to this in that it presents more specific information – for example, details – and/or more down-to-earth information – for example, photographs as documentary evidence, or maps, or statistics – and/or more practical information – for example, practical consequences, directions for action, etc.

Like given and new, ideal and real are multimodal concepts. The ideal–real structure can integrate different semiotic modes such as text and image into a single, unified multimodal design as well as integrate elements belonging to a single semiotic mode, for instance boxes and arrows in diagrams. A 1937 photo by the American photographer Arthur Rothstein shows, in the upper section, a wall with a large Frisian clock and a calendar. In the lower zone we see a railway clerk, slaving away at his desk, dwarfed and dominated by the clock. The clerk is the real, but the ideal and ideological essence of the photograph as a whole is the oppressive regime of clocktime, as symbolized by the clock and the calendar.

In figure 10.3 the headlines, traditionally ideal in any newspaper, have been demoted and replaced by the given–new structure I discussed earlier, that is by a combination of opinion and show business. However, they do remain the real without which a newspaper cannot be a newspaper. Within the bottom part of the page there is a further vertical division, with the headline as ideal, and some advertisements and announcements – practical matters, in other words – as real.

Centre and margin

So far I have discussed aspects of composition in which the semiotic space is polarized, in which one kind of thing is put on the left and another on the right, or one kind of thing on top and another at the bottom. The villages of the Winnebago Indians are polarized in this way (see figure 10.4). A line, running from north west to south east divides the village into two parts, the part where the *wageregi* ('those who are above') live and the part where the *manegi* ('those who are below') live. Lévi-Strauss called this a 'diametric' – as opposed to a 'concentric' – structure and noted that it is a

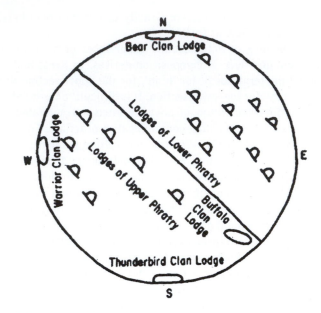

Figure 10.4   Winnebago village (from Lévi-Strauss, 1963)

common structure in North and South America and in Melanesia, and usually associated with inequality: 'We find words such as superior and inferior, elder and younger, noble and commoner, strong and weak, etc. ... used to describe them' (Lévi-Strauss, 1963: 139).

Composition does not always involve division and polarization. It may also gather its elements around a centre that will connect them and hold them together. In the villages of the Omarakana of northwestern Melanesia (figure 10.5), described by Malinowski (1929: 10), the centre of the village is the plaza, the space of the public and festive and sacred activities in which all participate. Around it are the yam storehouses, still strongly involved in sacred rituals and surrounded by taboos. On the outer edge are the huts of the married couples, the 'profane' part of the village, as Malinowski says. In other words, the more central a space, the more important, the more sacred, and the more public and integrative the activities which take place in it. But the centre is not opposed to the margin. It holds together what is arranged around it and creates a relationship of equality between the elements *within* a given concentric circle – for instance between the married couples in their huts.

Wherever people or things or buildings are arranged in space, there is a choice whether to polarize or to centralize. Sometimes both can exist at the same time. Lévi-Strauss (1963: 134–5) noted that different informants from the Winnebago tribe describe their villages differently. Those from the upper phratry stress the dividing line, those from the lower phratry stress centrality. And both are right, said Lévi-Strauss: these villages have a 'dual' organization. This should not surprise us. Many

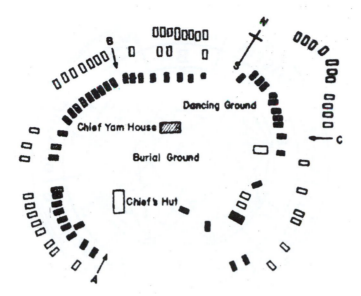

Figure 10.5   Omarakana village (from Malinowski, 1929)

modern cities have both a central business district to which people travel from the suburbs, and a dividing line with, say, the suburbs north of the river, or close to the coast, being more prestigious, and the suburbs south of the river, or further inland, less prestigious.

Centre and margin form another multimodal semiotic principle, a principle which can apply to the way buildings are arranged in a village, the way items of furniture are arranged in a room; to the way people arrange themselves in rooms or halls to tell stories, teach lessons, dance dances, perform music, etc. It can apply to the way objects are arranged in an exhibition or on a desk or table. It can also apply to the way things are arranged on a page or on a canvas or a screen. The traditional Hebrew scriptures, for example, had the oldest text, the Mishna in the centre, the Gemara written around it, and later, medieval commentaries again arranged around the Gemara. This creates relations between texts – and the activity of creating texts – that mirror the relations between people who are seated in concentric circles in a hall. Or look at the composition of paintings: in Byzantine art Christ would be placed in the centre, with Saints arranged around Him; in Buddhist art a central figure would be surrounded by subordinates (Arnheim, 1982: 207). The diagrams of the thirteenth century Spanish philosopher, Ramon Lull, were also based on the centre/margin principle. The one shown in figure 10.6, for instance, describes the attributes of God: the letter 'A' represents God, the other letters his divine attributes – B for *bonitas*, 'goodness', C for *magnitudo*, 'greatness', and so on. Other similar diagrams had 'virtue' in the centre, or 'wisdom'. Clearly in such diagrams there is no sense of opposition

Figure 10.6 Diagrammatic representation of God's attributes (Ramon Lull, c. 1235–1315)

between the concepts in the outer ring, between 'goodness' and 'greatness' for example. They all belong to, all gain their identity from, and lend their identity to, the central concept, just as the workers in the central business district both enact the sacred activity of 'work' and gain their social identity from it.

Precisely because its use extends over so many different semiotic modes, it is difficult to formulate the core meaning of the centre–margin model of composition. It is only in specific contexts that this meaning becomes fully defined. But perhaps it is possible to say this: if a composition makes significant use of the centre, placing one element in the middle and the other elements around it – or placing elements around an 'empty' centre – the centre is presented as the nucleus of what is communicated, and the elements that flank it, the margins, are presented as in some sense subservient to it, or ancillary to it, or dependent on it.

Note that there are degrees of marginality: just how marginal the margins are depends on their salience relative to the salience of the centre, and on their distance from the centre. Centrality, on the other hand, does not admit degrees. Even when the centre is empty, it will continue to exist *in absentia*, as the invisible pivot around which everything else turns. Think of sitting in a circle: physically there is nothing in the centre, but the topic discussed or the story told somehow fills the empty space and holds the group together in its shared orientation towards that 'empty' centre. It will be interesting to see whether the already quite noticeable trend towards circularity in postmodern architecture and industrial design will continue and expand beyond the merely symbolic – the curved gable, or the shape of a car radiator grille – and move into other domains where the rectangle used to rule.

In many cases the margins are identical or at least very similar to each other, so that there is no sense of polarization, no sense of division between given and new, or ideal and real. However, it also happens that centre and margin combine with given and new and/or ideal and real and in that case there is both centrality and polarization.

The most common mode of combining given and new with centre–margin is the triptych. In many medieval triptychs there is no sense of given and new. The centre shows a key religious theme, such as the crucifixion or the Virgin and Child, and the side panels show saints or donors kneeling in admiration. The composition is symmetrical rather than polarized. From the sixteenth century, altar pieces became more narrative and showed, for instance, the birth of Christ or the road to Golgotha on the left panel, the crucifixion in the Centre, and the resurrection on the right panel. This could involve some polarization, albeit subordinated to the temporal order, with the left, for instance, as the 'bad' side – for example, the transgression of Adam – the right as the 'good' side – for example, the ascent of the blessed – and the middle panel representing Christ's role as mediator and Saviour – for example, the crucifixion.

The triptychs in contemporary compositions, whether in art or elsewhere, tend to be polarized, with a given on the left, a new on the right and the central element as mediator, as bridge and link between the two extremes. Perhaps the tendency towards polarization has been a by-product of the bourgeois era and its emphasis on binary oppositions in many spheres of life, in government, in forms of reasoning and arguing, in forms of narrative structure and music, etc. Many of these are now being dismantled and it will be interesting to see whether a move towards less antagonistic and more holistic models will see centre–margin structures return to favour, perhaps in a form that allows the interlocking of multiple centres.

Figure 10.7 shows a triptych from a German social studies high-school textbook. 'production' is given, 'pollution' new. The everyday activities of the consumer form the mediator, the link between the two, in a structure that would seen to lay the blame primarily on the wasteful habits of the consumer: 'Was belastet die Umwelt, wenn Menschen essen?' asks the text, and 'Was belastet die Umwelt, wenn Menschen fahren?' and 'wenn Menschen wohnen?' – 'How do our eating habits affect the environment?' 'How do our driving habits affect the environment?' 'How do our homes affect the environment?'

The third dimension

So far I have considered the composition of two-dimensional semiotic spaces. Adding the third dimension provides further choices – the choice between placing an element on the front or the back, on the left or the right side, and so on. Each of these sides will of course be itself structured according to given and new and/or ideal–real and/or centre–margin. But each will also form part of a larger, three-dimensional structure.

Figure 10.7   Double page from V. Nitzschke, *Politics – Learning and Acting for Today and Tomorrow*, vol. 1

Consider first the information value of front and back. In our everyday experience of the world front and back are not always polarized. Trees do not have a front and a back – although leaves usually do. They are essentially the same from every side. If they acquire a front and a back, it is subjectively, in relation to something else which produces a favoured point of view for an observer. In the botanical garden the front will be the side which has the label with the Latin name of the tree. In the park it will be the side that faces the path. In the garden it will be the side that faces the house. The same can be said of many objects and buildings. Bottles and cans have a front and a back only if a label is applied to one side of the bottle – this then becomes the most semioticized and the most decorated side, the side that will face shoppers on the supermarket shelf. The Queen Victoria Building in Sydney, in its latest reincarnation as a shopping centre, does not have a front and a back. Every side is identical, with a central entrance and shop windows on each side. Many modern blocks of flats lack a clearly distinguishable front and back. Even sculptures may be composed in the round, offering essentially the same view from whichever side we approach them, for instance sculptures of the 'Three Graces'.

Other things in nature do have a front and a back, most notably (to us) the human body. There is no doubt that many semiotic uses of front and back derive from the difference between the front and the back of the human body. The front of the body is the side which announces our identity, which shows the world who we are and how we want to be read, and which expresses our reaction to and interaction with that world. It is also the side toward which all our sensory organs are oriented, the side that takes in the world as image, sound, smell, food. The back, by comparison, is semiotically poor. Even our clothes have few signs, few 'insignia' on the back. The back is also the side of the excretion of waste products. The use of front and back in the design of many of our buildings is modelled on this, with the front as the façade, the public side, the side which gives the world a message about who lives in the building or what activities go on in it, and the back as the private side, the side where there is no need for keeping up appearances, where the plumbing can be seen, and where the empty bottles pile up – which is why buildings that flaunt their plumbing, such as the Pompidou Centre, are such a strong example of architectural 'anti-language', almost as if they show us their bottoms. Computers, hi-fis, refrigerators, washing machines, and so on, are similarly only semiotic, only designed for display, on the front. The back is the non-semiotic side, the functional side, where cables and hoses are connected.

While this already begins to give a sense of the 'information value' of front and back, there are other possibilities to be considered. On the back of packages, for instance, we often find instructions for use, and/or more or less detailed descriptions or specifications of the content of the packages, or lists of ingredients. The back cover of books may have a table of contents, or a summary of the content of the book. But even here the back is still more functional than the front, still concerned with the use rather than the identity of the object.

In short, a three-dimensional composition may either:

1   not use the opposition between front and back, refuse to polarize, and so favour material, tactile semiotics over visual semiotics
2   weakly polarize, with front and back distinct, but both facing the world, both semiotic
3   have a distinct 'face', a side which defines the identity of the composition, and a distinct 'support', a side which is not meant for display, the side we turn to the wall when we display the composition.

This does not mean that it has to be entirely non-semiotic, like the back of a painting or a relief sculpture. It may be plain and unadorned, like the back of a souvenir T-shirt or coffee-mug, items which have a message on the front and are plain on the back.

There is still much that communicates here – colour, material, overall shape, but it is the same message that is also communicated by the front.

What about the right and the left side of three-dimensional objects? Remember first of all that many three-dimensional objects – trees, perfectly round buildings, bottles, balls – are the same all round and do not have distinct left and right sides. They can at best acquire sides in relation to a front – the front entrance of a round building for instance, or the label of a bottle. Second, if there are sides, they may be hidden from view in ways that fronts and backs rarely are, as in the case of terraced houses, Lego blocks, people linking arms in a barn dance. Even if the sides are visible, they are often symmetrical rather than a site for the creation of difference, semiotically poor, feature-less, empty spaces between front and back. Even freestanding buildings tend to have few features on their left and right sides, unless they lack differentiation between their sides, as in a fort or an Australian farmhouse with a verandah all round – isolated build-ings which must present an alert face in every direction.

In the human body, the arms (together with the ears) form the most lateral feature, and for this reason laterality is often associated with action. Clothes may have lateral pockets, and certain action-oriented objects – key rings, pistol holsters, swords – are worn on – and present their face to – the side, usually the right side. If the design of an object accords different functions and values to left and right, there is a tendency for the left to be associated with 'being', with what the object *is*, and with static acts such as 'holding', and the right with what an object can *do* or what you can do with an object, and with more dynamic acts such as 'using', 'opening, 'pouring', etc. Cups and jugs with a front, hence with a 'designed-in' left and right often – although by no means always – have the handle on the left and the spout on the right, and when packages open on the side it is often the right side. But the use of left and right is not as strictly coded as that of front and back, and there are so many variants and exceptions that it is difficult to capture the 'information value' of the left and right sides with labels of the kind that we have used for other zones of semiotic space. It is as if the functions of the sides derive from the functions of the front and the back which have spilled over to the flanks, in different degrees and with or without polarization. In other words, the sides may function as subsidiaries to either face or support, either meaning or function, either identity or operationality – or, if the face has a given–new struc-ture, as subsidiaries of that given and new. However, at times their use seems random, as if they are a place for putting things that do not have a clear space of their own – translations, patent numbers, addresses, etc. Perhaps the relative instability of left and right derives from their interchangeability. Whether the handle of a cup is on the right depends, after all, on where I put that cup. This can never be the case with front and back. If there is a front, it will remain the front even when it is turned away from me.

The bottom, the underneath, is a side we normally do not see. It is rarely semiotic. Even when elevated from the ground, as with the underneath of a table or a car, it is purely functional, not designed to be displayed or to communicate. At best, it carries a serial number or manufacturer's address. One of the reasons why we do not have any sense of a semiotics of the underneath may be that the human body has hardly any

Figure 10.8   Lexmark carton

underneath left: what was underneath, and hidden, became the front as we stood up and became bipedal.

As the 'crowning element', the top can be very significant. Few things are quite as elaborately and richly semiotic as hats, wigs, hairdos, etc. In addition, the top is often a cover, something which can be taken off to reveal an inside and a content. The lid of a jar can be taken off to give access to the jam. The lid of the box can be opened to reveal the jewellery. The hat can be taken off to reveal the person. But when the object is of equal size or larger than we are, the top will communicate only insofar as it can be seen from the front. So rarely do we have access to the top down angle that many objects are hard to recognize from this angle. Smaller objects, too, may be designed to be viewed from the sides. At the same time, in many other objects the top view replaces the front view. The face of the box, the biscuit tin, the bedspread and the coffin are all found on the top. Any decorations on the sides will be subsidiaries. This again shows that the information value of the various aspects of three-dimensional objects depends on the relation between the objects and those who 'read' and/or use them – the relative size of object and reader/user, the reader/user's point of view with regard to the object, the reader/user's actions on or with the object, etc.

To sum up, in any object in which front and back are polarized, there will always be a face and a support and they will spill over to the sides to different degrees. The left may be a subsidiary of the face, the right of the support, or the left of the given of the face, and the right of the new of the face. The underneath, finally, will never be semiotic.

The box containing the ink cartridge for my printer can serve as an example (figure 10.8). The front is the face, with the brandname/logo as the ideal, and a picture of the

Figure 10.9   Hour of the Traces (Alberto Giacometti, 1930)

product as the real. On the back the ideal is a text mixing description and praise of the product ('superior print quality') and the real two photographs to document this print quality. The sides carry practical information – such as printer compatibility and the word colour in 10 languages. The top doubles as face, carrying the brandname/logo – the packet has clearly been designed to be seen either from the front or from the top. The bottom carries the barcode and some further small print – the place of manufacture, the recyclability of the package.

Giacometti's *Hour of the Traces* (figure 10.9) is an open three-dimensional structure. Such a structure sets up the relation between an interior and an exterior, a 'core' and an 'enclosure'. The meaning of core and enclosure is not quite the same as that of centre and margin. The core is more than just the centre, it is the living heart, the animating principle. Giacometti's sculpture can be read as a representation of the body. The body is a rigid, rusty frame, with – as the ideal – a sensory organ, a kind of antenna with an abstract eye, and with – as its Core – a plaster heart, suspended on a thin string and moving slightly to and fro.

There are evidently degrees of openness. The core can be vulnerable and exposed within an open, or at least transparent, enclosure. This is the fascination of the treasure in its glass display case, the ship inside the bottle, the fossil embedded in amber. The core may also be invisible, yet known to be there, as in the Old Testament Tabernacle, where God's testimony rests inside the Ark and the Ark behind the veil of the most holy place in the Tabernacle – and as in the enclosures of countless other treasures and relics. In between there are, for instance, peepshows such as I made as a child from shoeboxes, with a small aperture to look through and coloured cellophane on top to bathe the core in a mysterious light. All these examples do, of course, reveal that core–enclosure is yet again a multimodal principle. In the case of the ark, for instance, words are the core, and an ark decorated with golden cherubs the enclosure. The opposite is equally possible.

A final aspect of three-dimensionality is foreground and background. As this can also be represented in two dimensions, the third dimension does not add new meanings here. The background is not only less salient than the foreground and, literally as well as figuratively, more 'distant' from the viewer, it is also acts as a context for the foreground, an environment that specifies its relevance and applicability. This is evident in the case of naturalistic images. But it is equally true when there is no naturalistic link between foreground and background, as when words are superimposed on a picture, or background pictures in a television news broadcast.

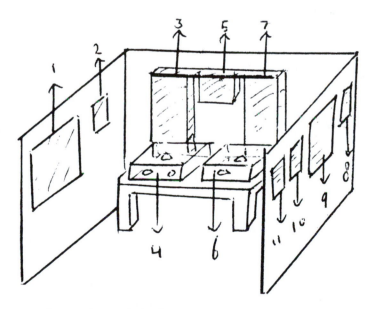

Figure 10.10   Composition of the first room in the Royal Observatory Museum, Greenwich

Composition and the viewer

Figure 10.10 sketches the composition of the first of the rooms of the Royal Observatory in Greenwich, London, which has been converted into a museum.

Entering the room, visitors face a kind of triptych. Two text panels flank a colour computer animation (5) of the building of the observatory. On the left, hence given (3), is a text panel explaining how King Charles II ordered the observatory to be built in 1675, in order to solve the problem of longitude by means of more accurate charts of the moon and the stars. On the right, hence new (7), is a text panel explaining the hazards of sea journeys at that time. The glass case below this triptych contains related artiefacts, on the left (4) documents and medaillons that once belonged to King Charles II, on the right (7) a ship's log from the period. With a very dark painting of the building of the observatory (1) and an engraved portrait of King Charles II, the left wall is a subsidiary of the given. The right wall is a subsidiary of the new, with a chart showing the erratic course of ships at that time (8), a gloomy painting of a storm at sea (9), and engraved portraits of Sir Christopher Wren (10) – the architect of the Observatory – and John Flamsteed (11) – the first Astronomer Royal. Overall, the room has a given–new structure. Given is the observatory itself and the English monarchy, new is what will become the theme of the museum as a whole: the solving of the problem of longitude.

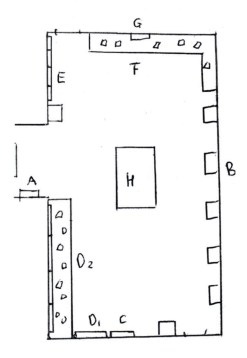

Figure 10.11   Composition of the final room in the Royal Observatory Museum, Greenwich

Figure 10.11 shows the composition of the last of the rooms in the part of the museum that deals with the longitude problem. This room has a centre–margin structure. The centre (H) is a very large turret clock, with a ship's bell ringing the hour. The mechanism is visible, encased in glass. Around it are various, only loosely related exhibits: an illuminated world map showing the time zones around the world (A), a short history of 'Greenwich Mean Time' (B), a short history of linear time (D), an overview of different ways of keeping time (F), and more. This room is much more varied, and much less tightly structured than the room shown in figure 10.10.

Observing how visitors negotiate these rooms is interesting. Here is a brief account of what 60 visitors did in each of the two rooms. On entering the room shown in figure 10.10 all but one of the visitors went straight to the triptych, watched the animation, read both panels, and glanced at the objects in the glass case. Only one visitor started with the left subsidiary, and looked at all the exhibits. Thirty-eight of the visitors did not even glance at the right subsidiary, 13 glanced briefly, on their way out, and nine studied exhibits 8 to 11 more carefully. Clearly the layout of this room played a large role in structuring how the visitors traversed it and what they did and did not look at.

Things were quite different in the room shown in figure 10.11. On entering this room, people immediately face the centre piece, but only nine visitors went up to it to have a closer look. The rest glanced at it for a brief moment and then either turned left (21 visitors) or right (30 visitors) – note that to see the two chronologically ordered exhibits, B and D, in the right order you would have to turn left. Here there was no common pattern either in what the visitors did and did not look at, or in the order in which they surveyed the exhibits. They criss-crossed freely through the room, everybody finding their own trajectory. It looks as if the 'non-polarized', circular centre–margin structure does not impose a single pattern of attention in the way the room shown in figure 10.10 does.

Earlier in this chapter I said that compositions structure the 'information value' of their elements, both in relation to each other and in relation to their viewers or users. The latter is difficult to observe in watching someone look at a picture, but, as my little experiment shows, it becomes clearly visible in looking at the way people negotiate the layout of spaces such as these museum exhibits.

Exercises

1   Choose two distinct magazines or types of magazine. What kinds of things tend to be given and new, and what kinds of things ideal and real in their single page advertisements? If there are any differences, how can they be explained?

2   Find examples of the use of centre and margin in the layout of pages – whether of books, magazines, papers or other printed materials. Can you observe any patterns as to what kinds of things tend to be centre, what kinds of things margin?

3   Compare and contrast the composition of corporate home pages and personal home pages.

4   Make photographs of objects and/or buildings in which the front, the back, the sides and the top have distinct information value, and photographs of objects and/or buildings in which they do not, in various permutations – (for example, front and back distinct, but sides not; front and back the same, but sides different, etc).
5   Design a poster for the tour of a musical group or single artist. It has to contain the following elements as a minimum: the name of the group or artist – and perhaps of the tour; a sentence to recommend the group or artist; a photo or other graphic; a list of venues and dates; information needed to book tickets; the URL of a website.
Reflect on the way you positioned these elements in the whole.

Note

The material in this chapter is based on two earlier publications, Kress and Van Leeuwen (1996), chapter 6, and Van Leeuwen (2003). Exercise 5 is inspired by a seminar paper by Sune Mortensen.

11   Information linking

Linking items of information

Information is often thought about in terms of 'bits', morsels of fact which have value in themselves, without reference to other pieces of information, and which are the more valuable the more information they pack in. Maruyama (1980) sees this 'isolationistic' view of information, as he calls it, as symptomatic for an equally isolationistic view of society, in which 'only the individual elements are real', 'society is merely an aggregate of individuals', and 'each question has its answers, unrelated to others'. It can also be linked to the increasing tendency in all information media to package information in strongly framed, individualized, bite-size morsels. The magazine genres discussed in chapter 6 are one example of the tendency.

In what Maruyama (ibid.: 29) calls 'contextual information', on the other hand, the value of information lies in its relation to its context: information can only be interpreted in the context of other pieces of information and of specific communicative interests and purposes. In this chapter I will explore how items of information, whether verbal, visual or otherwise, can be and are *meaningfully linked* to other items of information. In relation to the new media, 'links' are often seen as having value in themselves, again in terms of 'the more information, the better'. But the links between items of information not only have cumulative but also cognitive value. They link information in terms of such cognitive categories as causal or temporal relationships, and it is these categories that make items of information meaningful in relation to each other.

Different communicative situations require different understandings and uses of information. The items of information in 'how to do' texts – for instance, recipes – may have some meaning on their own but the information only becomes relevant if the items are linked in terms of the needs of people who want to find out how to do something – for instance, prepare a particular dish – and that means that they have to be placed in the chronological temporal framework of a step-by-step procedure. Without a temporal connection between the separate items of information, the recipe is, in practice, meaningless.

> Divide the mixed berries between two cocktail glasses
> ↓
> *(next event)*
> ↓
>
> Pour half the pink champagne or cava into a pan and bring to the boil
> ↓

(next event)
↓

Stir in the sugar and gelatine and warm over a very gentle heat until both have dissolved
(etc. ...)

In the example below, on the other hand, the elements also provide information about food, but the links between them are not temporal but *logical* because this is an advertisement, a persuasive text. A reason is given for 'starting with the finest ingredients', and the general label 'finest selection' is explained by more specific references. Persuasion not only favours value-laden terms such as 'finest', 'fresh', 'lush', 'real' etc., but also 'arguments' that hang together logically.

Start with the finest ingredients and keep it simple
↓
(reason)
↓

That's the inspiration for new Finest Selection from Dolmio
↓
(specification)
↓

Pasta sauces that combine a handful of fresh ingredients, harvested on lush Italian farms ...
↓
(further specification)
↓

Sun-ripened tomatoes, fragrant basil and real Italian olive oil ...
(etc. ...)

Links of this kind are needed, not only between the items of information in verbal texts, but also between the frames in a cartoon, the shots in a film, the pages of a website. In this chapter I will first explain some principles and types of verbal linking and then extend this to visual linking, to finally discuss how verbal and visual (and verbal-visual) linking works in documentary film and in educational CD-ROMs for children.

The logic of linking

Categories of verbal linking can be made explicit by means of conjunction. Temporal links, for instance, can be indexed by conjunctive words and phrases like 'then', 'next', 'after that', ' day later', or 'previously', 'before that', 'a day earlier', and so on. But explicit conjunction is not always necessary. Links can often be understood from the context, without explicit conjunction. For the purpose of analysis it is then possible to insert explicit conjunctions, to test how much sense they *would* make, and so decide what link obtains. For instance a temporal conjunction would make sense between the first two items of information in the recipe above – 'Divide the mixed berries between two glasses *and then* pour the pink champagne' – but a causal conjunction like 'because' – 'Divide the mixed berries between two glasses *because* pour the pink champagne' – would not.

Historians of language have shown that the use of explicit conjunction has increased during the past few centuries. Earlier, conjunction tended to remain implicit and '*and*' was used as a kind of universal link, serving all kinds of conjunctive purposes (Milic, 1970: 244). From the sixteenth century onward, the use of explicit conjunction increased, particularly in writing characterized by a spirit of scientific rationality. The eighteenth century philosopher and early semiotician John Locke, for instance, wrote:

> The words whereby the mind signifies what connexion it gives to several affirmations and negations, that it unites in one continued reasoning or narration, are generally called particles: and it is in the right use of these that more particularly consists the clearness and beauty of a good style ... To express ... methodical and rational thoughts, a man must have words to show what connexion, restriction, distinction, opposition, emphasis &c., he gives to each respective part of his discourse.
>
> (1972 [1706]: 72)

Others, however, thought that explicit conjunction made language less direct, and less colourful: 'Of all the parts of speech', said the eighteenth century rhetorician George Campbell, 'the conjunctions are the most unfriendly to vivacity' (quoted in Milic, 1970: 244). Attitudes like this cast a long shadow. Even now, academic writers tend to use a lot of conjunction, while journalists, who aim at 'vigorous, economical writing' (Evans, 1972: 23), tend to avoid it.

In the days of the silent movies the semantic links between the shots in films were explicitly signalled by title-cards: 'That night', 'Next day', 'Came the dawn', etc. When title-card writing became a prestigious and well-paid job, 'that night' transformed into '... inky black darkness, dotted with a myriad twinkling lights ...', 'next day' became '... comes another rising sun and the troubles of yesterday are forgotten in the brilliant new avenue of opportunities it unfolds ...', and so on. Explicit conjunction was necessary because image links were not always easy to understand for the audiences of the period. Linda Arvidson Griffith (1925: 23), wife of the film pioneer D.W. Griffith, has recounted people's reaction to Griffith's early use of parallel editing, in *Enoch Arden* (1908):

> When he suggested a scene showing Annie Lee waiting for her husband's return to be followed by a scene of Enoch cast away on a desert island, it was altogether too distracting. How can you tell a story jumping about like that?

Eventually parallel narratives would become commonplace and easily understood by audiences, even without title-cards.

Elaboration

In the remainder of this section I introduce the main categories of verbal linking, together with some of the conjunctions that can make them explicit.[1]

A given item of information can either *elaborate* or *extend* the information presented in other items of information. In the case of elaboration, it repeats or restates information for purposes of clarification. In the case of extension, it adds new information, linking it to the existing information in a particular way – for example, temporally, or logically.

There can be several types of elaboration. In the case of explanation, an item of information *reformulates* what was said in another item of information. Typical explicit conjunctions would be 'that is', 'in other words', 'to put it another way', etc. In the case of *exemplification*, clarification is given by means of an example. Explicit conjunctions could be 'for instance', 'for example', 'to illustrate', etc. In the case of *specification*, the information is made more specific – explicit conjunctions: 'more specifically', 'in particular' – and in the case of the *summary* it is generalized – explicit conjunctions: 'to summarize', 'in short', 'briefly', etc.). In the example below, the headmaster of a Muslim Community School in Perth, Australia, interviewed in a TV current affairs item, gradually dares to become more specific in the course of a series of elaborations:

We are giving the environment
↓
(explanation)
↓
We are giving the atmosphere
↓
(specification)
↓
We are giving the teaching of the Holy Koran
↓
(specification)
↓
We are giving them the feeling that everything you do is to please God

Temporal, logical and additive extension

If there is a relation of extension between two items of information, the second item will add new information, and the link between the two items will be temporal, logical or additive.

Temporal linking exists when the second of the two items tells us something that has occurred – or is occurring, or will occur – *after*, *before*, or *at the same time as* what the first item has told us. As the relation can often be understood from the context, the relevant explicit conjunctions – for example, 'then', 'next', 'after', 'meanwhile', 'previously' – are often left out. Another temporal relation is that of the 'conclusive event' – typical explicit conjunctions: 'finally', 'in the end', etc. Temporal relations are fundamental in stories and procedural – 'how to do' – texts, although they occur elsewhere as well. The recipe discussed earlier is an example of the use of temporal linking in procedural texts. Here is an example from a story, a thriller by Peter Corris (2000:10):

> Later, at home in the ranch style house he hated, Crawley sat with a hot rum and lemon juice and a photograph album
> ↓
> (*previous event*)
> ↓
> Mandy had gone to bed in her own room,
> ↓
> *(previous event)*
> ↓
> leaving Crawley with an invitation to visit if he chose
> ↓
> *(next event)*
> ↓
> Crawley had said he would.
> ↓
> *(next event)*
> ↓
> He sipped his drink and slowly turned over the pages

Logical linking exists when the information in the second of two items of information gives a reason for, a condition of, or a comparison with the information in the first item. Causal links include *result* – with conjunctions like 'in consequence', 'as a result', etc.; *reason* – with conjunctions like 'because', 'for that reason', etc.; and *purpose* – with conjunctions like 'for that purpose', 'with this in view', etc. Conditional links may be *positive* – conjunctions: 'if' 'in case', 'in that case', etc. – or *negative* – conjunctions: 'otherwise', 'if not', etc. Comparative links either index *similarity* – conjunctions: 'likewise', 'similarly', etc. – or *contrast* – conjunctions: 'by contrast', 'conversely', etc. These links are the mainstay of expository and persuasive texts, texts that argue for or against some idea or proposed action. In this excerpt from *The Document* (issue 3, 1995), an employee newsletter published by Xerox, the management is trying to persuade employees of their point of view – note the explicit conjunction: a purpose link is made explicit by '*the primary goal was*', a result link by '*so*', and a specification link by '*particularly*':

> A series of discussions began in July 1994 to raise the issues, identify causes and come up with solutions
> ↓
> *(purpose)*
> ↓

The primary goal was to improve product quality
↓
(result)
↓
and so raise consumer satisfaction levels
↓
(result)
↓
Significant advances were made,
↓
(specification)
↓
particularly in improving communications among the CBU, the supply chain and manufacturing

And in this example from Ivan Illich's *Deschooling Society* (1971: 48), Illich uses comparative linking to make his argument, comparing an aspect of schooling to an aspect of religion with which he assumes his readers will disagree – the comparison link is made explicit by '*I am reminded of*':

The school-leaving age in developed nations outpaces the rise in life expectancy.
↓
(result)
↓
The two curves will intersect in a decade and create a problem for Jessica Mitford and professionals concerned with 'terminal education'
↓
(comparison)
↓
I am reminded of the late Middle Ages, when the demand for Church services outgrew a lifetime, and 'Purgatory' was created to purify souls under the pope's control before they could enter eternal peace.

An *addition link* exists when an item of information does introduce new information, but without linking it either temporally or logically to already available information. There is no specific semantic dimension to the link. The new information simply adds more information – conjunctions: 'and', 'as well as', etc. – or *alternative* information – for example, 'or' – or *adversative* information – conjunction: 'but', 'however', etc. – information which in some way 'counters' the information in preceding item(s) of information. This is the kind of linking – or lack of linking – which dominates in contexts where people move from topic to topic on the basis of ad hoc associations, or in information media that adhere to the 'isolationistic' view of information as the accumulation of separate morsels of fact. This extract from a factual book for young children about reptiles (Bailey, 1988: 38), provides a lot of information, but does not do much to relate the separate items of information to each other.

Most crocodiles and alligators are found near fresh water
↓
(adversative)
↓
A few, like the saltwater crocodile in our picture, live in places where rivers flow into the sea and the water is salty
↓
(addition)
↓
These saltwater crocodiles grow up to six metres in length
↓
(Addition)
↓
They have long powerful tails and large mouths with many teeth

Spatial links form a final category, with conjunctions such as 'in front of', 'behind', etc. for spatial *proximity*, and 'here', 'where', 'in the same place' for links of *co-presence*. To summarize:

Type of connection	Subtypes	Typical explicit conjunctions	Typical environment
Elaboration	Explanation Example Specification Summary Correction	'that is', 'in other words' 'example', 'to illustrate' 'in particular', 'more specifically' 'in short', 'briefly' 'in fact', 'actually'	argumentation persuasion
Extension: addition	Addition Adversative Alternative	'and', 'moreover' 'but', 'however' 'or', 'alternatively'	description argumentation persuasion
Extension: temporal	Next event Simultaneous event Previous event Conclusive event	'then', 'next' 'meanwhile', 'just then' 'previously', 'hitherto' 'finally', 'in the end'	narrative procedure
Extension: spatial	Proximity Co-presence	'behind', 'in front', etc. 'in the same place', 'there'	description
Extension: logical	Similarity Contrast Reason Result Purpose Condition (positive) Condition (negative)	'likewise', 'similarly' 'by contrast', 'conversely' 'therefore', 'for that reason' 'as a result', 'in consequence' 'for that purpose', 'with this in view' 'in that case', 'in that event', 'if' 'otherwise', 'if not'	argumentation persuasion

Figure 11.1   Overview of verbal linking

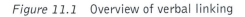

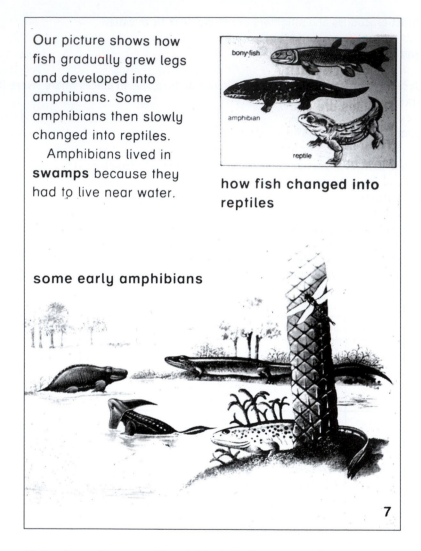

Our picture shows how fish gradually grew legs and developed into amphibians. Some amphibians then slowly changed into reptiles.

Amphibians lived in **swamps** because they had to live near water.

bony-fish

amphibian

reptile

how fish changed into reptiles

some early amphibians

7

Figure 11.2   A non-linear, multimodal text (Bailey, 1988: 7)

Linking images

All the examples so far are from linear texts in which each next item of information links to the previous one in one of the ways I have described – or several (it is possible to have ambiguous or deliberately multi-interpretable links).

In figure 11.2 the various items of information are simultaneously present on the page and can, in principle, be read in any order. I might start with the box top right and then move to the picture below, or first read the text top left, to mention just two possibilities. But this does not affect the way these items are linked. Whatever way I read the page, the semantic links stay the same. They have been pre-structured. It is certainly true that non-linear texts – of which this is a very simple example – provide more freedom of reading, but this freedom does not extend all the way. It does not, for instance, extend to the semantic linking between the items of information. I will return to this issue at the end of this chapter.

The text in figure 11.2 is not only non-linear, but also multimodal, and therefore has not just verbal, but also visual and verbal–visual links. The block top right, for instance, is a *specification* of (the first part of) the text top left: it provides more detail about the evolutionary process. Within the box there is a *next event* link between the pictures of the animals – after the appearance of the bony fish the appearance of the amphibian was the next evolutionary event, and that of the reptile the next one after that. But the link between the words and the pictures in the box is *explanatory* as the words label the pictures – an 'in other words', or rather 'in other semiotics' link – or, alternatively, a *specification*, as the pictures provide more detail. The link between the text box top left and the words 'some early amphibians' is an *addition* – 'have a look at some more amphibians' – and the picture at the bottom of the page is a *specification*: it makes the words 'some early amphibians' more specific by actually showing four of them.

In the next part of this section I will ask: Are all the links that are possible between words also possible between images, and between images and words? And if not, what links are possible? This will require a brief excursion into the history of the theory and practice of film editing, as it was in this context that the semantic linking of images was first explored.

Film editing theories of the 1920s

Because storytelling was, and still is, the dominant use of the film medium, temporal linking is its dominant form of 'conjunction'. But film time is not always linear. There can be previous events (flashbacks), future events (flash forwards) and simultaneous events, parallel stories intercut with each other, as first pioneered in the 1908 D.W.Griffith film *Enoch Arden* which I have already mentioned. The Soviet-Russian films of the 1920s began to explore other ways of linking images because in that period film was seen as an important propaganda tool. It was modern. It was progressive. It was thought to speak a universal language, thus overcoming the problem of the many languages spoken in the Soviet Union of the time. And it was thought of as addressing the emotions in a very direct way, as having the ability to 'shock' people into a revolutionary consciousness. The problem was how to use film for persuasive arguments rather than only for stories (Eisenstein even dreamt of filming Marx's *Das Kapital*). This problem was explored both in theory and in practice, as many of the filmmakers of the period also wrote theoretical papers. Pudovkin (1926) took what was still, basically, a narrative approach. What he called *structural montage* involved selecting actions and reactions to construct the narrative, while *relational montage* would introduce other material, not directly related to the story, and serve to interpret the story. To do so, relational montage involved logical linking, specifically contrast and similarity. Here is an example of the way Pudovkin explained his use of contrast. 'Suppose it is our task,' he said, 'to tell of the miserable situation of a starving man; the story will impress the more vividly if it is associated with mention of the senseless gluttony of a rich man' (Pudovkin, 1926: 47). As for similarity – he used the term 'symbolism' – here 'an abstract concept is introduced into the consciousness of the spectator without the use of a title' (ibid.: 49), for instance a scene showing workers is intercut with the slaughter of a bull to depict the destruction of the spirit of the working class by capitalism. Contrast and similarity linking was not restricted to the occasional insert, but might involve intercutting two narratively unrelated sequences, for instance a scene of a worker condemned to death for his part in a strike, with a scene showing an employer gradually getting drunk and falling asleep at the very point where the worker is executed.

In Eisenstein's theory of montage (1943, 1963), semantic links played a relatively minor role. His earliest theory, the theory of 'montage of attraction', was based on the idea of a *formal* clash between shots – for example, a clash between 'round' and 'square', 'horizontal' and 'vertical', or 'left-pointing' and 'right-pointing'. The 'shock effect', the 'agitation' this would produce, Eisenstein argued, could be used for political purposes as it would jar people out of the passive attitudes engendered by 'bourgeois' narratives. In his later theory of 'intellectual montage', the formal contrast would coincide with a contrast of content. 'Dialectical' montage, for instance, would involve putting contrasting shots together to create a 'thesis–antithesis' relation, which would then engender a synthesis in the viewer's mind. In the next section I will discuss some examples of the influence Eisenstein's ideas and practices had, and still have, on documentary film and television production.

Timoshenko (see Arnheim, 1933) also stressed the logical relations of contrast and similarity and added a form of cinematic 'elaboration', the link between a Close Shot and a Long Shot of the same subject – which he called 'enlargement' – and the link between a Long Shot and a Close Shot of the same subject – which he called 'concentration'.

Although this has not been studied as much as it might have been, there can of course also be spatial links between shots in a film. In what Metz (1974) has called a 'descriptive sequence', a place is 'described' by showing a series of details rather than a single overview shot. Needless to say, the details might in fact have been shot in different places. It is only through editing – and tonal cohesion – that the link of *co-presence* is created. Again, if we see 'matched angle' shots of two people, we understand these people as standing or sitting opposite each other, even if we never see them together in one shot, and even though the shots might have been taken in different places and/or at different times. Here the editing creates a *proximity* link, akin to the 'in front of', 'behind', etc. links between items of verbal information.

To summarize the types of visual linking reviewed in this section:

Type of connection	Subtypes	Realization	Typical environment
Elaboration	Overview	cut or other transition from CS to LS of *same* subject	description
	Detail	cut or other transition from LS to CS of *same* subject	
Extension: temporal	Next event	cut or other transition to next action or event	narration; procedure
	Previous event	cut or other transition to previous event	
	Simultaneous event	cut or other transition to simultaneous event	
Extension: spatial	Proximity	relative location indicated by matching angle	description
	Co-presence	series of two or more details	
Extension: logical	Contrast	contrasting subject (no narrative connection)	persuasion
	Similarity	similar subject (no narrative connection)	

Figure 11.3 Overview of visual linking

Clearly there are more verbal than visual types of logical and elaborative linking. But that is not to say that more logical links could never exist between images. If there is a need to develop a medium in a particular direction, as there was in the Soviet Union of the 1920s, the means will be found.

Word and image

The classic semiotic approach to the linking of words and images is that of Roland Barthes (1977: 39ff). His two key concepts are 'anchorage' and 'relay'. In the case of 'anchorage' words 'elucidate' pictures – 'the text directs the reader through the signifieds of the image, causing him to avoid some and receive others' and 'remote-controls him towards a meaning chosen in advance' (ibid.: 40). The concept of 'anchorage' is therefore very close to Halliday's concept of 'elaboration'. It is in fact a kind of *specification*. The words pick out one of the possible meanings of the image. In the case of 'relay', 'text and image stand in a complementary relationship' and are both 'fragments of a more general syntagm', to which each contributes its own, distinct information (ibid.: 41). The concept of 'relay' is very close to Halliday's concept of 'extension': two items – one verbal, one visual – provide different, but semantically related information.

While extension may also occur in the reverse direction – images extending words – 'anchorage' is uni-directional. Its reverse, according to Barthes, is 'illustration' – images 'anchoring' words. Clearly this approach presupposes linearity. Historically, says Barthes, images elaborated words, to be precise, the foundational words of society

– the Bible, Greek mythology, etc. Here many different pictures would exist, all illustrating the one text, to convey its content to the often illiterate audiences of the time. In the Renaissance a new approach emerged, in which images were founded on scientific rather than theological truth, and began to be seen as empirical evidence of the perceivable world and therefore still in need of interpretation. Here one picture would be open to many different interpretations, many different ways of being 'anchored':

> Formerly the image illustrated the text (made it clearer); today the text loads the image, burdening it with a culture, a moral, an imagination. Formerly, there was reduction from text to image, today, there is amplification from the one to the other.
>
> (Barthes, 1977: 26)

The approach taken in this chapter does not presuppose linearity. Every link is, at least in principle, reversible. However, in some cases there is symmetry between the two directions and in other cases there is no symmetry. In explanation, for instance, the 'in other words' link, is symmetrical: if a is a restatement of b, then b must also be a restatement of a. Specification, on the other hand, is not reversible: if b is a more specific version of a, then a is *not* a more specific, but a more general version of b.

Bill Nichols (1976, 1981) has discussed the relation between word and image in documentary film. Much of his account does not touch directly on the subject of this chapter. But some of the ideas in his discussion of the voice-over commentary are relevant. Images, he says, can 'confirm', 'counterpoint', 'ironically shade' or 'extend' verbal commentaries. Of 'extension' he gives an example that reminds us of Pudovkin: a commentary dealing with the exploitation of workers is accompanied by a shot of prisoners, and this metaphorically extends the meaning of the commentary. Clearly Nichols' categories are all similarity links ('confirm'), and contrast links ('counterpoint', 'extension', 'ironic shading'). The difference between 'counterpoint' and 'ironic shading' is perhaps that the one is strong and direct ('counterpoint') and the other more subtle and oblique ('ironic shading').

To summarize the word-image links reviewed here:

Image–text relations		
Elaboration	Specification	The image makes the text more specific (illustration)
		The text makes the image more specific (anchorage)
	Explanation	The text paraphrases the image (or vice versa)
Extension	Similarity	The content of the text is similar to that of the image
	Contrast	The content of the text contrasts with that of the image
	Complement	The content of the image adds further information to that of the text, and vice versa ('relay')

Figure 11.4   Overview of visual–verbal linking

Word and image in documentary film and television

In this section I use linking analysis to compare and contrast three excerpts from factual films and television programmes,[2] a classic documentary, a television current affairs item and a television news item. The first example is deliberately a historical example, and a film rather than a television example, to illustrate that the semiotic resources of information linking are used differently in different periods and different media.

Industrial Britain

Like the Soviet films discussed above, John Grierson's *Industrial Britain* (1933) was a propaganda film, aiming at bolstering the morale of the workers in a period of depression and massive unemployment. Also, like the Soviet films from which Grierson had learned a lot, it relied on non-narrative, 'argumentative' forms of image editing. The sequence reproduced in figure 11.5 is the beginning of the film. Images of traditional crafts are contrasted with 'the world that coal and steam have created'. From this 'thesis' and 'antithesis', a synthesis will emerge: traditional values can in fact continue in the 'world of coal and steam'. As the commentary has it, later in the film:

> But if you look closely enough you will find that the spirit of craftsmanship has not disappeared. William Gavin Broadcotton of Stoke on Trent, whom you see working now, is a young man of 26. But he is working exactly as the Greek potters worked, making the same beautiful things, using the same simple tools, Look at those hands ... That is the sort of thing that is being done behind these industrial chimneystacks.

Almost 70 years on, this commentary sounds very patronizing, yet the black and white images of the film have retained some of their poetry. In the transcript I have treated shots 1,2 and 3 (and shots 18, 19, and 20) as one visual item of information. These two series of three shots both show a process of 'coming down to earth' which would be more typically realized by a single downward camera movement, but is here realised by a 'montage' of three shots, a technique based on Eisenstein's filmmaking methods.

Three points. First, the links are for the most part *logical*. The sequence builds an argument, and uses similarity and contrast to do so. The first 7 shots visually 'say': all these things, people, places, activities – windmills, spinning and weaving by hand, working on the land, transporting things with barges and brigs – are similar. They are all traditional, non-industrial ways of doing things: slowly, manually, using natural sources of energy such as wind and water. This then contrasts to the next sequence – starting at shot 18 – which evokes the 'new world of coal and steam'. Note the symmetry in *form* between shots 1,2 and 3 and shots 18, 19 and 20. Contained within the 'traditional crafts' sequence there are some 'mini sequences', for example, the

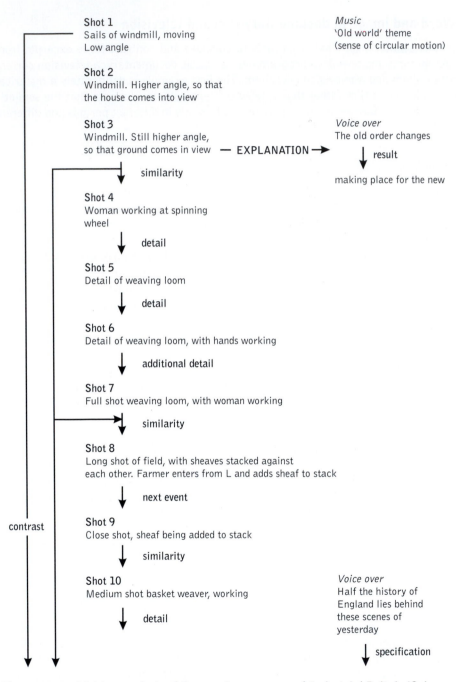

Figure 11.5   Linking analysis of the opening sequence of *Industrial Britain* (Grierson, 1933)

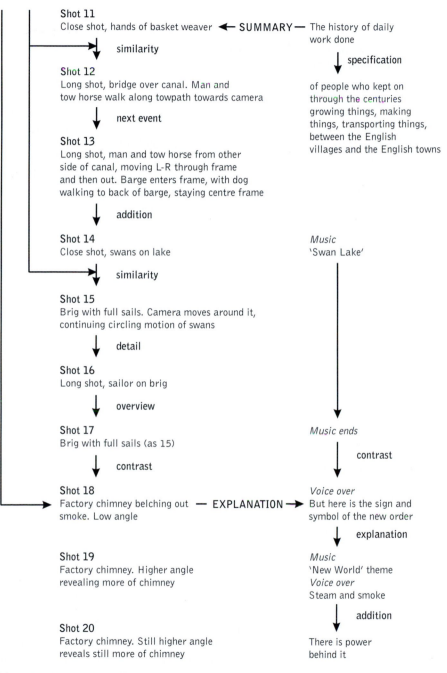

Shot 11
Close shot, hands of basket weaver ← SUMMARY — The history of daily
                                                work done

↓ similarity

↓ specification

Shot 12
Long shot, bridge over canal. Man and
tow horse walk along towpath towards camera

of people who kept on
through the centuries
growing things, making
things, transporting things,
between the English
villages and the English towns

↓ next event

Shot 13
Long shot, man and tow horse from other
side of canal, moving L-R through frame
and then out. Barge enters frame, with dog
walking to back of barge, staying centre frame

↓ addition

Shot 14
Close shot, swans on lake

Music
'Swan Lake'

↓ similarity

Shot 15
Brig with full sails. Camera moves around it,
continuing circling motion of swans

↓ detail

Shot 16
Long shot, sailor on brig

↓ overview

Shot 17
Brig with full sails (as 15)

Music ends

↓ contrast

↓ contrast

Shot 18
Factory chimney belching out — EXPLANATION → *Voice over*
smoke. Low angle   But here is the sign and
                                              symbol of the new order

↓ explanation

Shot 19
Factory chimney. Higher angle
revealing more of chimney

Music
'New World' theme
Voice over
Steam and smoke

↓ addition

Shot 20
Factory chimney. Still higher angle
reveals still more of chimney

There is power
behind it

Figure 11.5   continued

'weaving sequence' (shots 5 to 7), and the 'working on the land' sequence (shots 8 to 9). *Within* these 'mini sequences' other kinds of links can be found, for example, 'next event' and 'overview/detail' or 'detail/overview' links.

Second, the verbal commentary is sparse and intermittent. It restricts itself to underlining the key moments, reinforcing the similarity between the shots in the 'traditional crafts' sequence – but not until after the viewers have had a chance to look for themselves – and the essence of the 'new world' sequence ('coal and steam') and emphasizing the contrast between the two sequences ('but'). For most of the sequence the viewers just look and listen to the music, something which has become much less common in contemporary television documentaries. Note the shot of the swan (shot 14), a Pudovkian symbol of the beauty of the 'traditional ways', its movement continued by the brig, in the next shot.

The linking between the items of verbal information in the commentary itself, finally, is also mostly logical and elaborative. This commentary does not tell a story, it argues and persuades, quite openly.

Muslim Community School

The second example (figure 11.6) is an extract from an ABC (Australian Broadcasting Commission) current affairs programme, *7.30 Report*, broadcast in 1986. It deals with a Muslim Community School in Perth. The transcript shows that a single shot can sometimes contain several visual information items (for example, shots 19, 21, 26 and 27), connected for instance by a camera movement.

The image sequence is not as tightly structured as that of *Industrial Britain*, but, here too, it is mostly comparative and hence 'argumentative'. Immediately a contrast is made between 'praying' and 'playing' – the contrast between the Arabic sign and the clown picture (shots 19a and 19b), and between children participating in prayer (21b, 23) and children who are smiling and playing (24). There are similarities too, between people praying in a mosque and teacher Linda Walewski – both wearing traditional dress – and between smiling children and Linda Walewski – both wearing Western dress. Although these contrasts are more local and less emphatic than the contrasts in *Industrial Britain*, the sequence is nevertheless based on a similar method of visual argumentation. First 'praying' (thesis) is contrasted to 'playing' (antithesis), then Linda Walewski is presented as the synthesis, because she has a foot in both worlds and is thus able to guarantee the children's happiness, 'despite religion'.

The commentary is both more continuous and less sparse than that of *Industrial Britain*. Television may be a visual medium, but its staple fare is talk, rather than wordless images. It opens by emphasizing the contrast between 'praying' and 'playing': 'While religion and Muslim teaching remain foremost, the school conforms with educational guidelines in all other respects' – does this mean that 'Muslim teaching' does *not* conform to educational guidelines? The argument, meanwhile, is no longer presented by a single authoritative voice. Instead, statements by Magar and Walewski are carefully selected and edited into a single cohesive argument, linked by the reporter. And Linda Walewski gets the last word.

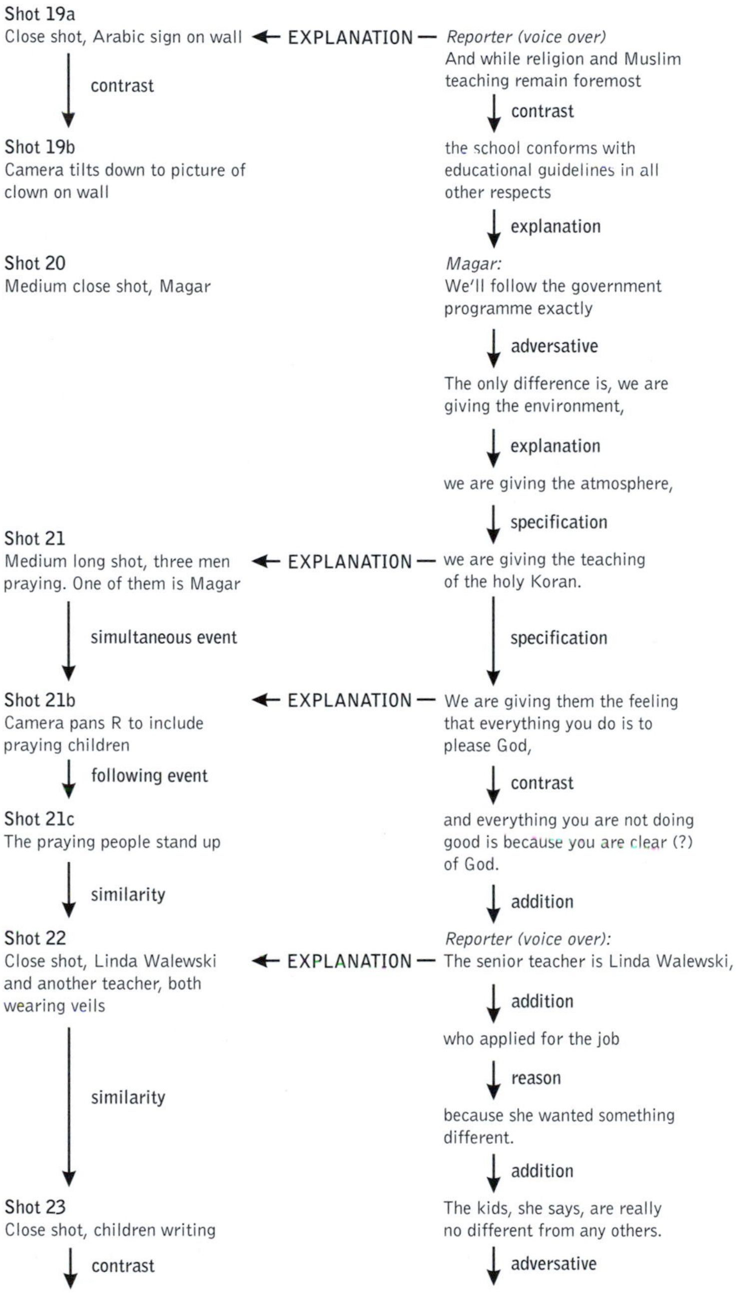

Shot 19a
Close shot, Arabic sign on wall ◄— EXPLANATION — *Reporter (voice over)*
And while religion and Muslim
teaching remain foremost

↓ contrast   ↓ contrast

Shot 19b   the school conforms with
Camera tilts down to picture of   educational guidelines in all
clown on wall   other respects

                                             ↓ explanation

Shot 20   *Magar:*
Medium close shot, Magar   We'll follow the government
                                             programme exactly

                                             ↓ adversative

                                             The only difference is, we are
                                             giving the environment,

                                             ↓ explanation

                                             we are giving the atmosphere,

                                             ↓ specification

Shot 21
Medium long shot, three men ◄— EXPLANATION — we are giving the teaching
praying. One of them is Magar   of the holy Koran.

↓ simultaneous event   ↓ specification

Shot 21b   ◄— EXPLANATION — We are giving them the feeling
Camera pans R to include   that everything you do is to
praying children   please God,

↓ following event   ↓ contrast

Shot 21c   and everything you are not doing
The praying people stand up   good is because you are clear (?)
                                             of God.

↓ similarity   ↓ addition

Shot 22   *Reporter (voice over):*
Close shot, Linda Walewski ◄— EXPLANATION — The senior teacher is Linda Walewski,
and another teacher, both
wearing veils   ↓ addition

                                             who applied for the job

                                             ↓ reason

↓ similarity   because she wanted something
                                             different.

                                             ↓ addition

Shot 23   The kids, she says, are really
Close shot, children writing   no different from any others.

↓ contrast   ↓ adversative

Figure 11.6   Linking analysis of an extract from 'Muslim Community School' (ABC,
1986)

Shot 24
Medium shot, smiling little girl

↓ similarity

Shot 25
Close shot, Linda Walewski in Western dress

Shot 26a
Medium long shot, children in cloakroom
hanging bags on coathooks

↓ overview

Shot 26b
Camera pans to full shot of classroom

↓ addition

Shot 27
Medium long shot, children in playground
eating lunch

Two children walk towards camera

↓ proximity

Shot 28
Long shot, children in playground

except that they share one
special quality.

↓ addition

Linda Walewski (voice over):
It comes from the family
basically;

↓ explanation

they have a terrific feeling
of community spirit,

↓ explanation

(sync.) family-mindedness
of sharing,

↓ explanation

caring for these children.

↓ example

(voice over) They were happy,
I've been told

↓ condition

if someone has no lunch at school
they will automatically share

their own things.

↓ reason

This is something that they're
taught in their religion,

↓ explanation

that you share;

↓ preceding event

before you can give yourself

↓ explanation

you give it to someone else
rather than yourself.

Figure 11.6   continued

Finally, while in *Industrial Britain* image and text are closely co-ordinated, here each seems to follow its own course. Only every now and again are there moments in which the two touch – just after Linda Walewski speaks of the 'special quality' of the children, we see a smiling child; as she states that 'they are happy', we see children going out to play. Such links are not as deliberate and tightly synchronized as the links in *Industrial Britain*. They just provide a loose, associative resonance between word and image. The message, meanwhile, is clear. A woman, a Western woman, is needed to guarantee a happy childhood for these children.

Strike

The television news item in figure 11.7 deals with a strike by airport baggage handlers, and was broadcast by Sydney's Channel 9 in 1986. The sequence analysed immediately followed the introduction by newsreader Brian Henderson:

> In a move that could have serious repercussions Ansett Airlines this afternoon sacked its striking airport baggage handlers. 370 people lost their jobs although Ansett chief Sir Peter Abeles is giving them one more chance in saying they'll be re-employed if they agree to toe their management line by 5 o'clock tomorrow afternoon. But the Transport Workers Union has warned of widening industrial action to ground the Ansett fleet.

In a classic documentary like *Industrial Britain*, there is tight logical linking between the images. In television news items the image track often hangs together like loose sand and would not make much sense on its own. Here the key principle behind the editing is spatial *co-presence*: all the shots have been taken in or around the airport. There is only the occasional sense of 'next event' and 'detail/overview' linking.

What there is in the way of structure is carried by the verbal text, which does provide some logical cohesion. The images merely serve as a kind of setting, which gives a spurious sense of authenticity to the news item. Spurious, because, although this item is about a strike, we do not see the workers striking, in fact we see them loading suitcases into a plane. Not the events are illustrated here, but only their actors (baggage handlers) and location (airport). This is by no means an exception. As I was writing this chapter I watched a television news item about sexually transmitted diseases. Apart from a shot of a document – just as in the 'Strike' news item: documents as 'proof' – all the shots show couples lying in the grass or walking in the park – again, the actors (couples), not the states, actions and events of the reported story.

Interactive linking

In film and television the links are created by the editor and the audience has no choice in the matter. In the new media, designers provide multiple links for users to choose from. Although the term 'link', which has of course come to the fore in

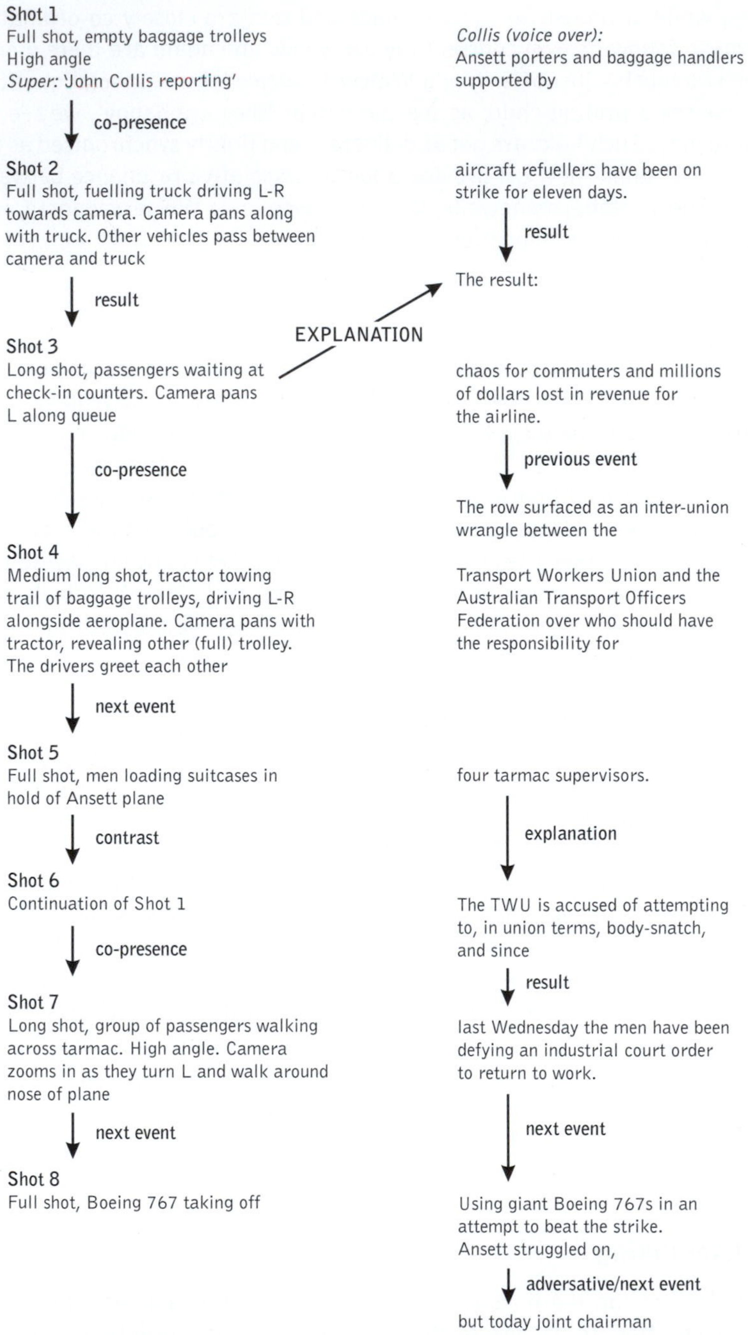

Shot 1
Full shot, empty baggage trolleys
High angle
Super: 'John Collis reporting'

↓ co-presence

Shot 2
Full shot, fuelling truck driving L-R
towards camera. Camera pans along
with truck. Other vehicles pass between
camera and truck

↓ result

Shot 3
Long shot, passengers waiting at
check-in counters. Camera pans
L along queue

↓ co-presence

Shot 4
Medium long shot, tractor towing
trail of baggage trolleys, driving L-R
alongside aeroplane. Camera pans with
tractor, revealing other (full) trolley.
The drivers greet each other

↓ next event

Shot 5
Full shot, men loading suitcases in
hold of Ansett plane

↓ contrast

Shot 6
Continuation of Shot 1

↓ co-presence

Shot 7
Long shot, group of passengers walking
across tarmac. High angle. Camera
zooms in as they turn L and walk around
nose of plane

↓ next event

Shot 8
Full shot, Boeing 767 taking off

EXPLANATION

Collis (voice over):
Ansett porters and baggage handlers
supported by

aircraft refuellers have been on
strike for eleven days.

↓ result

The result:

chaos for commuters and millions
of dollars lost in revenue for
the airline.

↓ previous event

The row surfaced as an inter-union
wrangle between the

Transport Workers Union and the
Australian Transport Officers
Federation over who should have
the responsibility for

four tarmac supervisors.

↓ explanation

The TWU is accused of attempting
to, in union terms, body-snatch,
and since

↓ result

last Wednesday the men have been
defying an industrial court order
to return to work.

↓ next event

Using giant Boeing 767s in an
attempt to beat the strike.
Ansett struggled on,

↓ adversative/next event

but today joint chairman

Figure 11.7   Linking analysis of a television news item

Shot 9
Long shot, boardroom with journalists
and cameramen silhouetted in foreground
and Abeles, under film lights, in background
at head of table

Sir Peter Abeles, decided enough
was enough.

↓ result

Shot 10
Full shot, letter of dismissal

This afternoon he authorised the
summary dismissal

↓ detail

SPECIFICATION

Shot 11
Close shot, letter ('A most serious
breach of your contract of employment ...
justifies summary termination. Accordingly ...
your employment with Ansett ... is terminated')

of all 370 strikers, representing
about one sixth of the airline's
Sydney staff.

↓ addition

Shot 12
Tight close shot, Abeles as he is talking,
in shirtsleeves

It was a decision, he said, taken
with regret.

↓ explanation

Abeles (sync.):
It was not easy for us to make this
decision,

↓ adversative

overview/next event

but, eh, we came to the conclusion
that we've given enough time;

↓ reason

we've tried everything

↓ additional reason

and we have to stand firm.

↓ addition

Shot 13
Continuation of Shot 9

Collis (voice over):
Sir Peter said the sackings were
with the knowledge but not necessarily
the support of the ACTU

↓ detail

↓ addition

Shot 14
Close shot, Abeles

which has already openly defended
Ansett in the dispute.

Shot 15
Close version of Shot 5

Figure 11.7   continued

precisely this context, is semantically neutral, hypertext links are in fact no different from the kinds of link I have discussed so far, as children learn from their earliest contact with computers. In *Max and the Machines,* an interactive learning CD-ROM for young children produced by Thomas Nelson in 1995, children are introduced to 'elaboration', 'addition', 'similarity' and 'next event' links in this order. A first game begins with three boxes with names on the screen: 'Selma' in the left-most box, 'Billy' in the middle box and 'Vicky and Ricky' in the right-most box. A cartoon bird then flies in, chirping:

> Selma, Billy, Vicky and Ricky
> Click on the name, that's the game
> Selma, Billy, Vicky and Ricky
> Tricky? Clicky!

Here clicking initially produces *elaboration*. The name of the child on the screen is replaced by a picture of the child. It also – and without further action by the user – produces *addition*, as the children in the boxes are soon joined by their parents, siblings, pets, etc. This use of clicking to provide elaboration and addition is then repeated in a range of different learning activities.

The next game – and the user cannot change the order of the games – introduces *similarity.* A cartoon presenter stands next to an easel displaying a picture of a yellow fork, a blue knife and an orange plate. Superimposed on the top of the screen are four coloured squares. The cartoon presenter then asks 'What colour is my plate? Click if you know'. The link the child is asked to make – the link between the displayed item and the selected item – is one of (colour) similarity.

The third game introduces *next event* linking. The cartoon presenter tells a 'story' with eight episodes: pouring tea, drinking tea, running a bath, sitting in a bath, brushing teeth, getting into bed, reading in bed and switching the bed-light off. A strip with eight pictures, each illustrating one of the episodes is superimposed on the top part of the screen, above the presenter's head. But the pictures are in random order. The presenter then asks: 'Now can you click on the pictures in the order in which they happen in the story? Go on, click!'

The next game begins with a picture of a park in which several things are going on at the same time. Two children are throwing a ball at one another, a boy is playing with his dog, and a girl is pushing her little brother – who clutches a teddy – on a swing. The user can then click on one of these scenes to produce the next event, which, in every case, is a complication. To take just one example, the little boy on the swing loses his teddy, which disappears into a rabbit hole. His sister tries to retrieve it but cannot reach far enough into the rabbit hole. At this point the user can again select the next event. Max, the cartoon presenter, had earlier introduced three pairs of magic boots, a pair of yellow boots to make him invisible, a pair of red boots to make him smaller and a pair of blue boots to make him larger. Selecting the red boots will allow Max to get into the rabbit hole to retrieve the teddy.

Thus the child learns that clicking produces meaningful links between items of information, although there is not much choice involved as yet. As soon as the child progresses to 'similarity' and 'next event' linking, the choice is either right or wrong. The child is merely testing him or herself against preset answers, against authoritative knowledge. There is not as yet a sense of explorative learning, of trying out different possibilities, as is the case in more advanced CD-ROMs such as *Dangerous Creatures*, produced by Microsoft in 1994.

Dangerous Creatures[3] is a database about wild animals which can be explored in three ways – through the alphabetically organized index, through particular themes such as 'habitats', 'weapons', etc., and through a 'guide interface'. Choosing the guide interface produces a screen displaying twelve guides, each able to provide a different 'tour' of the database – 'Amazon Adventure', 'African Safari', 'Coral Reef Dive', 'Native American Stories', 'Tales from Asia', etc. Figure 11.8 maps a small section of the tour of the 'Aboriginal storyteller'. To explain it I will need to describe the screens and their links in some detail.

The 'Death adder information screen' has a headline 'Death adders' top right, and includes two pictures showing more or less inert snakes against a neutral background. There are three boxes with written text. The main text box runs as follows:

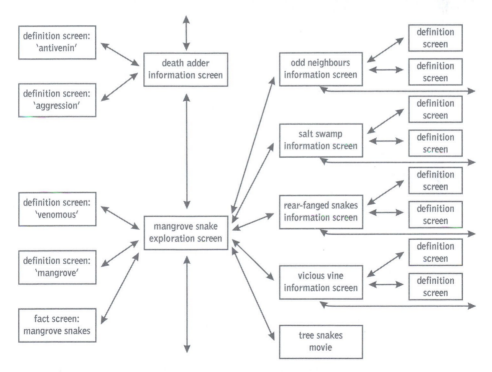

Figure 11.8 Section of 'Aboriginal guided tour' (Microsoft *Dangerous Creatures*, 1994)

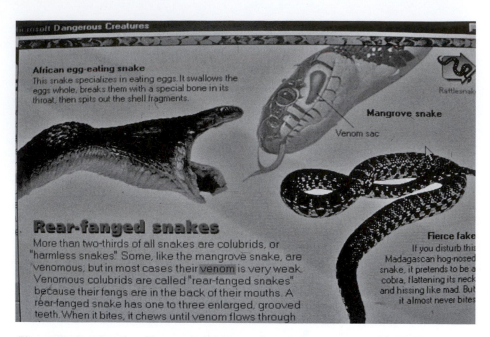

Figure 11.9 'Death adder screen' (Microsoft *Dangerous Creatures*, 1994)

Death adder
There is a good reason that this Australian snake is called the 'Death Adder'. Before an *antivenin* was developed, half the people bitten by it died. Luckily, the death adder is not very *aggressive* and bites only if touched.

The following is the text of one of the 'subsidiary' text boxes:

Not really an adder
Death adders aren't really adders, so the name is not very accurate. The death adder's closest relations include cobras, coral snakes and mambas, like this black mamba.

Like the reptile book (figure 11.2) this screen provides a range of separate morsels of information that are linked in one way only, that they all deal with snakes.

But there is also a *spoken* text, read by the female voice of the 'guide', the 'Aboriginal storyteller':

In that time there was not yet death. It was the fault of the first humans that death was led into the world (*didgeridoo music starts at this point*). For the moon came down to the earth and said to them: 'If you carry my pets across the river you will rise again after you have died and so live forever' (*didgeridoo music fades out*). But the humans refused. They were afraid of the moon's pets which were all deadly snakes. So the moon said: 'Silly humans, now when you die you will stay dead and I will always send you poisonous snakes to remind you that you disobeyed me.'

The 'death adder screen' links to two 'definition screens'. Clicking on the italicized words in the main text produces an *explanation* link, in the form of a superimposed text box with a spoken and written headline – for example, 'amphibians' – and an explanatory text:

Animals that are cold-blooded, lay eggs, and have moist skins. Frogs, toads, and salamanders are amphibians. When amphibians are babies, they have gills and must live in the water like fish. As they grow up, they lose their gills, grow lungs and eventually must live on land.

After returning to the death adder screen, the user can either go back or follow the guide to the 'Mangrove snake exploration screen' (fig. 11.10):

The 'Mangrove snake exploration screen' has a heading, 'Mangrove snake' and a picture that is both larger and more exciting than the pictures in the 'Death adder information screen'. It has a setting, and a snake which raises its head menacingly.

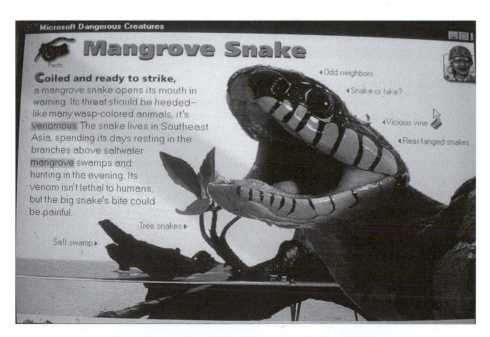

Figure 11.10 'Mangrove snake exploration screen' (Microsoft *Dangerous Creatures*, 1994)

The main text is more 'dramatic' than that of the 'Death adder information screen' and there are no 'subsidiary' texts:

> Coiled and ready to strike, a mangrove snake opens its mouth in warning. Its threats should be heeded – like many wasp-coloured animals, it's *venomous*. The snake lives in South-East Asia, spending its days resting in branches above salt-water *mangrove* swamps and hunting in the evening. Its venom isn't lethal to humans, but the big snake's bite could be quite painful.

At the same time the voice of the guide continues the story:

> One of those snakes was the mangrove snake. One day he sat complaining to his friend, the whipsnake: 'Yeah, I am very poisonous, but I am so slow, the humans are always chasing me and I must bite them when they catch me. It is quite exhausting.' The whipsnake, who was very fast, but perfectly harmless, said: 'Let me have your poison teeth, so the humans won't hate you anymore, and since I am too fast to catch, I won't need to bite them.' The mangrove snake agreed and ever since he has been only poisonous enough to kill his food and humans don't bother him.

What links these two screens? It depends on whether you focus on the speech or on the writing. From the point of view of the guide's story, this screen produces a *next event*. There is chronological order. From the point of view of the written text, there is only *addition*: 'yet more on snakes'. As for the link between written and spoken text, there does not seem to be any. The 'message' of the two could not be more different. The one emphasises caring and co-operation in nature, the other hunting and the survival of the fittest.

The 'Mangrove snake exploration screen' links to various other information screens. Again the links are *additions*. There is *more* information: you can look at more rear-fanged snakes, more items about saltwater swamps, and so on. The layout of these screens is similar to that of the 'Death adder information screen', but the Aboriginal story does not continue. Instead a male voice provides an item of information unrelated to the other information on the screen:

> How can you tell snakes and legless lizards apart? Look for eyelids.

There is also a link to a movie loop and a 'fact screen'. This 'fact screen' – every 'exploration screen' has one – contains a heading – 'Mangrove snake' – and three separate facts, each accompanied by an icon. To the right of the facts are three pictures, a representation of the snake itself, without setting; a map showing its habitats; and a picture comparing its size to a human being. The facts:

> (icon of skull and crossbones) Kills by injecting venom through its fangs

(icon of knife and fork) Birds, small mammals, frogs, lizards and other snakes

(large exclamation mark) Watch your head! A mangrove snake spends as much time slithering through the trees as it does hunting on the ground

Clicking an icon top left produces a spoken warning in a male voice.

There are no less than eight links to choose from, so the 'Mangrove snake exploration screen' does allow some 'free' exploration of the database. It is as if the guide lets the tourists shop around for a while on their own, before calling them back to the bus. But the links are shallow. Apart from the explanation links to the 'definition boxes', there is only addition, only an accumulation of more and more 'isolationistic' morsels of facts about snakes, except of course in the Aboriginal story which does link items of information in a meaningful way, and which does, in its own way, aim at understanding rather than knowledge.

The map in figure 11.8 does clearly allow for choice, for different trajectories, for instance those shown in figures 11.11 and 11.12:

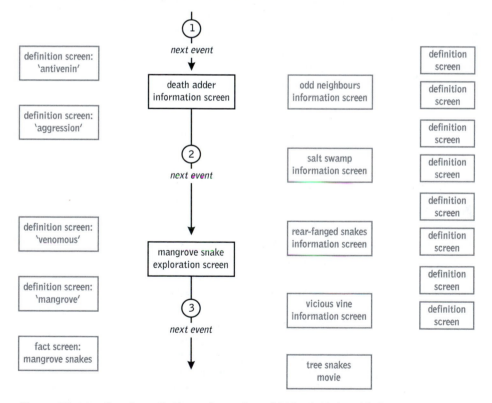

Figure 11.11 User's path through section of 'Aboriginal guided tour' (Microsoft *Dangerous Creatures*, 1994)

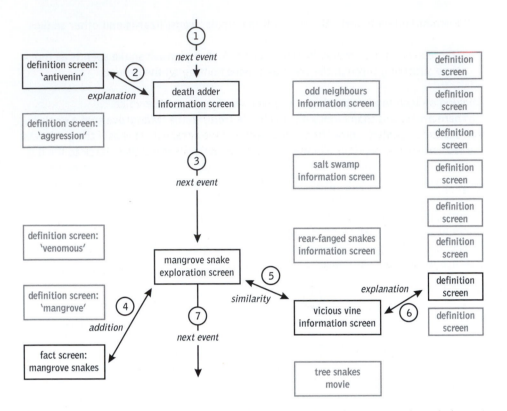

Figure 11.12   Alternative user's path through section of 'Aboriginal guided tour' (Microsoft *Dangerous Creatures*, 1994)

The path in figure 11.11, for instance, might be a more timid path, the path of a user who meekly follows the guide. Or would it be a user who is more interested in Aboriginal stories than in titbits of knowledge about snakes? The path shown in figure 11.12 perhaps shows more initiative, more interest and more curiosity. Definitions are sought out, options explored. Or is this user merely wandering about aimlessly? Questions like this cannot be answered without knowing more about the user. 'Contextual information' not only means linking items of information to each other, it also means linking them to the context, and this includes the user's interests and purposes. But one thing can be said. In *Dangerous Creatures* there are many links users can *not* make, and many questions users can *not* ask. Nor are the users in the position of an editor who can take the separate 'shots', the separate items of information, and marshal them into a meaningful whole of their own, using all the kinds of linking I have described in this chapter. If we disassembled the elements of the map in figure 11.5 and then tried to put them back together again, we would find that they only fit together in terms of one model, the model of the accumulation of unrelated facts about snakes. If databases like *Dangerous Crea-tures* are to play a role in education, children will need other resources as well if they are to learn to make the items of information coherent in relation to each other in such a way that they become *relevant*, that they become knowledge you can *do* something with, rather than quiz knowledge. By structuring knowledge according to this 'quiz' model, *Dangerous Creatures* controls meaning just as much – maybe even more – than other, more linear texts. As Umberto Eco has said (1979: 9): in the 'open text' 'you cannot use the text as you want, but only as the text wants you to use it ... an open text outlines a ''closed'' project of its Model Reader as a component of its structural strategy.'

Exercises

1   Choose two different types of publication – for example, a fashion magazine and a news magazine – and use the concepts introduced in this chapter to study the link between photographs and their captions. What explains the differences?
2   Record one or two television news items. Which aspects of the events recounted by the verbal text are illustrated? Which remain un-illustrated? Why?
3   Use the concepts introduced in this chapter to explore how information is linked in a website of your choice.
4   Observe how two children – differing for instance in gender, age or cultural back-ground – engage with the same 'edutainment' CD-ROMm or website. As they click to new information, ask them why they went where they went, and record the conversation. Try to explain any differences in the way they use the CD-ROM. Alternatively, observe two adults using a website of your choice, following the same method.
5   Design an educational website around five pictures showing different versions of the same tool – for example, five clocks, five cameras, five writing tools. For each tool write three different texts, for instance one placing it in its historical context, another describing how it works, and a third describing how it is used. Design the website in such a way that the pictures can be linked to each other and to the 'texts' in different ways, so that the user has a choice, for instance, between a historical overview, comparing and contrasting how different clocks – or cameras, or writing tools – work, or comparing and contrasting how they are used. The different texts can of course also contain non-verbal elements, for example, diagrams.

Notes

1   This section draws on Halliday (1985) and Martin (1992).
2   These excerpts were also used in Van Leeuwen (1991) an earlier paper on the subject.
3   This section draws in part on material published earlier in Kress and Van Leeuwen (2001).

12 Dialogue

The logic of dialogue

Multimodal cohesion can also be looked at in terms of interactional dynamics, of dialogue. Particularly through the influence of Vološinov, dialogue has become a central concept in social semiotics. According to Vološinov there is, alongside the semantic logic I have described in the previous chapter, another more emotive and interactive kind of logic, the logic of dialogue. He wrote (1986 [1929]: 38) that 'alternating lines of dialogue':

> are joined with one another and alternating with one another not according to the laws of grammar or logic, but according to the laws of *evaluative* (emotive) *correspondence*, *dialogical deployment*, etc., in close dependence on the historical conditions of the social situation and the whole pragmatic run of life.

It is this logic I will try to describe in this chapter – again, as a *multimodal* logic. There is no contradiction with the kind of logic I described in the previous chapter. Our brains are perfectly capable of understanding the same text or communicative event at two or more levels simultaneously. It is just that, in a book like this, I have to deal separately with what, in reality, is inextricably linked together.

To start, let us think back to the example I used in chapter 6, the 'apprenticeship' episode from Paddy Chayevsky's play *Printer's Measure'* (1994):

Mr Healey: Hey! Come here!	*Call to attention*
The boy looks up and comes scurrying down the shop, dodging the poking arm of the Kluege press, and comes to Mr Healey.	
Mr Healey pulls out a letterhead, points to a line of print	*Demonstration*
Mr Healey: What kind of type is that?	*Quizzing*
Boy: Twelve point Clearface	
Mr Healey: How do you know?	*Probing*
Boy: It's lighter than Goudy, and the lower case 'e' goes up	
Mr Healey: Clearface is a delicate type. It's clean, it's clear. It's got line and grace. Remember that	*Instruction*
Beat it!	*Dismissal*
The boy hurries back to the front of the shop to finish his cleaning	

As discussed in chapter 6, the overall cohesion of this interaction derives from the dynamic unfolding of its *generic structure*. But each stage of this structure has its own internal dynamics as a unit of dialogue or *exchange*, for instance the dynamics of question and answer, or of command and undertaking – or, more generally, of an *initiating move* and a *response*. In two cases the playwright has not actually indicated a response, but it is fair to assume that the actor playing Mr Healey will expect a response to his 'demonstration' – a nod, or a look of acknowledgement – and wait for a response to his 'instruction', a sign that he has been understood, before proceeding to the 'dismissal' stage.

Such exchange structures are multimodal in at least two ways, sequentially and simultaneously. Sequentially because, within them, the initiating move and the response need not be expressed by the same semiotic mode. The initiating move can be linguistic – 'Come here!' – and the response non-linguistic – 'scurrying down the shop'. Or the initiating move can be non-linguistic – 'pointing to a line of print' – and the response linguistic, for example, a 'Mmm'. But the exchange is also simultaneous, because in reality its moves do not just occur one after the other. While the boy scurries down the shop, Mr Healey might impatiently rap his fingers on his desk – the playwright has characterized him as a grumpy old man who only mellows when he talks about his beloved craft. Again, while Mr Healey talks, the boy will react, by looking at his boss with respect and at the typeface with a keen interest. When two people are involved in dialogue, there are always two simultaneous streams of events. That is why filmmakers, in dialogue scenes, often show the listener rather than the speaker, with the speech being heard off screen. Visually such 'reaction shots' allow us to hear the dialogue and see the simultaneous reaction at the same time. As discussed in chapter 9, partners in dialogue synchronize these two streams and create a joint rhythm between the speech and movements of each. These two streams of events – or three, or four, if more people are involved – may be in harmony with each other or in conflict. Instructor and learner may both look at the demonstrated object with the same rapt interest and attention. Or the learner may look away, eyes glazing over.

All this exists, not just in spoken dialogue, but also in music. Music, too, is almost always an interaction, for instance between the members of a band or orchestra or choir. These interactions also have both a sequential and a simultaneous aspect, although in the case of music the focus is usually on simultaneity, on whether the voices and instruments harmonize (consonance) or clash (dissonance), while in the case of spoken interaction the focus has usually been on sequentiality, at the neglect of simultaneous aspects. In this chapter I draw on both spoken dialogue and musical interaction for ideas about how modes cohere together in multimodal texts and communicative events. In other words, I will treat semiotic modes as though they are participants in a dialogue, or instruments in an orchestra. I will ask, for instance: Can I understand the interaction between the tracks in a movie – the image track, the dialogue track, the sound effects track(s), the music track – as similar to the interaction between musical instruments playing together? Can I understand the relation between the lyrics and the music of a song as a dialogue between two voices, which may either agree or disagree? And I can. The lyrics of the Simon and Garfunkel song *I Am a Rock*, for instance, begin on a wistful note:

> A winter's day
> In a deep and dark December
> I am alone
> Gazing from my window

They then move on to something like a refusal of love, out of fear of being hurt perhaps:

> I have no need of friendship
> I am a rock
> I am an island

The music on the other hand has a bright rhythm, shows no hint of sentimentality and has a melody which energetically rises in pitch. Clearly the clash between the message of the lyrics and the message of the music makes the song more interesting, makes it into a defiant, almost cynical piece, whereas, with a sad and sentimental melody, it would have been far more predictable and far less in tune with the mixture of ill-defined depression and eager enjoyment of life that characterizes the feelings of many teenagers and young adults.

In the next two sections I will look at some key ideas from the study of spoken and musical interaction. I will then try to show how these ideas can be used to understand some aspects of cohesion that I have not brought out so far.

Spoken dialogue

In this section I will discuss two aspects of spoken dialogue, *exchange structure* and *turn-taking*. As already mentioned, an 'exchange' – another common term is 'adjacency pair' – minimally needs two moves – another common term is 'turn' – an *initiating move* and a *response*, for instance:

> *Initiating move* [Instructor] What typeface is that?
> *Response* [Learner] Twelve point Clearface

In an important study of classroom interaction, Sinclair and Coulthard (1975) found that *classroom* exchanges usually have three moves. The response is *followed up* by the teacher (Sinclair and Coulthard's original term was 'feedback'). The teacher has both the first and the last word:

> *Initiating move* [Instructor] What typeface is that?
> *Response* [Learner] Twelve point Clearface
> *Follow up* [Instructor] Right.

Even when there is no explicit follow up, the silence will be interpreted as a follow up, for example, as indicating that the answer was wrong, as in this example from Coulthard and Brazil (1981: 89)

> *Initiating move* [Teacher] Can you think why I changed 'mat' to 'rug'?
> *Response* [Pupil] Mat's got two vowels in it.
> *Follow up* [Teacher] (*silence*)

Exchanges can be still further expanded. In the above example the exchange remains unfinished. The pupil has to respond again, this time hopefully with the right answer. Only then can the teacher move on to the next stage in the unfolding of the 'lesson' genre, for instance the next question or comment. If the pupil does not answer, the teacher will probe further – 'Is 't' a vowel?' – until the exchange can be concluded.

This three-part classroom exchange is a particular *type* of exchange. Sinclair and Coulthard called it 'eliciting', the case where a question is asked to which the person who asks the question already knows the answer. The same type of exchange occurs in other contexts as well, for instance, in doctor–patient interviews:

> *Initiating move* [Doctor] Whereabouts in your chest?
> *Response* [Patient] On the heart side here.
> *Follow up* [Doctor] Yes

> (Coulthard and Brazil, 1981: 90)

Clearly, 'eliciting' is an exchange that occurs in situations with an unequal relationship between the participants. Other types of exchange, too, may be characterized by inequality, for instance the 'informative' (Burton, 1980: 157), because statements seek acceptance from the respondent, or stronger still, explicit endorsement, an indication that he or she 'has heard and understood the previous utterance and is compliant' (ibid.: 158). Issues of equality and inequality play a key role in dialogue – and, as we will see, in music. If each party gets to ask roughly the same amount of questions, there is a sense of equality. If one party asks all the questions, as in the media interview or the courtroom, there clearly is not. Again, if each party gets to make roughly the same amount of statements, there is parity. If one party gets to make all the statements, and the other remains restricted to agreeing or disagreeing, there is not.

Finally, responses can be *supportive* or *challenging* – or, as is frequently the case in politics, refuse to do either and *hedge*. The terms 'supporting' and 'challenging' derive again from Burton (1980). To exemplify them we can again look at Halliday's classification of four basic types of exchange (1985: 69). It rests on two distinctions, that between 'giving' and 'demanding' and that between 'information' and 'goods and services'. Together these distinctions define the four types of exchange – the schema does not include 'follow up' moves, but these could of course be incorporated and would also be either supportive or challenging:

Giving information:	Initiating move:	Statement
	Supporting response:	Acceptance
	Challenging response:	Rejection
Demanding information:	Initiating move:	Question
	Supporting response:	Answer
	Challenging response:	Disclaimer
Giving goods and services:	Initiating move:	Offer
	Supporting move:	Acceptance
	Challenging move:	Rejection
Demanding goods and services:	Initiating move:	Command
	Supporting move:	Undertaking
	Challenging move:	Refusal

Needless to say all these moves can be made with different degrees of force. 'Acceptance' can run from 'bare acknowledgement' to 'enthusiastic endorsement', 'command' from 'polite suggestion' to 'brusque order', and so on. From the point of view of multimodality, finally, it can be noted that giving and demanding 'goods and services' is more often realized non-verbally than giving and demanding information (see for example, Burton, 1980: 134–6; Martin, 1992: 42).

The analysis of exchange structure is of course also an analysis of *turn-taking*, of the alternation that characterizes dialogue. Conversation analysts have paid close attention to 'turn-taking etiquette', to the way speakers start and end their turns, nominate the next speaker, and, above all, to whether or not they interrupt the previous speaker to start their turn. This again brings in issues of equality and inequality – speakers may try to dominate the floor by constantly interrupting other participants in the conversation. It has been well documented that this is done particularly often by men in conversations with women (see for example, Poynton, 1985). On the other hand, Deborah Tannen said:

> Claiming that an interruption is a sign of dominance assumes that conversation is an activity in which one speaker speaks at a time, but this reflects ideology more than practice. Most Americans *believe* one speaker ought to speak at a time, regardless of what they actually do. I have recorded conversations in which many voices were heard at once and it was clear that everyone was having a good time.
>
> (1992: 189–90)

According to Tannen, some conversations, for example, conversations between children, or between friends, especially women friends, are in the first place about 'enthusiastic involvement'. They are '*rapport* talk' rather than '*report* talk'. In such conversations, interruptions are not seen as rude, but as a sign of involvement. In

```
PEG:      The part I didn't like was putting everybody's snow pants and
          boots ┌and
MARGE:         └Oh yeah that was the worst part
PEG:                                          ┌and scarves
MARGE:                                        └and get them all
          bundled up in boots and everything and they're out for half an
          hour and then they come in and they're all covered with this
          snow and they get that *shluck* all over │
PEG:                                               │all that wet stuff
          and
JAN:      That's why adults don't like snow, huh?
MARGE:    That's right.
PEG:      Throw all the stuff in the dryer and then they'd come in and
          sit for half ┌an hour
MARGE:                 └and in a little while they'd want to go back out
          again.
PEG:      Then they'd want to go back out again.
```

Figure 12.1   Rapport talk (from Tannen, 1992: 204)

other conversations, for example, conversations between men and women or otherwise 'different' and/or unequal parties, or in adversarial conversations, interruptions will be seen as rude or aggressive. Figure 12.1 shows an example of 'co-operative overlapping' cited by Tannen:

Tannen comments that Peg and Marge 'play a conversational duet': they 'jointly hold one conversational role, overlapping each other without exhibiting (or reporting) resentment at being interrupted' (ibid.: 204). In other words, just as responses can be either supportive or challenging, so moments of simultaneity can be either supportive or challenging, and it is only in the latter case that we experience them as rude interruptions.

Drama scripts also follow the rule that conversation happens in turns. But expert scriptwriters know that interruption is not always aggressive and simulate simultaneity by means of 'dialogue hooks'. As described by a Hollywood scriptwriter (Herman, 1952: 205ff), this includes ending lines with 'and', so as to 'tie a series of speeches together', creating a joint production of meaning in precisely the way described by Tannen:

TONY
We can take in the Riviera, Sue and ...
SUE
(interrupting)
And Cannes, and Paris, and ...
TONY
(interrupting)
The whole works, yes!

Turn-taking is also common in music. In classical music it is called antiphony, in popular music 'call and response'. Musical duets also involve turn-taking. In the history of Western music, turn-taking has taken different forms. In early Christian psalms, two forms were recognized, the 'responsorial' form, in which the cantor sang the lines of the psalm and the choir answered after each verse with a single word, like 'Halleluiah or 'Amen', and the 'antiphonal' form in which the choir responded with a whole line – before the psalm, between the verses, and at the end. Nevertheless, even here the responses were formulaic and repetitive compared to the part of the cantor. There is clearly a relationship of inequality here, a relationship between a 'leader' and 'followers'. This inequality can be further enhanced by the degree to which there are respectful silences or overlaps between the 'call' and the 'response'. The anthropological musicologist Lomax (1968) has described how, in many smaller societies across the world, musical turn-taking characterizes ritual interactions between social groups and their leaders. In the royal assemblies of the Zulus, for instance, the King reached his decisions in public, with the whole tribe voicing its approval in musical fashion. Distance between the King and his subjects would diminish as the song proceeded. It would begin with the parts only just touching, but gradually the chorus would 'encroach upon the leader's time, until at last both are singing without letup in exciting rhythmic relationship to each other' (ibid.: 158). Much the same happens today in many advertising jingles, which start by alternating the sales pitch of a soloist with the responses of a choir of 'consumers' and end up with the two parties singing together. This shows that dialogic structure is not only about the parts of the whole, the brief exchanges that make up the whole, but also about the overall flow of the relationships. Does the same pattern of domination hold throughout or not? If not, is there a constant swapping of dialogic roles between the participants, as in a conversation between equals, or a gradual change from alternation and separateness to simultaneity and unity?

In the example below the soloist is a male voice, singing in a clownesque 'funny uncle' style, and the respondent a choir of children's voices who accept the leader's message by 'obediently' repeating it – all in humorous fashion, to take the sting out of it, so to speak. From the point of view of genre, the excerpt has two 'instruction' stages, each realized by a dyadic exchange:

> *Initiating move* [solo singer] You take a spoon on your lips
> *Response* [choir] Take a spoon on your lips
>
> *Initiating move* [solo singer] And then you lick your lips
> *Response* [choir] Then you lick your lips.

In The Who's *My Generation* the response is more independent – from the point of view of genre, the excerpt has two stages, a 'statement' and a 'reason' for this statement:

> *Initiating move* [soloist] People try to put us down
> *Response* [whole group] Talkin' 'bout my generation

Initiating move [soloist] Just because we get around
Response [whole group] Talkin' 'bout my generation

To summarize:

- The stages of a generic structure (see chapter 6) can be *exchanges*. In this case they have a dialogic structure and consist of a short series of dialogic moves and countermoves.
- There are four basic types of exchange: giving information, demanding information, giving goods and services, and demanding goods and services. Depending on the type of response each may either be supportive or challenging.
- Initiating moves have socially preferable responses. As a result initiators hold the balance of power in the exchange. Over a longer stretch of dialogue the initiator role may be monopolized by one participant, or more or less equally shared between several or all participants.
- The overlapping of the moves in an exchange, too, may either be supportive or challenging, depending on the nature of the exchange and the relations between the participants.
- Although exchange structure has mostly been studied in relation to spoken dialogue, it is also applicable to music.

Musical dialogue

In this section I introduce some musicological tools for describing dialogic interaction. Again, issues of equality and inequality play a role. But as this is music, they do so in an emotive way, testifying to Vološinov's point that the logic of dialogue is an affective, emotive logic.

Interlock

People may be involved in the same kind of musical activity at the same time and in the same place without actually playing or singing together, and yet get a sense of pleasure out of this, a sense of belonging to a larger whole, as in Charles Ives' composition *General Putnam's Camp*, as Mellers has described it:

> Several military and ragtime tunes are played together in different rhythms and tempi, and often in different keys, mixed with the huzzaing of the crowd and various a-rhythmic, non-tonal sounds of nature. The music evokes, with astonishing immediacy, the physical and nervous sensation of being present at a vast outdoor celebration

> (Mellers, 1964: 46)

It sounds chaotic, but can in fact be quite pleasurable and it is an everyday occurrence – it is there, for instance, in the simultaneous talking of many small groups of people at a party or reception, or in the simultaneous sounds of many different tools in a workshop, and, as Lomax has noted, it is also the most egalitarian of all models of human interaction, as everyone is allowed to do their own thing independently, so that it is impossible to ascribe a dominant role to any part.

Social unison

In social unison – the musicological term is 'monophony' – the participants in the musical dialogue sing or play the same notes, and in this way express a sense of belonging, of being united. Depending on the context this can lead to a positive sense of joint experience and belonging to a group, as for example, in community singing, or a negative sense of conformity, strict discipline and lack of individuality, as for example, in the case of soldiers marching in step.

An added factor is vocal or instrumental *blend*. Voices or instruments – for example, the strings in an orchestra – may blend so well together that individual timbres can no longer be distinguished, or, at the other end of the scale, sound 'heterophonic' with each voice or instrument standing out through individual variations in timbre, timing, embellishments, and so on. In between there are other possibilities. Vocal blend therefore makes individuality inaudible, and in societies that put strong value on individuality it tends to be avoided. In teaching children to sing, North Americans and Europeans put little emphasis on blending and seem charmed by childish heterophony. As Lomax has noted (1968: 171):

> Tonal unity is achieved among Anglo-Americans only by intensive rehearsal of carefully chosen personnel under the restrictive guidance of a director. Yet a casual assembly of comparative strangers in other cultures can immediately form a harmonious choir of voices that seem to melt together into a big, unified, colourful sound.

Advertising music often uses 'blending' to represent the consumer either as a unique individual or as united in preference for the advertised product. The male choirs in beer ads, for instance, tend to be rough, with individual voices standing out, while the female choirs in washing powder ads may be perfectly blended, as if women are less individuated than men.

In the case of social unison, all participants produce the same sounds, either in such a way that all sounds blend and individual sounds no longer stand out, or in such a way that individual sounds are unblended to a greater or lesser degree and can still be picked out from the whole.

Social plurality

In 'social plurality' – the musicological term is 'polyphony' – the various musical participants play or sing different parts. But these parts are equal in musical value and interest. They could stand on their own and still sound interesting, and they all contribute equally to the whole. No one is subservient to anyone else.

Lomax (1968) has shown that in many small societies across the world two-voiced polyphony symbolizes gender roles. This happens especially, he says, in societies where men and women do different work which is, however, equally valued. Indeed, Lomax believes that counterpoint and polyphony are 'very old feminine inventions':

> Subsistence complementarity is at its maximum among gatherers, early gardeners and horticulturists. Among gatherers, women generally bring in the major part of the food. In early hoe agriculture women outweigh or equal men in productive importance, probably because it was they who domesticated the plants and even the animals. In such societies women are not so likely to be shut away from the public centre of life; not so often are they passive witnesses of social events, but active participants at or close to the centre of the stage. It is in such societies that we find the highest occurrence of polyphonic singing.
>
> (Lomax, 1968: 167)

Early European music was monophonic. From about the ninth century onwards polyphony began to develop, first in the form of what we would now call 'harmony lines', where the participants still follow the same melodic line, but at 'their own' pitch levels, then, from about 1100 AD onwards, in the form of 'counterpoint' or inversion, where two voices are rhythmically in step but 'sing the opposite thing', one going down as the other goes up, and vice versa, with exactly the same intervals. YEt another hundred years later people gradually began to sing and play in full rhythmic and melodic independence. The culture, you could say, began to lose its unity, to grow more complex and diverse, but it could still 'sound harmonious'. In other words, it successfully managed to incorporate difference.

When the parts of the participants in a musical event are different, they may either be structured according to a hierarchical principle or not. In the case of 'social plurality' there is no hierarchy. All parts not only have value on their own, they also contribute equally to the whole. There is then the further possibility that they run parallel, 'saying the same thing in a different way' (at a different pitch level) or contrasting, 'saying opposite things' – and *both* principles can result either in harmonious, co-operative interaction or in disharmonious, competitive and conflictual interaction.

Social domination

In 'homophonic' music one voice or instrument, the melody, becomes dominant and the other voices or instruments become subservient to it, providing 'backing', accompaniment. The parts of these individual voices have no value in themselves and would sound incomplete and uninteresting if sung or played on their own. They are meaningful only in terms of their function with respect to the whole. Their role is 'harmonic', they must harmonize with the melody, the dominant voice.

The way in which this integrates musical participants is thus similar to that of the factory, where the work of individual workers became increasingly meaningless and repetitive compared to that of independent craftsmen – but contributed to increasingly complex and sophisticated wholes. Today this comparison may sound like sacrilege to lovers of classical music, but when it was first introduced, it did not. Arnold, in 1806, wrote this about the then new role of the conductor:

> The fusion of the individual members to the reproduction of a single feeling is the work of the leader, concert master, music director or conductor.
>
> (quoted in Koury, 1986: 61)

Lewis Mumford (1934: 173) quotes Andrew Ure, an early nineteenth century apologist for the factory system, who praised the role of factory overseers in much the same way. They 'had to overcome the difficulties', he said, in:

> the distribution of the different members of the apparatus into one cooperative body, impelling each man with the appropriate delicacy and speed.

But with harmony comes the possibility of disharmony and dissonance, of clashes between the melody and the accompanying voices – clashes which must then be 'resolved' by returning to the tonic, the key in which the piece of music is scripted. This kind of musical 'class struggle' between dominant and subservient voices would become one of the key sources of inspiration for the orchestral music of the nineteenth century.

In the case of 'social dominance' one voice – an individual or a group – can stand on its own and carries most weight in the interaction, while the others cannot stand on their own and are restricted to making limited contributions that only have value with respect to the whole. The relation between these two kinds of voices may be harmonious and supportive or disharmonious, challenging and conflicting.

To summarize:

- Four kinds of simultaneous dialogue can be discerned: interlock, social unison, social plurality and social dominance.
- In the case of *interlock* the parts are not co-ordinated with each other. In all other cases they are.

- In the case of *social unison* the parts of all participants are identical. In all the other cases they differ from each other. However, a certain amount of difference, and hence individuation, may be introduced through the degree to which the voices and/or instruments do not blend into one unified sound.
- In the case of social *plurality* the parts of the participants are different but equal. In the case of social *dominance* they are not.
- In all these cases simultaneous dialogue enacts social relationships – permutations of individuality and conformity, and of equality and inequality.
- Although simultaneous dialogue has mostly been studied in relation to music, it can also be applied to spoken dialogue, and to *polylogues*, dialogues with many participants – from the very informal simultaneous dialogues of 'interlock' to more formal and ritualized forms of joint speech.

Dialogic cohesion in a vocal duet

A vocal duet, such as the 'Elephant Medley' from Baz Luhrmann's film *Moulin Rouge* (2001) has both a sequential and a simultaneous dialogic structure.

Sequentially, it is a dialogue between Ewan McGregor, as the penniless poet who falls in love with a courtesan, and Nicole Kidman, as the courtesan whose services have been bought exclusively by a rich aristocrat in return for the funding of a Moulin Rouge musical spectacle written by Ewan's character and starring Nicole's character. The dialogue initiates a love that will threaten to sabotage the musical, as it amounts to a breach of Nicole's 'contract'.

Not surprisingly, Ewan makes the initiating move and Nicole responds – by rejecting his advances. Initially his moves belong to the category of 'giving information'. They take the form of statements about love, taken from a wide range of famous love songs – he begins, for instance, by declaring 'All you need is love'. At the same time, his body language leaves no doubt about the fact that he is not just 'giving information' but also 'demanding' love. The dialogue is therefore also simultaneous. Ewan speaks with two voices at once. The one is verbally expressed and makes general statements about love. The other is a non-verbally expressed declaration of love. The resulting whole is more than the sum of the parts. It allows the declaration of love to become a general statement about love, a theme for the film, albeit with ironic overtones, due to the bizarre set – the roof of a building in the form of an elephant – and the somewhat over-the-top acting style.

Nicole initially rejects his advances, at first directly – 'Please don't start that again' – then moving a step in Ewan's direction by joining into the 'discussion' mode he has set up, and contradicting his statements. But she is not yet *singing* along, and responds to his sung lines with spoken lines. Not for long. After a few exchanges she, too, begins to sing, taking over from Ewan in exactly the same way as the participants in the 'rapport talk' excerpt and the the film dialogue I quoted earlier:

Initiating move (giving information) All you need is love.
[Ewan, sung]
Response (rejection) A girl has got to eat.
[Nicole, spoken]

Initiating move (giving information) All you need is love.
[Ewan, sung]
Response (rejection) She'll end up on the street.
[Nicole, spoken]

Initiating move (giving information) All you need is love.
[Ewan, sung]
Response (rejection) Love is just a game.
[Nicole, sung]

In the next few exchanges Ewan shifts from 'giving information' to a more direct, 'demanding' approach – 'Give me just one night'. Nicole continues to reject him. But musically she now repeats Ewan's phrases in exactly the same way as the 'obedient' choir of children in the commercial jingle I quoted earlier. Musically – and hence emotionally – she is already 'with him'. In other words, Nicole also speaks with two voices. She is also involved in a (simultaneous) dialogue with herself. Verbally she rejects Ewan. Musically she already 'does everything he says'. The orchestra now joins in as well, and it, too, is a voice, a collective voice, the voice of the community. This voice is 'at one' with Ewan, playing in unison with his melody. It 'backs' the voice of love, as does the film as a whole, in which the real love of Ewan and Nicole must triumph over the mercenary love to which she is contractually obliged. In figure 12.2 I attempt to represent both the sequential and simultaneous aspects of this stage of the duet. Note that the orchestral voice is initially hesitant to support Nicole, but then gives full support to her musical compliance.

The duet continues along these lines for one more exchange, after which (see figure 12.3) Nicole takes over the initiating role, continuing to object to his advances. Two other things happen at the same time. The exchanges move back from the 'demanding' approach to the 'exchanging information' or 'discussion' approach, at least verbally, on the surface, and the orchestra stops doubling the melody and retreats to a more subdued chordal accompaniment, refusing to 'back' Nicole's objections in the way it backed Ewan's declarations of love. Initially Ewan responds by disagreeing only verbally, and musically 'following' her. But already in the second exchange he begins to respond in a musically more independent way, and then takes over the initiating role again, immediately acquiring the unanimous backing of the full orchestra.

Towards the end of the song, they move back to a more direct approach (see figure 12.4), but now in first person plural – '*We* should be lovers', '*We* can't do that'. Then, just as in the African call and response sessions described by Lomax, they suddenly

	lyrics	music	accompaniment
Initiating move [Ewan]	giving information	giving information	unison
	I was made for loving you baby You were made for loving me	(melody from *I Was Made For Loving You*	
Response [Nicole]	rejection	acceptance	unison
	The only way of loving me baby Is to pay a lovely fee	exact repeat of Ewan's melody line	(but lighter and softer
Initiating move [Ewan]	demanding 'goods and services'	demanding 'goods and services'	unison (more enthusiastic)
	Just one night Give me just one night	(melody from *One More Night*, Phil Collins)	
Response [Nicole]	rejection	acceptance	unison
	There's no way 'Cause you can't pay	exact repeat of Ewan's line but with raised pitch	

Figure 12.2 Multimodal dialogue analysis of an excerpt from *Elephant Medley*

reach consensus, suddenly begin to sing in unison and to complement each other in mid-sentence, just as in the 'vocal duet' I quoted in figure 12.1.

Clearly the semiotic resources of sequential and simultaneous dialogue play a crucial role in constructing the process of 'negotiation' taking place in this duet, with each individual sometimes in polyphonic counterpoint and sometimes in unison with him or herself, and the two initially divided and constantly challenging each other, but eventually becoming supportive, united in unison and 'rapport talk' style overlapping.

Dialogic cohesion in a film track

Can we look at the images and sounds of films in terms of 'simultaneous dialogue'? Can word and image be in social unison, or in a polyphonic relationship? The excerpt in figure 12.5 is the title sequence from Martin Scorsese's *Taxi Driver* (1976), which contains the last music score by Hollywood composer Bernard Herrmann, renowned for his collaborations with Alfred Hitchcock. It has only two tracks, the image track and the music track. The images convey a haunting atmosphere, but they do not yet set the story into motion because they have to serve as a background for the titles. Images and music therefore function in very similar ways. They both set the scene, introducing the theme and the mood of the film. As a result there is a kind of equality between them. They are in 'unison'. Of course, image and music are two very different semiotic modes, but voices and instruments singing and playing in unison can be very different too.

The music juxtaposes two themes, two voices, in a kind of duet in which each voice 'challenges' the other: (1) a hollow, lifeless drum roll and two bleak, haunting chords that alternate without going anywhere, and (2) a sleek jazz theme with a flowing saxophone melody. The images also juxtapose two themes: (1) images of the city at night – yellowish smoke rising from manholes in the street, enveloping the taxi, backlit by yellow light; coloured lights reflecting in the wet surface of the street – and

	lyrics	music	accompaniment
Initiating move [Nicole]	giving information	giving information	subdued accompaniment
	You think that people would have enough of silly love songs	(melody of *Silly Love Songs*, McCartney)	
Response [Ewan]	rejection	acceptance	(continues)
	I look around me and I see it isn't so ... oh no	exact repeat of Nicole's line	
Initiating move [Nicole]	giving information	giving information	(continues)
	Some people wanna fill the world with silly love songs	(melody continued)	
Response [Ewan]	rejection	rejection	(continues)
	Well, what's wrong with that I'd like to know 'Cause here we go again	(different melody)	
Initiating move [Ewan]	giving information	giving information	unison
	Love lifts us up where we belong *Where eagles fly* *On a mountain high*	(melody of *Up Where We Belong*)	(very loud)

Figure 12.3   Multimodal dialogue analysis of an excerpt from *Elephant Medley*

(2) a very close shot of De Niro as Travis, the insomniac taxi driver, lit by red light, with every now and again a brighter, white light gliding across his face, as if from the headlights of a passing car. As the image cuts from shots of the city to De Niro's face, the music also cuts from the alternating chords to the saxophone melody. Thus both music and image alternate between depicting the nocturnal city as a place of bleak desolation and brooding menace, and depicting De Niro's inner space – the close up

	lyrics	music	accompaniment
initiating move [Ewan]	giving information	giving information	subdued accompaniment
	We should be lovers And that's a fact	(melody from *Heroes*, David Bowie)	
response [Nicole]	rejection	acceptance	(continues)
	No, nothing could keep us together	repeat of Ewan's line	
initiating move [Ewan]	giving information	giving information	unison
	We could steal time	(*Heroes* continued)	(very loud)
response [Ewan and Nicole]	acceptance	acceptance/unison	(continues)
	Just for one day We could be heroes Forever and ever We can be heroes Forever and ever We can be heroes	(*Heroes* continued)	
initiating move [Ewan]	giving information	giving information	(continues)
	Just because I and I will always love you	(melody from *I Will Always Love You*, Dolly Parton)	
continuation [Nicole]	completes Ewan's line	completes Ewan's musical line	(continues)
	I only can't help		
continuation [Ewan and Nicole]	completes Nicole's line	completes Nicole's musical line	(continues)

Figure 12.4   Analysis of final section of *Elephant Medley*

image	dialogue	music	sounds
1 Smoke, lit up by an orange yellow glow billows up, filling the screen		A hollow drum roll and two bleak chords that alternate without going anywhere	
Out of the smoke a yellow taxi appears and drives through frame		Repeat	
Once out of frame, the frame fills up with smoke again.		Repeat	
Superimpose main title (A range of titles is superimposed on the shot)		Repeats, with 4-note bass pattern added	
DISSOLVE TO		*CUT TO*	
2 Very close shot of De Niro's eyes, scanning the environment. A red glow lights his face. Every now and again a stronger, white light glides over his face, as if from a passing car		Nightclub jazz, with medium tempo, flowing saxophone melody	
DISSOLVE TO		*CUT TO*	
3 Shot of the road from behind windscreen of moving taxi, coloured neon lights reflecting in the wet road surface.		Back to original pattern, with hollow drums and alternating chords	
(more titles)			
DISSOLVE TO			
4 Footpath, seen from the road. Neon lights and skimpily dressed women		Repeat	
(more titles)			
DISSOLVE TO		*CUT TO*	
5 Very close shot De Niro, lit by red glow		Repeat of saxophone melody	
DISSOLVE TO		*CUT TO*	
6 Billowing yellow-orange smoke		Repeat of hollow drums and chord alternation	

Figure 12.5   Title sequence from *Taxi Driver*

image	dialogue Travis (voice over):	music	sounds
1 Long shot Travis walking along street, towards camera		Repetitive bass patterns and alternation of bleak chords – background level	Sounds of traffic
2 Camera travels into Travis' room and pans around to reveal, first a sink with some pans hanging from nails and a bare lightbulb, then a bed covered with newspaper clippings, then Travis writing, seated at a small table in front of a barred window	May 10th Thank God for the rain which has helped wash away the garbage and the trash off the sidewalks. I'm working long hours now. Six in the afternoon to six in the morning, sometimes even eight in the morning, six days a week, sometimes seven days a week. It's a long hustle, but it keeps me busy. I can take in 3,350 a week, sometimes even more when I do it off the meter	Music continues	A woman's voice speaking Spanish comes closer and then fades out as camera travels into Travis' room.
3 Close shot front fender and headlight of yellow taxi, low angle, as it moves through rainy streets. Coloured lights of cinemas and bars in the background.		Music fades up and continues throughout next section	
4 Close shot back window of taxi			Rain fades up

Figure 12.6 Excerpt from *Taxi Driver*

image	dialogue Travis (voice over):	music	sounds
5 Close shot bonnet of taxi, windscreen visible top right, with wipers going			Rain fades out
6 Close shot side mirror with droplets. Change of focus to wet surface of road			
7 Long shot street through windscreen of moving car. Coloured lights reflect in the wet surface of the road.			
8 Medium long shot footpath, with young men loitering in shadowy foreground and women dressed in skimpy clothes in background. Camera pans along with three women	**Travis (voice over):** All the animals come out at night. Whores, skunks, pussies, buggers, queers, fairies, dopers, junkies.		

Figure 12.6   continued

shows only his eyes. In the film De Niro is a 'nobody who dreams of being a somebody', who, from his taxi, unshaven and with dark rings under his eyes, looks up at Cybill Shepherd, as she is at work in a brightly lit office, blonde, dressed in immaculate white, unreachable. Perhaps shot 3 anticipates the way in which she briefly and inter-mittently touches his world like a ray of bright light — as does the flowing saxophone melody, in multimodal unison with the image.

The scene represented in figure 12.6 has four tracks: image, verbal commentary, music and sound effects — the latter could be further subdivided into ambient sounds and momentary 'effects'. Initially all of these tracks, in their own way, evoke the bleak atmosphere of the city. But the level of the music is lower here than in the title sequence. Although we still hear the same two alternating chords, the musical evocation of hopeless, trapped city lives is now relegated to the background, as a kind of accompaniment to the story of Travis' life. Also in the background, to be 'heard but not listened to', are the sounds of the street – and, a moment later, of the apartment block in which Travis lives – which give a naturalistic sense of presence to the scene. So here the image track is dominant, forming the melody, so to speak, and the music and sound tracks provide two different kinds of accompaniment: (1) symbolic interpretation and emotive atmosphere, and (2) naturalistic presence – each harmonizing with the story in its own way.

Then, in the middle of shot 2, things begin to change. Now the dialogue track tells one story, the story of Travis' daily life as a taxi driver, and the image track another, the story of the environment in which he lives. Two separate streams of information, equal but different, in a cinematic polyphony. Meanwhile the music continues its interpretive and mood-setting background role.

In shot 3 we return to the 'unison' of the title sequence. The music fades up and the naturalistic atmosphere sounds disappear, with the exception of a brief rain effect which is in fact rather unnaturalistic – because it also rains in the preceding and following shots – and which therefore perhaps underlines the symbolic significance of rain in this sequence – the verbal commentary will end with Travis musing: 'Some day a real rain will come and wash all this scum off the streets'. When, finally, the commentary returns, in shot 8, it is no longer in a polyphonic relation to the image track, but in 'unison'. Here we see what we also hear.

Clearly dialogic structure is not restricted to dialogues in the narrow sense of the word, but exists whenever several 'voices' are seen or heard, whether sequentially or simultaneously – and this, given the multimodality of all communication, is perhaps always.

Exercise

1 Record some commercials targeted at children – or another category of consumers – that use jingles with a 'call and response' structure. What kind of voices play the roles of 'callers' and of 'respondents'? Can you use concepts introduced in this chapter to describe these roles and their interactions?

2 Contrast and compare the interaction between the voices in two instances of simultaneous speech – a school playground, a church service, a reception, etc.

3 Transcribe a short section from a film or television programme in which one track counterpoints another.

4 Use ideas from this chapter to study programmed dialogues – instances of human–computer communication that use spoken or written dialogue (perhaps combined with other responses, such as pressing buttons).

5 Choose a poem, 'score' it for several voices and/or groups of voices, and then record it. What patterns of sequential and/or simultaneous dialogue did you use and why?

Recommended reading

Arnheim, R. (1974) *Art and Visual Perception*, Berkeley and Los Angeles, University of California Press

Arnheim, R. (1982) *The Power of the Center*, Berkeley and Los Angeles, University of California Press

Arnheim's work has been a key influence on social semiotic theories of visual communication. I draw in particular on his ideas about framing, colour and composition. Although he writes from a psychological perspective, he emphasizes the communicative functions of these aspects of visual communication throughout.

Barthes, R. (1973) *Mythologies*, London, Paladin

Barthes, R. (1977) *Image, Music, Text*, London, Fontana

Barthes, R. (1983) *The Fashion System*, Berkeley and Los Angeles, University of California Press

Roland Barthes was the first truly multimodal and social semiotician, despite the fact that he saw all non-linguistic semiotic modes as dependent on language and worked within a structuralist paradigm. In this book, I draw especially on his concepts of 'myth' and 'connotation', his ideas on the relations between image and text, and his masterful account of the 'fashion system'.

Eggins, S. (1994) *An Introduction to Systemic Functional Linguistics*, London, Frances Pinter

A very clear account of some key ideas from the work of Halliday and Martin.

Fairclough, N. (1992) *Discourse and Social Change*, Cambridge, Polity

Fairclough, N. (2000) *New Labour, New Language*, London, Routledge

Fairclough's work has been another key influence on this book, particularly his approach to discourse, genre, style and social practice. Fairclough (1992) also contains a lucid account of Foucault's theory of discourse and its importance for a social theory of discourse, hence also for social semiotics.

Foucault, M. (1971) 'Orders of Discourse', *Social Science Information* 10(2): 7–30, also in Shapiro, M., ed. (1982) *Language and Politics*, Oxford, Blackwell

Foucault, M. (1977) *The Archeology of Knowledge*, London, Tavistock

Foucault's theory of 'discourse', and his emphasis on discourse history, have strongly influenced the account of discourse presented in this book.

Halliday, M.A.K. (1978) *Language as Social Semiotic*, London, Arnold

Halliday, M.A.K. (1985, 1994) *An Introduction to Functional Grammar*, London, Arnold

Halliday's work has been a fundamental departure point for social semiotics, particularly his notions of language as 'resource' and 'meaning potential', and his functional and systemic approach to the study of language, which has since been extended to the study of other semiotic modes. My chapters on modality and 'linking' also draw strongly on his work.

Hodge, R. and Kress, G. (1988) *Social Semiotics*, Cambridge, Polity

The book that put social semiotics on the map. I draw in particular on their approach to modality and style, and on their comparison between different semiotic theories, in chapter 2.

Iedema, R. (2001) 'Resemiotisation', *Semiotica* 37(1/4): 23–40

Iedema, R. (2003) 'Multimodality, resemiotisation: extending the analysis of discourse as multi-semiotic practice', *Visual Communication* 2(1): 29–58

Rick Iedema's concept of 'resemiotization' captures the way in which discourses are resemiotized as part of a larger, staged process of sign production. What starts as talk – for example, a script meeting – may then become a written document – for example, a script – and eventually a product in yet another medium – for example, a movie.

Kress, G. and Van Leeuwen, T. (1996) *Reading Images – The Grammar of Visual Design,* London, Routledge

A social semiotic approach to visual communication, and the first book to introduce some of the key concepts used in this book, particularly in relation to composition, modality and framing.

Kress, G. and Van Leeuwen, T. (2001) *Multimodal Discourse – The Modes and Media of Contemporary Communication,* London, Arnold

This book presents the outline of a general theory of multimodality, defining key concepts such as 'mode' and 'medium' and laying particular emphasis on the role of semiotic technology.

Lakoff, G. and Johnson, M. (1980) *Metaphors We Live By*, Chicago, Chicago University Press

Lakoff and Johnson's cognitive theory of metaphor has been an important influence on recent work in social semiotics and multimodality, even though they did not themselves explore the multimodal potential of their theory.

Laurel, B., ed. (1990) *The Art of Human–Computer Interface Design*, Reading, MA, Addison-Wesley.

Several chapters in this book show how semiotic concepts and methods – metaphor, narrative, conversation, non-verbal communication – can be, and have been used as creative tools by computer interface designers. See especially the section titled 'New Directions'.

Lomax, A. (1968) *Folk Song Style and Culture*, New Brunswick, NJ, Transaction Books

Based on a very large survey of singing styles across the world, this book relates forms of music to their social contexts and has been one of the main inspirations for the chapter on dialogue in this book.

Malinowski, B. (1928) 'The Problem of Meaning in Primitive Language', Supplement to C.K. Ogden and I.A. Richards, *The Meaning of Meaning*, London, Routledge and Kegan Paul

A classic account of the relation between language, action and social context.

Martin, J.R. (1992) *English Text – System and Structure*, Amsterdam, Benjamins

Martin's work has been another key influence on this book, particularly his account of genre, discourse and 'linking'.

Nöth, W. (1995) *Handbook of Semiotics*, Bloomington, Indiana University Press

A very thorough and comprehensive encyclopaedic dictionary of traditional semiotics, and hence useful background to the discussion of traditional semiotic concepts in Part I of this book.

O'Toole, M. (1994) *The Language of Displayed Art*, London, Leicester University Press

An application of Halliday's ideas to visual communication which highlights some aspects of visual communication that remain undeveloped in Kress and Van Leeuwen (1996).

Van Leeuwen, T. (1999) *Speech, Music, Sound*, London, Macmillan

A social semiotic approach to the analysis of speech, music and sound. The current book draws on many of the ideas about rhythm, modality and dialogue which I first developed in this earlier book.

Vološinov, V.N. (1986 [1929]) *Marxism and the Philosophy of Language*, Cambridge, MA, Harvard University Press

A classic forerunner of social semiotics which advocated relating language to the 'concrete forms of social intercourse' as early as 1929.

Glossary of key terms

Abstract See 'narrative genre'.

Abstract modality A type of modality* in which the truth criterion is cognitive, based on whether the representation represents a general pattern underlying superficially different instances, or the deeper 'essence' of what is represented.

Addition Addition is a transformation* in which elements are added to representations of social practices*, for instance evaluations*, legitimations* or purposes*. Addition is also a form of linking* – see 'extension'.

Adversative linking See 'extension'.

Affordance Affordances (Gibson) are the potential uses of a given object, stemming from the perceivable properties of the object. Because perception is selective, depending on the needs and interests of the perceivers, different perceivers will notice different affordances. But those that remain unnoticed continue to exist objectively, latent in the object, waiting to be discovered.

Alternation linking See 'extension'.

Anchorage See 'elaboration'.

Arbitrary A sign is arbitrary when there is no apparent reason why its particular signifier* should be used to signify its particular signified*.

Background See 'information value'.

Centre See 'information value'.

Challenging Speech acts*, whether initiating moves (see rhythm*) or responses*, are challenging when they withhold agreement or co-operation from the other party in a dialogue.

Coda See 'narrative genre'.

Communicative act See 'speech act'.

Communicative practices See 'social practices'.

Complication	See 'narrative genre'.
Composite of connotation	A composite of connotations* is a combination of connotative signs (see 'connotation') deriving from different domains. For instance, a writing style combining elements from the style of advertising and the style of casual conversation can connote both informality and allegiance to the values of consumer society and designer taste. Composites of connotation are particularly favoured by the semiotic regime* of the role model*, in connection with signifying lifestyles (see 'style').
Composition	Composition is the fundamental cohesive principle of space-based texts and semiotic artefacts and arrangements, the counterpart of rhythm* in time-based texts. It incorporates three aspects: information value*, framing* and salience*.
Conative function	See 'interpersonal function'.
Conclusive event	See 'extension'.
Condition	See 'extension'.
Conformity	Conformity is a type of semiotic regime* in which semiotic practices are governed by conforming to the semiotic behaviour of other participants in the given communication situation.
Conjunction	See 'linking'.
Connotation	Connotation occurs when a semiotic resource is imported from one domain into another where it is not normally used. It then stands for the ideas and values which those who import the resource associate with the domain from which they have imported it. Connotative signs generally signify ideas and values, rather than refer to concrete specific people, places and things.
Contrast linking	See 'extension'.
Co-presence	See 'extension'.
Core	See 'information value'.
Demanding goods and services	See 'speech function'.
Demanding information	See 'speech function'.

Denotation   Denotation is the use of a semiotic resource to refer to concrete people, places, things, actions, qualities and events.

Dialogue   An interaction between two or more participants. Social semiotics has extended this notion beyond speech, applying it also, for instance, to music or to the interaction between the different tracks of a film, and recognizes both sequential dialogues – in which the participants take turns – and simultaneous dialogues, in which they speak, or musically interact, at the same time.

Discourse   Discourses are resources for representation, knowledges about some aspect of reality which can be drawn upon when that aspect of reality has to be represented. There may be several discourses about a given aspect of reality, making sense of it in different ways, including and excluding different things, and serving different interests. Any given discourse may be realized by different genres* and different combinations of semiotic resources.

Discourses combine two kinds of elements, representations of social practices* and evaluations* of, purposes* for, and legitimations* of these social practices.

Double articulation   The use of a semiotic resource is organized according to the principle of double articulation if it has two layers: (1) a layer in which basic meaningless building blocks or 'atoms' such as speech sounds are combined to form meaningful units such as words, according to one set of rules, and (2) another layer in which these larger units are combined into yet larger units – such as sentences – according to another, separate set of rules. In the case of single articulation there is only one layer and one set of rules.

Elaboration   A form of linking* in which an item of information contains the same information as the preceding item. There can be several types of elaboration. An *explanation* reformulates the preceding item of information, a *specification* makes it more specific, an *exemplification* provides an example, and a *summary* generalizes it.

Barthes' concepts of *anchorage* and *illustration* apply 'specification' to the relation between words and images. In the case of 'anchorage' words make the meanings of an image more specific, in the case of 'illustration' images make the meanings of words more specific.

Emotive function   Jakobson's term for the semiotic function of expressing an attitude toward what is represented.

Enclosure   See 'information value'.

Evaluation   Evaluations of social practices* or parts of social practices
                       form part of discourses* about these practices. The same
                       practices or parts of them may be evaluated differently in
                       different discourses.
                       Also see 'narrative genre'.

Exchange   A unit of dialogue*, minimally consisting of an initiating
                       move (see rhythm*) and a response*. There may be other
                       elements as well, for example, a 'follow-up', that is, an act of
                       confirming a response. The term 'exchange structure' then
                       refers to the structure of such an exchange.

Exclusion   Exclusion is a transformation* in which elements are deleted
                       from representations of social practices*, for instance certain
                       actors or actions, and/or certain details of manner or time or
                       place.

Exemplification   See 'elaboration'.

**Experiential   A metaphor is understanding one thing in terms of another
metaphor**   thing with which it has a relation of (partial) similarity.
                       According to Lakoff and Johnson, our understanding of the
                       world is based on metaphors. In this way we are able to under-
                       stand complex and abstract ideas on the basis of our concrete
                       experiences. In social semiotics, experiential metaphor is one
                       of the ways, along with connotation*, in which a sign can be
                       motivated, and through which semiotic innovation can be
                       achieved.

Expertise   Expertise is a type of semiotic regime* in which semiotic
                       practices are governed by following the advice of experts.

Explanation   See 'elaboration'.

Extension   A type of linking* in which an item of information adds new
                       information to the preceding item. The link between the items
                       can be temporal, spatial, logical or additive. Roland Barthes'
                       term *relay* applies 'extension' to the relation between words
                       and images.
                       In temporal links between items of information, one item
                       relates an event that happened before ('previous event'), after
                       ('next event'), or at the same time ('simultaneous event') as
                       another item of information. Another temporal link is the
                       'conclusive event', the last event in a series.

In spatial linking one item describes something that is close to ('proximity') or at the same place as ('co-presence') what is described in another item.

In logical links between items of information one item of information provides the reason for ('reason'), result of ('result'), purpose of ('purpose'), or condition of ('condition') another item, or the two items may be compared to one another in terms of 'similarity' or 'contrast'.

If there is neither a temporal nor a logical relationship between two items of information, the relation is that of an 'addition' (an 'and' relation), an 'alternative' (an 'or' relation) or an 'adversative' (a 'but' relation).

See also 'information value'.

Framing
Framing is one of three key aspects of composition*. It creates a sense of disconnection or separateness between the elements of the composition, for instance by means of frame-lines, empty space, or discontinuities of various kinds.

The concept also includes the creation of a sense of connection between the elements of a semiotic artefact or event, for instance by the absence of framing devices or by means of similarities between the elements.

The significance of this is that the disconnected elements will be understood as in some sense separate and independent, perhaps even contrasting, while connected elements will be understood as in some sense belonging together.

Frequency modality
Linguistic modality can be expressed in terms of frequency. This rests on the principle that the more often something occurs or is the case, the higher its truth value, and is expressed through sets of adjectives and adverbials such as *always/often/sometimes, most–many–some*, etc.

Function
Vladimir Propp's term for the generalized events that make up the plot structure of specific kinds of stories.
See also 'semiotic function'.

Genre
A type of text defined in terms of its structure as a communicative event. Genres are ways of achieving communicative goals, such as telling a story, persuading people to do or believe things, instructing people in some task, and so on. They are analysed as consisting of stages which are given functional labels such as 'Identifying a problem', 'Proposing a solution', and so on. Each stage is a step on the way towards fulfilling the overall communicative goal of the genre, and is typically homogeneous in terms of

the speech acts it contains, for instance a stage in a story will typically contain speech acts of 'recounting events', although other speech acts may be embedded – for instance descriptions. Genres can thus be seen as the actions of communicative social practices*. A given genre can, in principle, combine with any discourse because genres are, as it were, templates for communicative action. In practice, not all combinations of genre and discourse are socially acceptable.

Given   See 'information value'.

Guide rhythm   In a film the rhythm of one of the tracks – for example, the rhythm of action, or of dialogue, or of the music – can become a guide rhythm with which the rhythms of the other tracks, and the placement of sound effects, editing points, etc., are synchronized.

Homophony   See 'social dominance'.

Ideal   See 'information value'.

Ideational function   Halliday's term for the semiotic function* of constructing representations of what is going on in the world. Jakobson uses the term 'referential function'.

Illocutionary act   See 'speech act'.

Illustration   See 'elaboration'.

Impersonal authority   Impersonal authority is a semiotic regime* in which semiotic practices are governed either by explicit written rules, or by customary law, or tradition.

Individual style   See 'style'.

Information value   Information value is one of the three main aspects of composition*. It provides different values for a number of different zones in the semiotic space.
Given and *new* are the information values of the left (given) and the right (new) of the semiotic space, when these zones are polarized*. The given is presented as something already known to the reader or viewer, and hence not in question, the new as something not yet known to the reader or viewer, and hence the important part of the message.
Ideal and *real* are the information values of the upper part (ideal) and the lower part (real) of a semiotic space, when these zones are polarized*. The ideal is presented as the generalized and/or idealized essence of the information, the real as more specific – for example, details – and/or more

realistic – for example, documentary evidence – and/or more practical information – for example, directions for action.

Centre and *margin* are the information values of the centre (centre) and the periphery (margins). The centre is presented as the nucleus of what is communicated, and the elements that flank it, the margins, are presented as in some sense subservient to it, dependent on it, or complementary to it.

Many triptychs combine given–new with centre–margin. The central element then becomes a *mediator* which bridges and links the two polarized* elements.

When the third dimension is taken into account, further zones need to be taken into account. *Face* and *support* are the information values of the front and the back, if both are used as semiotic spaces and polarized*. The front (face) then presents the identity and meaning of the composition, and the back (support) contains more functional elements, such as the lists of ingredients on food packaging, the table of contents on journals, and so on. The sides, if used at all, tend to be subsidiaries, extending either the face or the support. The top, if used, has similar functions as the face.

Objects may also display an inside (*core*) and an outside (*enclosure*). The core intensifies the value of the centre. It functions as the 'heart', the animating principle, or represents a treasure, or something secret or magic.

The meaning potential of *foreground* and *background*, finally, is that of being 'close' to, and hence important for the viewer, or far from, and hence less important for, the viewer.

Initiating move   The communicative act that opens a unit of dialogue, for instance the question in a question–answer pair. Initiating moves may be 'supportive' – for instance agreement with the answer to a preceding question – or 'challenging' – for instance disagreement with a preceding question.

Interlock   A form of simultaneous dialogue* in which the parts of the participants are not co-ordinated with each other.

Interpersonal function   Halliday's term for the semiotic function* of constituting communicative interactions. Jakobson uses the term 'conative function'.

Langue   Langue is the traditional semiotic term for the system of language – as described by grammars and dictionaries – or of some other semiotic mode, as separated from its use. In social semiotics this term is replaced by semiotic resource*.

Legitimation	Legitimations of social practices* or parts of social practices form part of discourses* about these practices. They provide reasons for why the practice (or part thereof) exists and why it takes the form that it does. The same practices or parts of practices may be legitimated differently in different discourses.
Lifestyle	See 'style'.
Linking	The linguistic term conjunction is used for the meaningful links between items of information. In social semiotics, the term linking is used to extend the concept beyond language and relate it to the way items of information are linked in hypertext.
	The two main types of linking are elaboration*, in which an item of information contains the same information as the preceding item, and extension*, in which an item of information adds new information to the preceding item.
Locutionary act	See 'speech act'.
Main phrase	See 'rhythm'.
Main pulse	See 'rhythm'.
Margin	See 'information value'.
Measured time	Measured time is time with a regular pulse. Unmeasured time is time in which no regular pulse can be discerned. Its meaning potential is 'out of time' and it is therefore often used to signify the 'eternal', the 'sacred', the 'supernatural', or the 'uncanny'.
Measures	See 'rhythm'.
Mediator	See 'information value'.
Metalingual function	Jakobson's term for the semiotic function of communicating about communication itself.
Metaphor	See 'experiential metaphor'.
Metonym	A metonym is a metaphor (see experiential metaphor*) in which one thing is understood in relation to another thing on the basis of a temporal or spatial connection between the two. For instance the word 'hand' is understood as referring to a whole person, or a picture of a sheep as referring to wool.
Metronomic time	Metronomic time is a form of measured time* with very precise and unvarying timing, often aided or produced by mechanical or electronic technology. In non-metronomic time, metronomic timing is subverted by anticipating or

delaying the beat, or by other means, for example, local increases and decreases in tempo.

Modality
The term modality refers to semiotic resources* for expressing *as how true* or *as how real* a given representation should be taken. Modality resources allow both degrees and kinds of modality to be expressed.

Language has modality resources for expressing the truth of utterances in terms of probability*, frequency*, and in terms of whether the truth of the utterance is subjective or objective (see objective modality*).

In visual communication modality can be naturalistic*, abstract*, technological* and sensory*.

Monophony
See 'social unison'.

Monorhythm
See 'polyrhythm'.

Motivation
A sign* is said to be motivated when we can see why a particular signifier* is used to signify a particular signified*.

Move
See 'rhythm'.

Multimodality
The combination of different semiotic modes – for example, language and music – in a communicative artefact or event.

Narrative genre
Labov describes the stages (see genre*) of the genre* of narrative as follows:

The *abstract* begins the story and contains a brief summary or indication of the topic, to attract the listener's attention and interest.

The *orientation* introduces the setting – who is involved, when, where – and the event that kicks off the story. Elements of orientation may also occur later in the story, when new people, places and things are introduced.

The *complication(s)* are the event(s) that make up the core of the story.

Evaluations may occur at various moments in the story, when the storyteller answers the unspoken (or spoken) question 'Why should we find this interesting?'

The *resolution* provides the final event and outcome of the story.

The *coda* – which does not always occur – moves from the time of the story to the time of the telling of the story, and provides the story's relevance for the storyteller and the listeners or readers.

Naturalistic modality
When the modality* of a visual representation – or a sound – is naturalistic, the truth criterion is perceptual and rests on

the idea that the more a visual representation resembles what we would see if we saw the represented things in reality the truer it is. In effect, this also depends on the state of the art of naturalistic imaging technology.

New   See 'information value'.

Next event linking See 'extension'.

**Non-metronomic   See 'metronomic time'.
time**

Objective modality Linguistic modality can be expressed objectively – for example, through phrases such as 'It is certain that … ' – or subjectively – for example, through phrases like 'I am certain that … '.

**Offering goods and   See 'speech function'.
services**

**Offering   See 'speech function'.
information**

Orientation   See 'narrative genre'.

Parole   Parole is the traditional semiotic term for the way language ('langue'*) or some other semiotic system is used.

Perlocutionary act See 'speech act'.

Personal authority The rule of personal authority is a semiotic regime* in which semiotic practices are governed by the will of one or more powerful people. For instance, in the case of fashion, the decisions of key fashion designers determine what will be in fashion and what will not.

Phatic function   Jakobson's term for the semiotic function of communicating for the sake of communication, communication aimed only at 'keeping the channel open' rather than at imparting information or achieving some other communicative goal.

Phrase   See 'rhythm'.

Poetic function   Jakobson's term for the semiotic function of communicating aesthetic pleasure.

Polarization   The term polarization is used when two elements in a composition* – one placed on the left, the other on the right, or one placed in the upper, the other in the lower zone of the semiotic space – are different from, or opposed to each other.

Polyphony   See 'social plurality'.

Polyrhythm	Monorhythmic time is a form of measured time* in which all the sounds and movements of a text or communicative event synchronize to the same pulse (see rhythm*). In polyrhythmic timing this does not happen. The participating sounds and movements use different, overlapping rhythms, without the whole becoming rhythmically incoherent.
Previous event linking	See 'extension'.
Probability modality	Linguistic modality can be expressed in terms of probability, for instance through modal auxiliaries such as *may–will–must* and related adjectives, adverbials and nouns (for example, *possibility–probability–certainty*).
Proximity linking	See 'extension'.
Pulse	See 'rhythm'.
Purpose	Purposes of social practices* or parts of social practices form part of discourses* about these practices. The same practices or parts of practices may be given different purposes in different discourses. The term is also used to refer to a type of linking* in which one element of a text supplies the purpose of another.
Real	See 'information value'.
Rearrangement	Rearrangement is a transformation* in which the order of the actions that form part of a social practice* is changed in representations of that social practice.
Referential function	See 'ideational function'.
(Rhythmic) Regularization	The patterning of rhythm* by means of one or more of the following: (1) regularizing tempo; (2) regularizing the amount of sound per measure (see rhythm*); (3) regularizing the amount of measures per phrase (see rhythm*); (4) regularizing the amount of phrases per move (see rhythm*).
Resolution	See 'narrative genre'.
Response	The second move in a unit of dialogue, for instance the answer in a question–answer pair. Responses may be 'supportive'* or 'challenging'* See also 'speech function'.
Result	See 'extension'.
Rhythm	Rhythm is the fundamental cohesive principle of all time-based texts and communicative events, the counterpart of composition* in space-based texts, environments, etc.

Rhythm divides the flow of time into *measures* of equal duration. *Tempo* results from the duration of these measures.

Each measure has one *pulse,* which is perceptually more prominent than the other element(s) of the measure. The pulses mark the elements which have the greatest information value in the measure.

Measures are grouped together into *phrases* of up to seven or eight measures, marked off by boundaries, breaks or changes in the regular rhythm. The phrases demarcate communicative acts (see speech acts*).

Each phrase has a key pulse, the *main pulse,* which marks the most important item of information in the phrase.

Phrases are grouped together into *moves* of up to seven or eight phrases, marked off by perceptually more salient boundaries. The moves demarcate stages (see genre*) in the generic structure of the text or communicative event. One phrase will be the *main phrase* of the move, and carry the communicative act that is most crucial for what the stage seeks to achieve.

Role model

The rule of the role model is a type of semiotic regime* in which semiotic practices are governed by following the example of admirable people, for instance peer group leaders, or media stars and celebrities.

Salience

Salience is one of the three key aspects of composition*. It creates difference between the elements of a composition in terms of the degree to which they attract the viewer's attention.

This is caused by differences between the elements in terms of one or more of the following, absence or presence of movement, size, amount of detail and texture shown, tonal contrast, colour contrast, placement in the visual field, and specific cultural factors such as the appearance of a human figure.

Semiotic function

The term 'semiotic function' may refer to the role of a semiotic 'part' in a semiotic 'whole', for instance the role of a word in a sentence, or to the role of a semiotic mode in society. Halliday calls the former 'function in structure' and the latter 'function in society'. Halliday's 'metafunctions', the 'ideational' function*, the 'interpersonal' function* and the 'textual' function* merge the two as they are both functions of language in society and functions of certain linguistic systems within language. While Halliday has three functions, Jakobson posited six functions. In addition to functions that are closely

related to Halliday's 'ideational' and 'interpersonal' functions, he recognized the 'emotive' function*, a 'poetic'* function, a 'metalingual'* function and a 'phatic'* function.
Semioticians have also applied these functions to semiotic systems other than language, and this has led to debates over questions such as whether music can fulfil the ideational function, or whether semiotic modes other than language can fulfil the metalingual function.

Semiotic regime Semiotic regimes are the ways in which the uses of semiotic resources are governed in specific contexts. They include personal authority*, impersonal authority*, conformity*, role models* and expertise*.

Semiotic resource Semiotic resources are the actions, materials and artefacts we use for communicative purposes, whether produced physiologically – for example, with our vocal apparatus, the muscles we use to make facial expressions and gestures – or technologically – for example, with pen and ink, or computer hardware and software – together with the ways in which these resources can be organized.
Semiotic resources have a meaning potential, based on their past uses, and a set of affordances* based on their possible uses, and these will be actualized in concrete social contexts where their use is subject to some form of semiotic regime.

Semiotics The study of semiotic resources* and their uses.

Sensory modality When the modality* of a visual representation (or sound) is sensory, the truth criterion is emotive, based on the effect of pleasure or displeasure created by the visual or sound. This is conveyed by a 'more than real' type of image or sound, in which there is more vivid colour, greater sharpness, and so on – or in the case of sound, greater rendition of textural detail, acoustic perspective, etc. – than in standard naturalistic* representations.

Sign An instance of the use of a semiotic resource* for purposes of communication, for example, the action of frowning, used for the purposes of communicating disapproval, or the use of the colour red, for purposes of warning against some danger.

Signified The meaning we express with a signifier*, for example, 'disapproval' in the case of a frown, 'danger' in the case of red.

Signifier The observable form we use to communicate something – for example, a facial expression, a colour.

Similarity linking   See 'extension'.

Single articulation   See 'double articulation'.

Social dominance   A form of simultaneous dialogue* in which the contributions of the various participants are different and unequal, with one voice or instrument, or one group of voices or instruments, dominating the others, and the others playing an accompanying role which may be supporting* – consonant, in the case of music – or challenging* – dissonant, in the case of music. The musicological term is *homophony*.

Social plurality   A form of simultaneous dialogue* in which the contributions of the various participants are different but equal. The musicological term is *polyphony*.

Social practice   Social practices are the things people do to, for, or with each other insofar as they follow recognizable patterns. The main elements of social practices are the actions that constitute them, the manner in which these actions are performed, the actors participating in the actions, the resources needed to perform the actions and the times and places of the actions. When the actions are represented, whether linguistically or otherwise, this will be mediated by a discourse* which will involve transformations*.
Social practices can be divided into communicative practices, that is practices that include the representation of other practices ('genres'*), and practices that do not.

Social style   See 'style'.

Social unison   A form of simultaneous dialogue* in which the contributions of the participants are identical. A certain amount of difference may be introduced through the degree to which the voices and/or instruments blend into one unified sound, or remain differentiated. The musicological term is *monophony*.

Specification   See 'elaboration'.

Speech act   The linguistic utterance seen as a unit of social action with three simultaneous elements, the locutionary act, an act of referring to something that exists or is going on in the world or the mind, the illocutionary act, an act of communicating some kind of interactive intent, such as 'persuading' or 'teaching', and the perlocutionary act, the act of achieving some communicative goal, such as 'convincing' or 'imparting knowledge'.

In social semiotics this concept is broadened to include all communicative acts and as realized by a combination of semiotic modes.

Speech function   Halliday's term for the four basic speech acts* that are realized by specific grammatical categories and have specific responses*: offering information, which is realized by statements, has 'agreement' or 'acknowledgement' as its preferred or 'supportive'* response, and disagreement as its 'challenging'* response; demanding information, which is realized by questions and has answers as its preferred or 'supportive' response, and refusals to answer as its 'challenging' response; offering goods and services, which is realized by various idioms such as 'Here you are', has acceptance as its preferred, 'supportive' response and rejection as its 'challenging' response; and demanding goods and services, which is realized by commands, has 'undertakings' as its preferred, 'supportive' response, and 'refusals' as its 'challenging' response.

An intermediate kind of response is also possible, for instance noncommittal responses to 'offering information', 'disclaimers' – for example, 'I don't know' – to 'demands of information', and so on.

Each of these speech functions has many different subtypes which are realized by combinations of linguistic and other features.

The concept of speech function has also been used in social semiotic theories of visual communication, where permutations of the gaze in images of people are interpreted as realizing 'demands' – people looking at the viewer – or 'offers' – people not looking at the viewer – of information (Kress and Van Leeuwen, 1996).

Stage   See 'genre'.

Style   The manner in which a semiotic artefact is produced, or a semiotic event performed, as contrasted with the discourse and genre it realizes.

The meanings conveyed by style differ. In the case of individual style, style marks the identity and character of an individual person. In the case of social style it indexes social categories such as provenance, class, profession, etc. In the case of lifestyle it indicates individual lifestyle identities and values which are, however, socially produced and shared with others, forming a new kind of social identity.

Subjective modality   See 'objective modality'.

Subsidiary   See 'information value'.

Substitution   Substitution is a transformation* in which elements of social practices are substituted for by other elements in representations of that social practice. Examples include the substitution of specific actors by types, or of concrete actions by abstractions. Because all representation involves the substitution of the 'real thing' by a representation, substitution is a fundamental aspect of representation – but it can be done in many different ways.

Summary linking   See 'elaboration'.

Support   See 'information value'.

Supporting   Supporting speech acts*, whether initiating moves* or responses*, offer agreement or co-operation with the other party in a dialogue.

Technological modality   When the modality* of a visual representation is technological, the truth criterion is pragmatic, based on the practical usefulness of the visual, as for example, in maps, patterns for dress making, architectural blueprints, etc.

Textual function   Halliday's term for the semiotic function* of creating texts, complexes of signs* which cohere both internally with each other and externally with the context in and for which they are produced.

Transformation   When a social practice* is represented through a discourse*, it undergoes certain transformations: elements – for example, certain actions or actors – may be deleted ('exclusion'), the order in which the actions of the practice take place may be rearranged ('rearrangement'), actions, actors or other elements may be replaced by other elements ('substitution'), and elements may be added, for example, evaluations, or purposes ('addition'). Such transformations tend to be motivated by the interests the discourse represents.

Unmeasured time   See 'measured time'.

References

Allen, G.D. (1975) 'Speech rhythm: its relation to performance universals and articulatory timing', *Journal of Phonetics* 3: 75–86

Aristotle (1954) *The Rhetoric and the Poetics*, New York, Random House

Arnheim, R. (1933) *Film as Art*, Berkeley and Los Angeles, University of California Press

Arnheim, R. (1974) *Art and Visual Perception*, Berkeley and Los Angeles, University of California Press

Arnheim, R. (1982) *The Power of the Center*, Berkeley and Los Angeles, University of California Press

Arthur, L.B., ed. (1999) *Religion, Dress and the Body*, Oxford, Berg

Arvidson Griffth, L. (1925) *When the movies were young*, New York, E.P. Dutton

Austin, J.L. (1962) *How to Do Things with Words*, Oxford, Oxford University Press

Bailey, D. (1988) *Reptiles*, London, Macmillan

Barnouw, E. (1966) *A Tower of Babel: A History of Broadcasting in the United States to 1933*, New York, Oxford University Press

Barthes, R, (1967a) *Writing Degree Zero*, London, Cape

Barthes, R. (1967b) *Elements of Semiology*, London, Cape

Barthes, R. (1973) *Mythologies*, London, Paladin

Barthes, R. (1977) *Image, Music, Text*, London, Fontana

Barthes, R. (1978) *A Lover's Discourse: Fragments*, London, Penguin

Barthes, R. (1983) *The Fashion System*, Berkeley and Los Angeles, University of California Press

Beck, U. (1994) *Risk Society – Towards a New Modernity*, London, Sage

Beckham, D. (2000) *Beckham: My World*, London, Hodder & Stoughton

Bell, P. and Van Leeuwen, T. (1994) *The Media Interview – Confession, Contest, Conversation*, Sydney, New South Wales University Press

Bellantoni, J. and Woolman, M. (1999) *Type in Motion – Innovations in Digital Graphics*, London, Thames and Hudson

Benjamin, W. (1972 [1931]) 'A Short History of Photography', *Screen* 13(1): 5–27

Bennett, N. (1978) 'The organisation of teaching and curriculum in open plan schools', in J. McNicholas, ed. *Open Plan Primary Schools*, special issue of *Aspects of Education* 21: 35–49

Bennett, N., Andreae, J., Hegarthy, P. and Wade, B. (1980) *Open Plan Schools*, Windsor, NFER

Berger, J. (1972) *Ways of Seeing*, Harmondsworth, Penguin

Bergson, H. (1965) *La Pensée et le mouvant*, Paris, Presses Universitaires

Bernstein, B. (1971) *Class, Codes and Control*, Vol I, London, Routledge

Bernstein, B, (1972) 'Social Class, Language and Socialisation', in P.P. Giglioli, ed. *Language and Social Context*, Harmondsworth, Penguin

Bettelheim, B. (1978) *The Uses of Enchantment*, London, Penguin

Blum-Kolka, S. (1997) 'Discourse Pragmatics' in T.A. van Dijk, ed. *Discourse as Social Interaction*, London, Sage

Bocock, R. (1993) *Consumption*, London, Routledge

Bogatyrev, P. (1971 [1937]) *The Function of Folk Costume in Moravian Slovakia*, The Hague, Mouton

Boje, A. (1971) *Open Plan Offices*, London, Business Books Ltd

Bourdieu, P. (1977) *Outline of a Theory of Practice*, Cambridge, Cambridge University Press

Brace-Taylor, B. (1972) 'Le Corbusier at Pessac', in P. Serenyi, ed. (1975) *Le Corbusier in Perspective,* Englewood Cliffs, New Jersey, Prentice-Hall.

Brown, R. and Gilman, A. (1960) 'The Pronouns of Power and Solidarity', in T.A. Sebeok, ed. *Style in Language*, Cambridge, Mass, Harvard University Press.

Browne, E.J. (1970) *The Open Plan Office – Principles and Design*, London, The Institute of Office Management.

Buffon, G.L. de (1971) *De l'Homme*, Paris, Duchet

Bühler, K. (1934) 'Die Axiomatik der Sprachwissenschaft', *Kant Studien* 38: 19–90

Bunton, R. and Burrows, R. (1995) 'Consumption and health in the "epidemiological" clinic of late modern medicine', in Bunton, R., Nettleton, S. and Burrows, R., eds. *The Sociology of Health Promotion: Critical Analyses & Consumption, Lifestyle and Risk,* London, Routledge

Burton, D. (1980) *Dialogue and Discourse*, London, Routledge and Kegan Paul

Caldas-Coulthard, C.R. and Van Leeuwen, T. (2002) 'Stunning, shimmering, iridescent: toys as the representation of gendered social actors', in I. Litosseliti and J. Sunderland, eds. *Gender Identity and Discourse Analysis*, Amsterdam, Benjamins

Cardiff, D. (1989) 'The Serious and the Popular: Aspects of the Evolution of Style in the Radio Talk 1928–1939', *Media Culture and Society* 2: 31

Chaney, D. (1996) *Lifestyles*, London, Routledge

Chayevsky, P. (1994) *The Collected Works of Paddy Chayevsky: The Television Plays,* New York, Applause Theatre and Cinema Books

Chernoff, J.M. (1979) *African Rhythm and African Sensibility – Aesthetics and Social Action in African Musical Idioms*, Chicago, University of Chicago Press

Conrads, U., ed. (1975) *Programs and manifestoes on 20th century architecture*, Cambridge, Mass, MIT Press

Cook, G. (1992) *The Discourse of Advertising*, London, Routledge

Cooke, D. (1959) *The Language of Music*, Oxford, Oxford University Press

Corris, P. (2000) *The Vietnam Volunteer*, Lismore, Southern Cross University Press

Coulthard, M. and Brazil, D. (1981) 'Exchange Structure' in M. Coulthard and M. Montgomery, eds. *Studies in Discourse Analysis*, London, Routledge and Kegan Paul

Crystal, D. and Davy, D. (1969) *Investigating English Style*, London, Longman

Daneš, F. (1964) 'A three-level approach to syntax', *Travaux Linguistiques de Prague* 1: 225–40

Davis, K. (1942) 'A Conceptual Analysis of Stratification', *American Sociological Review* 7(3): 309–21

Davis, K. and Moore, W.E. (1945) 'Some Principles of Stratification', *American Sociological Review* 10: 242–9

Descartes, R. (1972 [1649]) *Oeuvres et Lettres*, Paris, Gallimard

Douillard, J. (1994) *Body, Mind and Sport*, New York, Three Rivers Press

Durand, J. (1970) 'Rhétorique et Image Publicitaire', *Communications* 15: 70–93

Durkheim, E. (1964 [1912]) *The Elementary Forms of the Religious Life*, New York, Collier

Durkheim, E. and Mauss, M. (1963) *Primitive Classification*, London, Cohen and West

Eco, U. (1976) *The Role of the Reader*, Bloomington, Indiana University Press

Eggins, S. (1994) *An Introduction to Systemic Functional Linguistics*, London, Frances Pinter

Eisenstein, S. (1943) *The Film Sense*, London, Faber

Eisenstein, S. (1963) *Film Form*, London, Dennis Dobson

Eley, J. and Marmot, A.F. (1995) *Understanding Offices – What Every Manager Needs To Know About Office Buildings,* London, Penguin

Elias, N. (1978) *The Civilising Process: The History of Manners*, Oxford, Blackwell

Evans, H. (1972) *Newsman's English*, London, Heinemann

Erdmann, K.O. (1900) *Die Bedeutung des Wortes*, Leipzig, Avarius

Fairclough, N. (1993) 'Critical discourse analysis and the marketization of public discourse', *Discourse and Society* 4(2): 133–69

Fairclough, N. (2000) *New Labour, New Language*, London, Routledge

Fish, S. (1980) *Is There a Text in This Class? The Authority of Interpretive Communities*, Cambridge, Mass., Harvard University Press

Fiske, J. (1989) *Understanding Popular Culture*, London, Unwin Hyman

Forceville, C. (1996) *Pictorial Metaphor in Advertising*, London, Routledge

Foucault, M. (1977) *The Archeology of Knowledge*, London, Tavistock

Foucault, M. (1978) *The History of Sexuality*, Vol I, Harmondsworth, Penguin

Foucault, M. (1979) *Discipline and Punish*, London, Peregrine

Freud, S. (1977 [1905]) *On Sexuality*, Harmondsworth, Penguin

Gage, J. (1999) *Colour and Meaning – Art, Science and Symbolism*, London, Thames and Hudson

Gibson, J.J. (1979) *The Ecological Approach to Visual Perception*, Boston, Houghton Mifflin

Giddens, A. (1976) *New Rules of Sociological Method*, London, Hutchinson

Goethe, J.W. von (1970 [1810]) *Theory of Colour*, Cambridge, Mass, MIT Press

Graybill, B. and Arthur, L.B. (1999) 'The Social Control of Women's Bodies in Two Mennonite Communities', in L.B. Arthur, ed. *Religion, Dress and the Body*, Oxford, Berg

Grisham, J. (1996) *The Runaway Jury*, London, Century

Guiraud, P. (1972) *La Stylistique*, Paris, Presses Universitaires de France

Gurley-Brown, H. (1962) *Sex and the Single Girl*, London, Muller

Hall, E.T. (1983) *The Dance of Life – The Other Dimension of Time*, New York, Anchor Press

Halliday, M.A.K. (1973) *Explorations in the Functions of Language*, London, Arnold

Halliday, M.A.K. (1975) *Learning How To Mean*, London, Arnold

Halliday, M.A.K. (1978) *Language as Social Semiotic*, London, Arnold

Halliday, M.A.K. (1985) *An Introduction to Functional Grammar*, London, Arnold

Halliday, M.A.K. and Martin, J.R. (1993) *Writing Science – Literacy and Discursive Power*, London, Falmer Press

Hamilton, J.A. and Hawley, M.H. (1999) 'Sacred Dress, Public Worlds: Amish and Mormon Experience and Commitment', in L.B. Arthur, ed. *Religion, Dress and the Body,* Oxford, Berg.

Hanke, R. (1989) 'Mass media and lifestyle differentiation: an analysis of the public discourse about food', *Communication* 11: 221–38

Hartkopf, V., Loftness, V., Drake, P., Dubin, F., Mill, P. and Ziga, G. (1993) *Designing the Office of the Future: The Japanese Approach to Tomorrow's Workplace*, New York, John Wiley and Sons

Hasan, R. (1979) 'On the Notion of Text', in J.S. Petöfi, ed. *Text vs sentence: basic questions of text linguistics,* vol II, Hamburg, Helmut Buske

Hausmann, C.R. (1989) *Metaphor and Art,* Cambridge, Cambridge University Press

Hawkes, T. (1972) *Metaphor*, London, Methuen

Herman, L. (1952) *A Practical Manual of Screenplay Writing for Theatre and Television Films*, New York, New American Library

Heyman, A. (1974) *Growing Up Female: A Personal Photojournal*, New York, Holt, Rinehart and Winston

Hitchcock, H.-R. and Johnson, P. (1932) *The International Style*, New York, W.W. Norton

Hodge, R. and Kress, G. (1988) *Social Semiotics*, Cambridge, Polity

Honeywill, P. (1999) *Visual Language for the World-wide Web*, Exeter, Intellect

Illich, I. (1971) *Deschooling Society*, Harmondsworth, Penguin

Jakobson, R. (1960) 'Closing Statement: Linguistics and Poetics' in T.A. Sebeok, ed. *Style in Language*, Cambridge, Mass, MIT Press

Joas, H. (2003) *War and Modernity: Studies in the History of Violence in the 20th Century*, Cambridge, Polity

Knowledge Adventure Inc (1995) *3D Body Adventure*

Koury, D. (1986) *Orchestral Performance Practices in the Nineteenth Century,* Ann Arbor, UMI Research Press

Kress, G. (1993) 'Against arbitrariness: the social production of the sign as a foundational issue in critical discourse analysis', *Discourse and Society* 4(2): 169–93

Kress, G. and Hodge, R. (1979) *Language as Ideology*, London, Routledge

Kress, G. and Van Leeuwen, T. (1996) *Reading Images – The Grammar of Visual Design*, London, Routledge

Kress, G. and Van Leeuwen, T. (2001) *Multimodal Discourse – The Modes and Media of Contemporary Communication*, London, Arnold

Kress, G., Jewitt, C., Ogborn, J. and Tsatsarelis, C. (2000) *Multimodal Teaching and Learning*, London, Continuum

Labov, W. (1972a) 'The logic of non-standard English', in W. Labov, *Language in the Inner City*, Philadelphia, University of Pennsylvania Press

Labov, W. (1972b) 'The transformation of experience in narrative syntax', in W. Labov, *Language in the Inner City*, Philadelphia, University of Pennsylvania Press

Lacy, M.L. (1996) *The Power of Colour to Heal the Environment*, London, Rainbow Publications

Lakoff, G. and Johnson, M. (1980) *Metaphors We Live By*, Chicago, Chicago University Press

Lawson, J. and Silver, H. (1973) *A Social History of Education in England*, London, Methuen

Leech, G. (1969) *English in Advertising*, London, Longman

Leech, G. (1974) *Semantics*, Harmondsworth, Penguin

Leitner, G. (1980) 'BBC English and Deutsche Rundfunksprache: A Comparative and Historical Analysis of the Language of the Radio', *International Journal of the Sociology of Language* 26: 75–100

Lévi-Strauss, C. (1962) *The Savage Mind*, London, Weidenfeld and Nicholson

Lévi-Strauss, C. (1963) *Structural Anthropology*, Harmondsworth, Penguin

Locke, J. (1972 [1706]) *An Essay Concerning Human Understanding*, Vol. II, London, Dent

Lomax, A. (1968) *Folk Song Style and Culture*, New Brunswick NJ, Transaction Books

Lyons, J. (1977) *Semantics*, Vol. I, Cambridge, Cambridge University Press

Machin, D. and Van Leeuwen, T. (2003) 'Global Schemas and Local Discourses in *Cosmopolitan*', *Journal of Sociolinguistics* 7(3): 493–513

Machin, D. and Van Leeuwen, T. (2004) 'Global Media: Generic Homogeneity and Discursive Diversity', *Continuum* 18(1): 99–120

Malinowski, B. (1929) *The Sexual Life of Savages in Northwestern Melanesia*, New York, W.W. Norton

Malinowski, B. (1935) *Coral Gardens and Their Magic*, Vol. II, London, Allen and Unwin

Malinowski, B. (1939) 'The Group and the Individual in Functional Analysis', *American Journal of Sociology* 44: 938–64

Marothy, J. (1974) *Music and the Bourgeois, Music and the Proletarian*, Budapest, Akademiai Kiado

Martin, J.R. (1992) *English Text – System and Structure*, Amsterdam, Benjamins

Martinec, R. (2001) 'Interpersonal resources in action', *Semiotica* 135–1/4: 117–45

Maruyama, M. (1980) 'Information and Communication in Poly-epistemological Systems', in K. Woodward. ed. *The Myths of Information: Technology and Postindustrial Culture*, London, Routledge

McConnell-Ginet, S. (1977) 'Intonation in a Man's World', *Signs* 3: 541–59

McLean, R. (2000) *Manual of Typography*, London, Thames and Hudson

McNicholas, J. (1978) 'The Development of Primary School Design', in J. McNicholas, ed. *Open Plan Primary School Design*, special issue of *Aspects of Education* 21: 1–10

Mellers, W. (1964) *Music in a New Found Land – Themes and Developments in the History of American Music*, London, Faber and Faber

Metz, C. (1974) *Film Language*, Oxford, Oxford University Press

Meyer, H. (1928) 'Building', in Conrads, U., ed. (1975) *Programs and manifestoes on 20th century architecture,* Cambridge, Mass, MIT Press

Michman, R.D. (1991) *Lifestyle Market Segmentation*, New York, Praeger

Midwinter, E. (1978) 'Open Plan – Open Door'; in J. McNicholas, ed. *Open Plan Primary Schools*, special issue of *Aspects of Education* 21: 58–63

Milic, L. (1970) 'Connectives in Swift's Prose Style' in D.C. Freeman, ed. *Linguistics and Literary Style*, New York, Holt, Rinehart and Winston

Mill, J.S. (1843) *A System of Logic*, London, Longman

Mole, J. (1992) *Brits at Work*, London, Brealey

Mouzelis, N. (1995) *Sociological Theory – What went wrong?,* London, Routledge

Mumford, L. (1934) *Technics and Civilization*, New York, Harcourt, Brace and World

Nakano, Y. (2002) 'Who initiates a global flow? Japanese popular culture in Asia', *Visual Communication* 1(2): 229–53

Neuenschwander, B. (1993) *Letterwork – Creative Letterforms in Graphic Design*, London, Phaidon

Nichols, B. (1976) 'Documentary Theory and Practice', *Screen* 17(4): 34–9

Nichols, B. (1981) *Ideology and the Image*, Bloomington, Indiana University Press

Nöth, W. (1990) *Handbook of Semiotics*, Bloomington, Indiana University Press

Ong, W.J. (1982) *Orality and Literacy – The Technologizing of the Word*, London, Methuen

Paolucci, G. (1996) 'The Changing Dynamics of Working Time', *Time and Society* 5(2): 145–67

Papatheodorou, F. and Machin, D. (2003) 'The Umbilical Cord That Was Never Cut – The Post-Dictatorial Intimacy between the Political Elite and the Mass Media in Greece and Spain', *European Journal of Communication* 18(1): 31–54

Parret, H. (1974) *Discussing Language*, The Hague, Mouton

Parret, H. (1995) 'Synaesthetic Effects', in T.A. Sebeok and J. Umiker-Sebeok, eds. *Advances in Visual Semiotics*, Berlin, Mouton de Gruyter

Peirce, C.S. (1965) *Collected Papers*, vols I, II, Cambridge, Mass, Harvard University Press

Poynton, C. (1985) *Language and Gender: Making the Difference*, Oxford, Oxford University Press

Price, D. (2000) 'Surveyors and surveyed: Photography out and about' in L. Wells, ed. *Photography: A Critical Introduction*, London, Routledge

Propp, V. (1968 [1927]) *Morphology of the Folktale*, Austin, University of Texas Press

Pudovkin, V. (1926) *Film Technique and Film Acting*, New York, Bonanza Books

Rifaterre, M. (1971) *Essais de Stylistique Structural*, Paris, Flammarion

Riley, C.A. (1994) *Color Codes – Modern Theories of Color in Philosophy, Painting and Architecture, Literature, Music and Psychology*, Hanover, University Press of New England

Ritchin, F. (1990) 'Photojournalism in the age of computers', in C. Squiers, ed. *The Critical Image*, Seattle, Bay Press

Sassoon, R. (1999) *Handwriting of the Twentieth Century*, London, Routledge

Saussure, F. de (1974 [1916]) *Course in General Linguistics*, London, Peter Owen

Schafer, R.M. (1986) *The Thinking Ear*, Toronto, Arcana Editions

Scheflen, A.E. (1963) 'The significance of posture in communication systems', *Psychiatry* 27: 316–31

Scollon, R. and Scollon, S.W. (1998) 'Literate Design in the Discourses of Revolution, Reform and Transition: Hong Kong and China', *Written Language and Literacy* 1(1): 1–39

Selander, S. and Van Leeuwen, T. (1999) 'Vad gör en text?' in C.A. Säfström and L. Östman, eds. *Textanalys*, Lund, Studentliteratur

Sinclair, J. McH. and Coulthard, M. (1975) *Towards an Analysis of Discourse*, Oxford, Oxford University Press

Sontag, S. (1979) *Illness as Metaphor*, London, Allen Lane

Tagg, P. (1984) 'Understanding Musical Time Sense – Concepts – Sketches and Consequences' in *Tvarspel – Festskrift for Jan Ling (50 år)*, Göteborg, Skriften fran Musikvetenskapliga Institutionen

Tagg, P. (1990) 'Music in Mass Media Studies: Reading Sounds for example', in K. Roe and U. Carlsson, eds. *Popular Music Research, Nordicom-Sweden* (2): 1093 – 115

Tannen, D. (1992) *You Just Don't Understand – Women and Men in Conversation*, London, Virago

Teige, K. (1929) 'The Mundaneum' in P. Serenyi, ed. *Le Corbusier in Perspective*, Englewood Cliffs, New Jersey, Prentice-Hall

Thompson, P. and Davenport, P. (1982) *Dictionary of Visual Language*, Harmondsworth, Penguin

Tortora, G.J. and Grabowski, S.R. (1996) *Principles of Anatomy and Physiology*, New York, HarperCollins

Uspensky, B. (1975) 'Left and Right in Icon Painting', *Semiotica* 13(1): 33–41

Vachek, K. (1966) *The Linguistic School of Prague*, Bloomington, Indiana University Press

Van den Berg, J.H. (1961) *Het Menselijk Lichaam*, Vols I and II, Nijkerk, Callenbach

Van Doesburg, T. (1924) 'Towards a plastic architecture', in U. Conrads, ed. (1975) *Programs and Manifestoes on 20th-century architecture*, Cambridge, Mass, MIT Press

Van Leeuwen, T. (1984) 'Impartial Speech – Observations on the Intonation of Radio Newsreaders', *Australian Journal of Cultural Studies* 2(1): 84–99

Van Leeuwen, T. (1985) 'Rhythmic Structure of the Film Text', in T.A. van Dijk ed. *Discourse and Communication – New Approaches to the Analysis of Mass Media Discourse and Communication*, Berlin, de Gruyter

Van Leeuwen, T. (1991) 'Conjunctive Structure in Documentary Film and Television', *Continuum* 5(1): 76–114

Van Leeuwen, T. (1992) 'Rhythm and Social Context', in P. Tench, ed. *Studies in Systemic Phonology*, London, Frances Pinter

Van Leeuwen, T. (1999) *Speech, Music, Sound*, London, Macmillan

Van Leeuwen, T. (2003) 'A multimodal perspective on composition' in T. Ensink and C. Sauer, eds. *Framing and Perspectivising in Discourse*, Amsterdam, John Benjamins

Van Leeuwen, T. and Jewitt, C. (2001) *Handbook of Visual Analysis*, London, Sage

Verschueren, J. (1985) *What People Say They Do With Words*, Norwood NJ, Ablex

Vološinov, V.N. (1986 [1929]) *Marxism and the Philosophy of Language*, Cambridge, Mass., Harvard University Press

Vosnesenskaja, J. (1987) *Women's Decameron*, London, Methuen

Warde, B. (1995) 'Printing should be invisible', in R. McLean, ed. *Typographers on Type*, London, Lund Humphries

Whorf, B.L. (1956) *Language, Thought and Reality*, Cambridge, Mass, MIT Press

Williams, R. (1974) *Television, Technology and Cultural Form*, London, Fontana

Williams, R. (1976) *Keywords*, London, Fontana

Wright, W. (1975) *Sixguns and Society – A Structural Study of the Western*, Berkeley and Los Angeles, University of California Press

Zablocki, B.D. and Kanter, R.M. (1976) 'The differentiation of lifestyles', *Annual Review of Sociology* 2: 269–98

Index

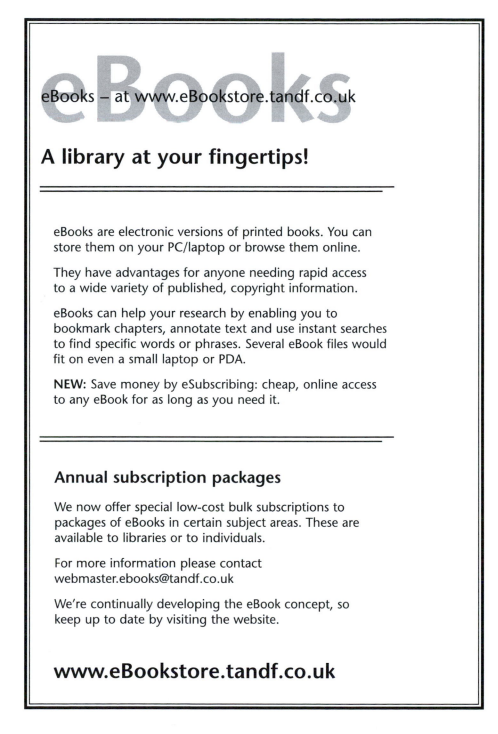